# Beauty Up

# Beauty Up

Exploring Contemporary
Japanese Body Aesthetics

## Laura Miller

UNIVERSITY OF CALIFORNIA PRESS

*Berkeley / Los Angeles / London*

University of California Press, one of the most distinguished university presses in the United States, enriches lives around the world by advancing scholarship in the humanities, social sciences, and natural sciences. Its activities are supported by the UC Press Foundation and by philanthropic contributions from individuals and institutions. For more information, visit www.ucpress.edu.

Parts of this book appeared earlier in different form in the following publications and are printed here by permission of their original publishers: parts of chapter 1 as Miller, 2000, "Media Typifications and Hip *Bijin*," *U.S.-Japan Women's Journal* 19: 176–205; chapter 3 as Miller, 2003, "Mammary Mania in Japan," *Positions: East Asia Cultures Critique* 11 (2): 271–300, by courtesy of Duke University Press; parts of chapter 4 as Miller, 2004, "Youth Fashion and Changing Beautification Practices," in *Japan's Changing Generations: Are Young People Creating a New Society?*, ed. G. Matthews and B. White, 83–97, by courtesy of Routledge/Curzon Press; and chapter 5 as Miller, 2003, "Male Beauty Work in Japan," in *Men and Masculinities in Contemporary Japan: Dislocating the Salaryman Doxa*, ed. J. Roberson and N. Suzuki, 37–58, by courtesy of Routledge Press/Taylor & Francis.

University of California Press
Berkeley and Los Angeles, California

University of California Press, Ltd.
London, England

© 2006 by The Regents of the University of California

Library of Congress Cataloging-in-Publication Data
Miller, Laura, 1953–
    Beauty up : exploring contemporary Japanese body aesthetics / Laura Miller.
        p.      cm.
    Includes bibliographical references and index.
        ISBN-13 978-0-520-24508-2 (cloth : alk. paper), ISBN-10 0-520-24508-3 (cloth : alk. paper)
        ISBN-13 978-0-520-24509-9 (pbk. : alk. paper), ISBN-10 0-520-24509-1 (pbk. : alk. paper)
        1. Body, Human—Social aspects—Japan.     2. Beauty, Personal—Japan.     3. Beauty culture—Japan.     4. Body image—Japan.     5. Philosophy, Japanese.     6. Japan—Social life and customs.     I. Title.
GT497.J3B43    2006
306.4'0952—dc22                                                                    2005016386

Manufactured in the United States of America
15   14   13   12   11   10   09   08   07   06
10   9   8   7   6   5   4   3   2   1

# Contents

# Illustrations

# Tables

# Preliminaries

The dollar amounts used in the book were calculated on the basis of ¥107 to US$1, although the average exchange rate fluctuated over the course of my research.

Japanese names in the text and bibliography are given in the Japanese style, with surname first, followed by given name. The exception is when a Japanese author publishes in English. Except for well-known Japanese names and terms (e.g., Tokyo, Shiseido, Shinto), the long vowel is denoted with a macron for *a, u, o,* and *e.*

The names of the aesthetic salons and treatments are real, but Japanese beauty workers are identified with pseudonyms.

All translations from Japanese are my own.

# Acknowledgments

I began thinking and writing about Japan's aesthetic salons and related beauty industries in 1995 but never envisioned them as a book topic until Takie Sugiyama Lebra urged me to do so. I am grateful to her for that initial push. Many people were helpful in furnishing assistance, artifacts, feedback, or stimuli over the years I have intermittently worked on this project. I'm sure I have forgotten several people when I thank Ruth Beckman, Linda Chance, Tina Chen, Rebecca Copeland, Yuka Fukunaga, Diane Grams, Dawn Grimes-Maclellan, Joseph Hawkins, Laura Hein, Jeffry Hester, Hiroko Hirakawa, Yuko Hoshino, Shuhei Hosokawa, Masakazu Iino, Hiroko Kawazoe, Susan Lindquist, Gordon Mathews, Brian McVeigh, Yukihiro Nagaoka, Debra Occhi, Shigeko Okamoto, Lou Perez, David Plath, Linda Arlene Schwartz, Carolyn Stevens, Nobue Suzuki, Jeannine Takaki, Roger Thomas, Kazuko Watanabe, Wei Wei, and Paola Zamperini. For their insightful and constructive comments on early drafts of the manuscript, I am grateful to Paul Breidenbach, Scott Clark, Sharon Kinsella, Barbara LeMaster, James Roberson, and Chris Yano. Jan Bardsley and William Kelly in particular were terrifically generous and helpful in providing extensive advice and for urging me to shore up the arguments in the book. Deep thanks go to Reed Malcolm, Kalicia Pivirotto, Laura Harger, and Elizabeth Berg at the University of California Press for their patience and expertise.

Funding to support a chapter of the book came from the Northeast Asia Council (NEAC), Association for Asian Studies, Short-Term Research Travel to Japan. A one-semester teaching leave from Loyola University in 1999 allowed me to work on a chapter of the book. I did much of the fieldwork for the project while I was a visiting professor at Kanazawa Institute of Technology during the summer of 1997, and I thank Scott Clark for the introduction to that lovely city and school. I also thank Teruko Ohno and Kyomi Iwata of the National Women's Education Center in Saitama for their permission and assistance in using the center's library in 1999.

Versions of different chapters were presented at academic meetings since 1996, and I thank those audience members who gave me feedback, especially the participants in the Midwest Japan Seminar and the CosnumAsia Workshop on Asian Advertising and Media hosted by Lise Skov and Brian Moeran in Hong Kong in 1998. I thank those who gave permission to republish some sections of this book: parts of chapter 1 from *U.S.-Japan Women's Journal* and earlier versions of chapter 3 in *positions* and chapter 5 in *Men and Masculinities in Contemporary Japan*.

I would like to thank the following for kindly granting permission to use images: Pauline Strong, assistant registrar, Honolulu Academy of Art; Tomiya Masayuki, senior editor, *Men's Egg* Magazine; Kase Hirotada, Bunkasha Publishing, publisher of *Ranking Dai Suki!* magazine; Fukuda Toshiyuki, illustrator, and *Asahi Shimbun;* Hayashi Yasunari, editor of *Bidan* magazine; Inoue Masaharu, public relations officer for Slim Beauty House Corp.; Ishiyama Terumi and Shogakukan Publishing Company, publisher of *Can Cam* magazine; Tanaka Tomoya, manager of publications; Kinki Nippon Tourist Company; and Yasuhiko Suzuki, Sonoko Corporation. Every effort has been made to contact copyright holders for their permission to reprint images in the book. The author would be grateful to hear from any copyright holder who is not here acknowledged and will undertake to rectify any errors or omissions in proper credit in future editions of the book.

Most of all, I am especially indebted to my wonderful friends in Japan studies for their ongoing and enthusiastic encouragement. My partner, Roland Erwin, and our feline children, Lucy and Raquel, provided a warm haven that made research and writing possible.

# Introduction

*Approaches to Body Aesthetics and the Beauty System*

Sachiko glided the metal rollers, which were connected by cable to an electromassage unit, over the backs of my legs. The sensation was ticklish but not painful. She was a Japanese beauty worker at an aesthetic salon and wore a reassuring nurselike uniform. After several passes with the roller, she applied a thick jelly and massaged it into my skin. My legs were then wrapped in revolutions of latex. She set a timer and left me alone for ten minutes, and then returned to remove the plastic and the jelly. At the conclusion of this beauty treatment for "leg slimming," Sachiko looked at me with poorly disguised exasperation when I declined to purchase the aftercare products or to schedule the follow-up treatments that she assured me would turn my legs into thin, elegant "charm points." We parted with pleasant formulaic expressions, but I could tell that she was disgruntled by my refusals.

I had seen Japanese advertisements that featured skinny groomed women who proclaimed the efficacy of beauty treatments like this one. Descriptions of services with suggestive names—"Egyptian Slimming" or "Hip Up"—piqued my interest as something extraordinarily new in Japanese culture. I suspected that these treatments were no different from some questionable ones sold outside Japan (consider the guano-based Nightingale Facial offered at a spa in Santa Fe), but I still had questions. What do they actually do to you? What methods do Japanese beauty workers and promoters use to sell you services and products? Why are Japanese paying for them? I also began to wonder about the nature of the beauty industry in general. What new practices have become part of everyday beauty work? What parts of the body have become the objects of beautification? What is driving these efforts at surface change? Are there empowering effects of doing beauty work?

In this book I present the voices of Japanese advertisers and consumers, but I also use myself as the object of beauty services in order to understand them as cultural and consumption activities. Beauty culture and how it changes provide an excellent example of the way cultural values and attitudes shape and are discursively shaped by consumerism, and how rapidly and readily they become entrenched as "natural" and "good." At one time it was normal Japanese beauty practice to blacken the teeth to eliminate their ghoulish whiteness, a practice now thought strange. When I lived in Japan in the late 1970s and had multiple ear piercings, a typical response was "*yādā*," the Japanese equivalent of "ick"; by 2000, ear piercing and body piercing had become established as acceptable fashion among younger Japanese.

In writing this book, I aim to provide a preliminary portrait of the culture of body aesthetics and the beauty system during the mid-1990s to early 2000s by exploring its images, practices, products, and services. When scholars of Japan write about "business," they rarely think of beauty. Studies of service industries usually look at spheres such as banking, automotive, computer, telecommunications, and health. Yet there are more people working in the beauty industry and more businesses that deliver beauty than there are software, auto repair, and wedding and funeral services. The point is easy to grasp if we compare actual numbers of some seemingly ubiquitous businesses with beauty industries. According to government statistics, the industry category "beauty parlors" included 173,412 establishments. By contrast, that same year there were 7,530 wedding and funeral services, 67,789 auto repair shops, and 14,136 software businesses (*Asahi Shimbun* 2003: 173). Sachiko's aesthetic salon workplace is such an enormous and growing business that the Ministry of Economy, Trade, and Industry is in the process of creating a separate industry classification for it (Ministry of Public Management, Home Affairs, Posts, and Telecommunications 2002). The cosmetics market in Japan, of which men's cosmetics account for about 10 percent, is the second largest in the world after the United States. It is estimated that sales of perfume, hair-care products, skin-care products, and makeup accounted for around $15 billion in 2002 (Japan External Trade Organization 2003).

What makes the beauty industry worth exploring is not simply its staggering profit but its position at the center of many contemporary concerns, particularly ideas about gendered identity and its relationship to new forms of consumer capitalism. Aspects of the beauty industry point to recent changes in social altitudes and thinking, and provide an ideal locus for looking at a number of overlapping themes. As I examine topics such as breast enhancement, men's beauty work, and the aesthetic salon, I consider whether certain conceptions should be viewed as native, foreign-inspired, syncretic, or part of a shared transnational beauty system. I also note that beauty practices are presented in often contradictory ways, as cutting-edge technology and as ancient wisdom. A third argument relates to claims about the relationship between self-esteem and appearance, and whether the pursuit of beauty is a form of empowerment or enslavement to media-delivered normalization. A fourth idea found in the book has to do with cultural models of self-improvement and beauty work as an acceptable way to display admired effort and discipline.

## Conceptualizing Contemporary Beauty

A study of the Japanese beauty industry presents a good case for evaluating theories of globalization. In interpreting recent changes in beauty ideals, many critics see in these developments a straightforward process of Western domination. When I show my students photos of J-Pop stars with dyed hair and colored contact lenses, they automatically ask, "Why do they want to look like Americans?" One scholar wrote that "the Japanese woman paying for the face job has had a race change. . . . She has altered her appearance until she appears to be white" (Halberstam 1999: 131). In this book I hope to provide a critique of this trope of emulation. The eagerness to see everything as a Western import obscures the historicity of particular practices and suggests an ethnocentric stance.

More than twenty years ago, an influential article in the *Harvard Business Review* stated that the age of globalization would eradicate all vestiges of indigenous cultural tastes and replace them with homogenized products and services. Characterizing local consumer preferences as befuddled and idiosyncratic, the author had this advice for global corporations: "Instead of adapting to superficial and even entrenched differences within and between nations, it will seek sensibly to force suitably standardized products and practices on the entire globe" (Levitt 1983: 102). Scholars have effectively countered the idea that cultural diversity will be completely submerged by globalization in their ethnographic accounts of what actually happens to rationalized products and services at the point of consumption. There are modifications to business practices and offerings, as in McDonald's in East Asia (Watson 1997), and local responses to transnationally circulated images, as in bridal photography in Taiwan, which is "full of Taiwanese agency" (Adrian 2003:12). Condry (2000) shows how American hip-hop is mediated in Japan thorough local sites and language. These and other studies illuminate the manner in which borrowed elements are given new meanings, uses, and values when they arrive at a new cultural setting (Howes 1996), highlighting the agency and innovation enabled by consumption activities (D. Miller 1995). A new focus on breasts as an aspect of female beauty, which I believe is linked to American beauty imaging, nevertheless did not result in massive numbers of women going to surgeons for implants. Instead they seek noninvasive alternatives, including prayer at a Shinto shrine. The ways in which beauty is formulated in Japan are complex, and there are at least four dimensions that take us beyond simplistic notions of uninvited homogeneity and avid imitation.

One point to keep in mind is that some contemporary beauty practices reflect indigenous ideas. Pale skin was valued during the premodern period among male and female nobility, but over time the white face became a marker of ideal womanhood for middle-class women (Ashikari 2003). Contemporary Japanese consumption of skin-lightening products is linked to ideas with their own local history, so to claim that a desire for pale skin is merely a new form of postwar deracialization brought about by hegemonic Euroamerican beauty ideology is a failed analysis based on a belief that the West is always in an ascendant position. Within the Japanese beauty industry, many products and services, including knowledge about skin care, are described as superior to foreign ones by virtue of their presumed status as natively Japanese.

A process of cultural blending has been going on for more than a century, as Japanese have engaged in creative syncretism within mass culture forms since the 1800s. During the prewar period, people of all classes were actively struggling over the meanings, symbols, and images they encountered through consumption of new mass-produced goods, which even then were not synonymous with global homogenization. During the 1920s Japanese scholars began the study of "modernology" and were producing analyses that worked against a simple dichotomy between West and East (Silverberg 1992). This process continues today, as many forms of beauty meld East Asian and foreign (most often Euroamerican) ideas. Tobin (1992) uses the idea of "domestication" for this phenomenon, but I think the concept of creolization formulated by Hannerz (1987) also provides a framework for discussion of this dimension. Creolization (I also use the terms *syncretic* and *syncretization* in this book) is a process of cultural interpenetration, an intermingling of two or more discrete traditions or cultures to form a unique outcome. One example is an aesthetic salon treatment called the Royal Hawai'ian Facial, which includes face exfoliation using a small electrical unit that looks something like a mini-sander, a beautifying device I doubt was a traditional part of Hawai'ian massage.

In addition, it is not only that "outside" ideas are combined to create new creolized forms. Together with creolization is co-occurrence of the Japan-created Other and a reinvented notion of the traditional in unblended coexistence. Goldstein-Gidoni (2001) presents a refined thinking about the processes in which the foreign and the local interact through examination of patterns and changes in the modern Japanese wedding ceremony. What she describes is neither cultural homogenization nor creolization, but rather a complex domain where imaginary or contrived Western and Japanese constructions commingle. The artificial wedding cake and fake chapel are Japanese abstractions of Western ritual, and the traditional Shinto wedding is not rooted in legend but is a Meiji-era (1868–1912) invention. Similarly, "French" or "South Asian" beauty industry goods and services often do not "arrive" in Japan but are created there. Thus we find an aesthetic salon treatment based on Western astrological signs and Shiseido's faux-French Clé de Peau Beauté series of skincare products. Aesthetic salons are always busy inventing putatively indigenous beauty treatments, such as the Ama Massage, named after Japanese women shellfish divers. Despite its venerable Taoist name, the Yin Yang Five Elements treatment originated in the minds of the marketing staff at an aesthetic salon, not in the ancient Chinese past.

Although some aspects of Japan's beauty culture are unique, many beauty concerns are no different from the defects women all over the world are taught through global advertising and imagery to hide or correct. Thus the Japanese beauty industry participates in an arena of transnational body aesthetics and practices. Appadurai (1996) sees this as a process of "deterritorialization" that impacts local experience. Cultural encounters are not unidirectional, nor do they have predictable outcomes. He brings to our attention the existence of multiple centers and peripheries and the hybrid products that circulate internationally through the media. I think Appadurai's idea of transnational "flows" and "scapes" is one way to understand what happens to concepts and images as they move around in the world of beauty, but there is more to it than his idea of sameness versus difference. For example, seaweed is a common staple in Japanese cuisine, but it was not a normal ingredient in Japanese cosmetics prior to 2000.

Yet some salons began offering sea algae mud packs for the body in the mid-1990s, modeled after Euroamerican "seaweed" spa treatments. (Interestingly, these are usually referred to in Japan as *arugo,* the loanword for algae, rather than with a native Japanese term.) Euroamerican advertising touted seaweed as an exotic and natural Asian beauty skin agent, and by 2004 a Japanese company began to make and sell skin-care products with seaweed as an important ingredient, using a discourse of seaweed as a traditional Asian remedy.

This leads to another theme of the book: tracking how the beauty industry draws on idioms of ancient knowledge and naturalness, as well as modern technological rationality. Aesthetic engineers like Sachiko, who deliver beauty expertise, are fashioning it in novel ways, often as scientifically based skills and techniques. The electromassage unit used in the slimming treatment described above is just one of numerous machines routinely used in the aesthetic salon. At the same time, many aspects of beauty culture rely on a discourse of the natural or traditional, such as the Yin Yang Five Elements treatment. Yet these categories and the interplay between them do not necessarily correlate with notions of an ancient East versus a rational West. It is often Japan that is said to possess the latest scientific answer, and the West that provides the ancient beauty knowledge. Thus sometimes facial treatments are presented as a resurrection of Renaissance uses of special Italian mud, while eyelid glues are based on Japanese advances in medical science.

A third theme found throughout this book is the tension between the location of beauty in a restricting gendered system and its possibility as a form of human agency. Feminism has a long history of writing about the politics of the body, beginning in 1792 with Mary Wollstonecraft, who described the production of the docile body of the upper-class woman (Poston 1988). Women's Studies literature on femininity and beauty in particular has always been sensitive to the systematic grip of cultural norms on the body. Bordo (1993) traces the development of feminist thinking about the body, noting that initially writers were responding to the widely accepted folk model of women as "naturally" concerned with superficial matters like appearance. It was commonly believed that women were willing to suffer in order to be fashionable and so were responsible for their subordination to beauty norms. Feminists criticized this model for ignoring how a patriarchal culture of male desire has a role in the sexualization and commodification of female bodies. However, this critique often relied on an oppressor/oppressed model that positioned women as densely unaware of the beauty system and powerless to resist its privileging of male desire. As Bordo (1999: 250) said, "Women are not 'cultural dopes'; usually they are all too conscious of the system of values and rewards that they are responding to and perpetrating." Later writers wanted to acknowledge how collusion works and to recognize that men too are enmeshed in a cultural system not of their own making. Older feminist writing was criticized for not considering the subversive potential of beauty work. Some feminists appropriated Foucault's (1978) notion of impersonal power and the idea that forms of selfhood are maintained not through coercion but through surveillance. Of course, the influential sociologist C. Wright Mills (1959: 40) said something similar years earlier, when he stated that one form of power is to manage and manipulate consent without the awareness of the obedient.

I see evidence of youth, subcultural, and gender resistance in some aspects of Japan's changing beauty ideology. Young men and women use new beauty technologies to make their bodies look different from those of their parents. At the same time, I wonder how the contribution of new beauty technologies to individual self-image and self-confidence balances out against the pressures to conform to mass-mediated models of appearance. Perhaps new forms of beauty work merely create new forms of gender oppression—"cheerful robots" (Mills 1959: 171). Are Japan's changes in beauty ideals only a strategy to feed consumerism? In 1954, American members of the Socialist Workers Party debated the relationship between women's use of cosmetics and female oppression (Hansen and Reed 1986). One side viewed cosmetics as undermining women's economic power and heightening their experience as objects of patriarchal desire. The other side saw beauty work as both an economic necessity and an expression of aesthetic urges and individuality. Sixty years later, scholars are still debating whether beauty work represents individual agency (Davis 1995) or positions women as dupes of capitalist hustlers (Bordo 1993, 1997). Paraphrasing others (Friedan 1982; Kilbourne 1999; Wolf 1992), is the function of beauty portrayals in the media and in other cultural productions simply to get women to buy more things to reproduce these images in themselves? Some critics of this idea point out that everywhere from ancient times, women have spent time and effort on beauty work (ignoring the fact that men have as well).

There have always been writings specifying what beautifully gendered bodies should look like, but never the type or quantity of visual forms we see today. A major difference from the past is that the ideals for culturally sanctioned beauty attributes are on display in new and unavoidable forms of media everywhere, with precise details of what the consumer should strive for. To be sure, because of a thriving print media culture, women during the Edo era (1600–1868) were also exposed to popular prints of demimonde beauties who were considered models of fashion. But these images were not found in nearly every space that greets the eye, as they are today. Wolf (1992: 14) wrote that "before the Industrial Revolution, the average woman could not have had the same feelings about 'beauty' that modern women do who experience the myth as continual comparison to a mass-disseminated physical ideal." For example, the Japanese cosmetics firm Shiseido began contributing to the construction of femininity before the Pacific War through publication of the magazine *Hanatsubaki,* which included details on hair, fashion, and makeup needed to create desirable gendered looks. This constant bombardment with normalizing images, which Bordo (1997: 37) calls a "pedagogy of defect," keeps consumers engaged in eternal work to "correct" the flaws the media have revealed to them. In this sense, beauty is an attribute of the social system and not simply an individual enterprise. A consequence of media beauty vigilance is that there is virtually no woman who doesn't already know her skin type and perhaps even the ideal temperature of water for washing her face.

Beauty efforts benefit the status quo because they forestall other forms of agency, including social protest over class and gender inequality. However, the two primary notions in feminist theorization of the body—the focus on aspects of self-determination and choice and the view of beauty practices as forms of containment and control—are not necessarily contradictory. An individual may perceive her particular beauty work as self-defining and empowering, even though her choices are limited and molded by her culture. Bordo (1985), for example, described anorexia nervosa as grounded in feminine practices that train the female body in obedience to cultural demands, although it is a disorder that is experienced in terms of individual control.

Another difference in the pursuit of beauty past and present is the amount of money and time spent on beauty work that targets more extensive parts of the body. It was only in the late 1800s that Japan and the United States began to manufacture cosmetics for mass consumption. Prior to that, women in both countries relied on what Peiss (1998: 7) termed "kitchen physics." In the late Meiji, only a few mass-produced goods, such as Kaō Soap, Shiseido cosmetics, and Lion Dentifrice, became brand names and could command a higher price than bulk generic goods. A few decades ago, a Japanese woman could use a facial cleanser made with powdered azuki beans from the kitchen, exfoliate her face with a homemade pouch of rice bran (called *nukabukuro*), and moisturize using a do-it-yourself lotion of cucumber and gourd juice. Now there are thousands of brands to replace homemade physics. Instead of cucumber lotion, women are urged to buy a jar of Creme Ex Cello Chanter for $400 or Kose's Cosme Decorte AQ Cream Meliority face cream, made with carrots, Siberian ginseng, and soybean extract, which costs $761 for 45 grams (Iigarashi 2002).[1] Conformity to current beauty ideals requires more extensive body modifications, and the areas of the body targeted for beauty work have expanded dramatically. These days, women are sold products that are far more specialized, for many more types of body "problems." Every inch, down to the fingernail, is plucked and pumiced, and failure to engage in new beauty practices would, according to advertising rhetoric, result in a woman being judged decidedly frumpish. In the struggle against natural and unworked flesh, the entire geography of the body, including the pigmentation of the nipples, comes under the control of new beauty regimens.

Such detailed and extensive focus on the body creates new anxieties among women, which are in turn reflected in countless polls. Depending on how the question is asked and what micromarket is targeted, the key body worries are always connected to fatness, hairiness, breast size, and facial attributes. A 1997 survey of body worries revealed that hairiness was the top concern for respondents (*Sankei Shimbun* 1997). In another mini-poll, younger women who were asked about beauty "repair" work they do listed the entire face, management of body hair, head hair, skin, underarm hair, legs, and eyebrows as the areas of the body most frequently targeted for attention (*Ranking Dai Suki!* 1999a). However, in a different survey, when asked, "If you could correct one place on your body, where and what would you do?" respondents listed, in order, a "bigger bust," "longer and thinner legs," and a "thinner face" (*Fine Surf & Street Magazine* 1999a). In a poll of women's body worries by region, the top two concerns were clear skin and a thin face (Mizuki 1991: 118–19). The bare leg fad *(nama ashi būmu)* of the late 1990s spawned a consumer demand for bronzing gels, self-tanning lotions, and leg foundation makeup to cover imperfections. One can buy Miss Walk Leg Firming Gel, Foot Cool Slimming Lotion, Leg-o-Slim leg cream and binding tights set, Aesthetic Shoes intended to make the legs look straight, and Bodii Sera (body cellophane), a type of wrap used to straighten and slim the legs. These products illustrate how body anxieties are directed at specific parts of the body and how these body locations become the object of increasingly specialized products and technologies.

A fourth theme in the chapters to follow relates to the folk model of beauty work as a form of socially sanctioned self-improvement. Normativities that govern the body are brought about by rigorous self-monitoring and training. One reason the beauty industry has been so successful, despite some of its fraudulent excesses, is that it fits well with long-standing Japanese ideas about self-development and discipline. Scholars often note that there has never been a radical philosophical separation in Japan between body and mind (Kasulis 1993). This unity of the corporeal and spiritual is illustrated in the concept of *kata*. *Kata* are standardized postures and movements that accompany spiritual or aesthetic activities, such as martial arts, the tea ceremony, and the execution of calligraphy. *Kata* are also important in Japanese social contexts; bowing may be considered one type of interactional *kata*. If one can say there are *kata* for female comportment, they would entail consciously controlled movements of limb and torso, a stiff and confined posture and body orientation. For instance, whenever hands are used in gestures, the fingers should be held together and pointed straight, with unthreatening thumbs tucked behind. Just as *kata* in the traditional arts make it possible to study precise, rational, exact movement, women may study "beauty *kata*" through consumption of routines and practices described in minute detail in beauty manuals and fashion magazines. One article in an aesthetic salon's in-house publication speaks about beauty as a matter not only of the body, but as "mental aesthetics" *(mentaru esute)*, a "spiritual matter" *(seishin-teki na mono)* that contributes to self-development (Baba 1997: 18).

The culturally salient notion of *gambaru* (effort) as the drive needed for continuing self-development is ubiquitous in daily life. The lexicon of self-help and mighty exertion usually reserved for moral development has been adopted by the beauty industry, where women (and men) are urged to work hard at aesthetic progress. The beauty industry also represents body maintenance as a form of good social manners. Beauty is therefore extended outside the private domain into the sphere of public life. In a similar vein, for women of reproductive age in the United States, pregnancy has become a public health issue with laws that prosecute drug-addicted women for fetal abuse (Terry 1989). While there are no laws about being unlovely in Japan, public surveillance of appearance is no less intense, eroding the distinction between pursuit of beauty as a private or public matter. Beauty has become as aspect of social responsibility and etiquette.

## Beauty in Modernity

It is said that modernity marks a change from birth-determined identity to self-fashioned identity (Giddens 1991). Many contemporary scholars locate the roots of Japan's early modern past in the latter part of the Edo period. It was during the Meiji period, however, that the modernization project was wholeheartedly embraced. The Meiji state's endorsement of social position based on merit rather than birth meant the elimination of sumptuary regulations that had proscribed clothing and appearance, and many people began to adopt accoutrements such as pocket watches, Western-style umbrellas, gloves, and French boots. Urban men who ostentatiously displayed the new fashions and affectations became an object of satire in works such as Kanagaki Robun's *Aguranabe* (Cross-legged at the beef pot). His vignettes of social strata at a beef restaurant included the character of the "Westernist," a new type who is impossible to place in a class, occupational, or regional slot because of his adoption of Western clothing and mannerisms (Mertz 1996). The Meiji shift to an ideology of the self-made man resulted in increased concern with surface manners and appearance (Kinmouth 1981). Even so, men and women were ultimately judged on their characters and social achievements. It is in late modernity that the role of appearance has taken on critical meanings, and thus we find the movement of subjectivity more frequently deflected from placement in a social matrix and onto the surface of the body.

According to Giddens (1991: 187–201), modernity allows new expressions of the self, but these are molded under conditions strongly influenced by the standardizing effects of commodity capitalism. In the logic of capitalism, everything may be transformed into a product or consumer good with value, including beauty. In consumer societies our relationship to consumption rests on the ability to incite desire, and increased attention to appearance becomes constitutive of self-identity. The closer the body comes to resembling prevailing prototypes, the higher its "exchange value" (Featherstone 1991: 177). Changes are made to the body in order to bring it into line with prevailing models of gender, class, and age (Balsamo 1996; Bordo 1993; Featherstone 1991; Shilling 1993). This constant effort is a way of thinking about the body as a "project" that requires attention and work (Featherstone 1991). Such body transformation-work subsequently takes on other symbolic meanings, and consumption operates as a means of differentiation and self-definition. The self-management and discipline required to achieve an appropriate body indicate good character and self-control. Sculpted bodies symbolize perseverance or determination, while an untamed body means that the person lacks control, is slovenly, weak, and inadequate. Although a shift to the body and appearance as constituting the self is a common social formation in capitalist societies in late modernity, the particular forms it takes are local. By looking at Japanese body aesthetics, we further our understanding of identity construction in late modernity by addressing shortcomings in this literature, which currently focuses on this process in Euroamerican societies.

## Beauty as a Focus of Research

When I mentioned my interest in the Japanese beauty industry to an older male Japanese academic, he said, "What a waste." Why was I not using my knowledge of Japanese language and culture to research something important, he asked, like "real" business or the economy? However, an industry that involves billions of dollars and trillions of hours, and in some cases drastic revision of appearance, is anything but trivial. His view reflects a deeply held sexist bias that beautification activities are unworthy of serious research precisely because they primarily concern women. Beauty industries are commonly viewed as "seemingly frivolous, superficial, and female" (Peis 2001: 7). I recall the classic feminist article "If Men Could Menstruate: A Political Fantasy" (Steinem 1983), in which Steinem highlighted the point that the characteristics and traits of the powerless are always negated, ignored, or ridiculed. Beauty as an object of research is sneered at because it is primarily a concern of women (although, as I show in chapter 5, it is also a male concern), yet it has enormous economic and cultural weight.

Scholars are increasingly called on to display an awareness of their own role and position in their research projects, a form of introspection known as reflexivity. I have been asked how, not being Japanese or of Japanese ancestry, I could dare to discuss such a personal topic as Japanese beauty and body aesthetics. I am particularly vulnerable to criticisms that, as an outsider with some presumed status vis-à-vis the Japanese, I am unavoidably implicated in an existing power relation in which Westerners have hegemonic dominance. Robertson (2002) discusses this problem of identity politics in academe, and relates her frustration with reviewers of her book who asked that she position herself as a specific category of person, with unequal power between her and her research subjects. Although Robertson brings to our attention the problem of this sort of "self-stereotyping," I will at least note that my status as an American woman did not confer any sort of privilege while doing this research.[2] For one thing, I did not conform to stereotypes about what an American woman ought to look like. I am shorter than almost every Japanese woman under forty I met, and have the stocky peasant body and frizzy hair of my Californio ancestors.[3] My middle-aged hybrid body was never a target of comparison as an imagined "American" body.

When I told friends and colleagues about the topic of my research, I invariably received snide comments about how "difficult" it must have been getting "pampered" for the sake of research. The reality is that I was terribly uncomfortable having my body become the object of scrutiny and labor. I sensed in the salon workers an almost palpable disappointment that I did not have the blond hair, long legs, and enormous breasts of their imagined foreigner. I was also not accustomed to having someone else perform beauty work of any sort on me (as an unreformed hippie, I have been to a hair salon only once in my life). Because of my age, prior to my encounters with beauty practitioners I had expected to be exempt from exhortations to conform to beauty standards, yet this did not prove to be the case. The intense evaluation of my physical shortcomings and the humiliating documentation of my flaws, diagrammed and measured by disapproving strangers, no doubt influenced my portrait of the beauty industry.

As I worked on this project, I sometimes gave invited talks on its content at universities all over the United States. I learned from this experience that adding some information about non-Japanese beauty practices was essential. Non-Japanese audiences consistently "forget" about the cultural nature of their own beauty constructions. For example, an American company named Koremlu sold a depilatory made with rat poison during the 1930s (Gavenas 2002), and in the 1980s American men concerned about baldness had carpet fibers implanted on their heads (Hurley 2004). In the United States, radiation from an X-ray machine was commonly used for facial hair removal until around 1940. Women were urged to submit their chins and upper lips to its harmful rays every two weeks. In the year 2002 alone, nearly a quarter of a million American women had foreign material surgically inserted into their breasts (American Society for Aesthetic Plastic Surgery 2004). When I write about Japanese beauty practices, I want readers to keep non-Japanese examples like these in mind. I believe that including reminders of the cultural construction of beauty and gender in other places will help readers *denaturalize* it. American breast implants and Botox injections are no less exotic than Kayapo nose plugs or Japanese nipple bleaching. My hope is that in recognizing the often strange things they do to their own bodies, readers will have empathy for the Japanese women and men who are the consumers and targets of the beauty industries and beauty work I describe.

It may seem odd that someone who spent her graduate student years and the majority of her professional life studying inbreathed fricatives, diminutive suffixation, and other aspects of linguistic anthropology is now writing about breast enhancement, facials, and cupping treatments. My interest in the topic came about quite by accident. Until 1994, I had only occasionally glanced at Japanese women's magazines, and when I did, I saw glossy images of young, crisp, cute, impeccably groomed debutantes. The young models in their twenties looked naive and sometimes babyish, with round faces and flat-chested frames. I later inherited a huge stack of women's magazines from a graduate student's project and decided to spend part of a summer plowing through them in search of interesting neologisms and other linguistic examples. I was initially concerned solely with language but was increasingly perturbed by the visual images I saw. Since when, I wondered, did Japanese women fret over heel texture and feces odor? And the new models no longer looked all that innocent. I know that what we see in magazines is not often a reflection of what exists in the real world, but the amount and scope of print media devoted to body appearance indicated that something significant and new was going on in Japanese culture. New types of youth fashion that incorporated radically revised body styles were also apparent in other forms of popular culture. Thus I began to peer into the world of *esute,* or body aesthetics.[4] During the 1980s the concept of "aesthetics" or *esthétique* (in French) was borrowed from Europe and used to create a four-hundred-trillion-yen beauty industry that came to be known simply as esute.

Mabel Bacon wrote more than one hundred years ago, "It seems necessary for a new author to give some excuse for her boldness in offering to the public another volume upon a subject already so well written up as Japan" (1891: vii). Since her time, there has been a rich and detailed scholarship on Japanese society from scholars in numerous disciplines. Even so, up until the mid-1990s the paramount model of a "typical" Japanese, which carried intense ideological force in both scholarship and Japanese media representation, was the white-collar salaryman (see Kelly 1986; Roberson and Suzuki 2003; and L. Miller 1998a, 1995 for critiques of this view). Although Sugimoto (1997) debunks the idea of the male white-collar worker as the norm, it remains a potent symbol of Japanese national identity outside Japan. This model of typicality was grounded in the intense economic competition with the United States during the 1970s and

1980s. The male corporate worker stood for Mr. Everyman, and the main body of scholarship centered on the media men read, the places they frequented, and their work and sex lives. More recently we find books and documentary films devoted to the subject of Japanese women, their life trajectories over time (Rosenberger 2000), their internationalism (Kelsky 2001), their college education (McVeigh 1997), and their experience with menopause (Lock 1993).[5] These authors bring a fresh understanding to our portrait of contemporary Japanese life. As anthropologists, they firmly ground their studies in the fieldwork method. I hope someday a woman with more youth and fortitude than me will write an ethnography of the Japanese aesthetic salon industry along the lines of Goldstein-Gidoni's (1997) detailed and engaging analysis of the creation of the Japanese bride, or Spielvogel's (2003) study of Japanese fitness clubs.

In order to get a sense of how beauty is produced, I did fieldwork in the summer of 1997 in the city of Kanazawa and in Tokyo in the summer of 1999, where, among other things, I visited aesthetic salons, *kanpō* apothecaries, drugstores, and makeup showrooms. To see how beauty is promoted, I read magazines, brochures, flyers, and other print media published between 1994 and 2004 (up-to-date Japanese beauty guides and fashion magazines are easily obtainable in Japanese bookstores near my home in Chicago; Miller 2003c). In place of a traditional ethnographic study I offer a collection of essays in which I take a cultural studies approach. I am not a "social science voyeur" who stands apart from what is observed or described, and therefore I do not view industrial figures as the most interesting or important data. While traditional social science that relies on positivist empirical support is certainly important, I am also persuaded by the multidimensional nature of cultural studies, which is more accepting of interpretations and readings of data that allow provocative critiques. Within cultural studies, there is broad acceptance of diverse practices of knowledge and multiple methodologies. This book deliberately melds observation, interviews, historical background, and textual/linguistic interpretation of media images and products as legitimate support for my ideas. Similar to other cultural studies scholars, I am suspicious of unidimensional theories and accept multiple explanations, meanings, and interpretations.

For models of how to approach the topic of beauty imaging and consumption, I have found feminist writing to be useful. Bordo (1997, 1999) forwards my understanding of beauty's meanings in discussion of how the body comes under social control. Foucault (1978) and others make the mistake of using men and the male body as the unmarked or "normal" category of analysis and omit gender as an aspect of the power configurations they analyze (Diamond and Quinby 1988). In contrast, Brumberg (1997), Douglas (1994), and Bordo (1993, 1997) speak to issues of beauty and the gendered body with insight and humor and without theoretical prescriptivism, and I have found inspiration and stimulation in their work.

## Chapter Outline

If millions of Japanese now think it is important to spend hours of time and massive amounts of money on beauty treatments, we should attend to why beauty work is an integral part of cultural practice. These days Japanese women and men are rewarded for looking a certain way and are penalized when they ignore the pressure of beauty ideals. The images, products, and services I examine do not appear sui generis; each has its own cultural history and trajectory. One way to begin exploring these issues is to review some changes in beauty values, as I do in chapter 1, "Changing Beauty Ideology."

Chapter 2, "Aesthetic Salons," examines one of the primary venues women (and increasingly men) visit for the purposes of body transformation. Drawing on participant observation, interviews with salon aestheticians, and a reading of promotional literature, the chapter discusses how the salon differs from the beauty parlor or spa, the model of beauty it offers for emulation, and those aspects of the body that are targeted for fixing. The aesthetic salon industry, while participating in a global market of goods, services, and images, also reflects and creates domestic concepts of body and beauty. Aesthetic salons are a site where abuses of the consumer seem to be especially problematic. This is followed by a discussion of changes in breast fashions and symbolism in chapter 3, "Mammary Mania." A new focus on the breast as an aspect of female beauty is reflected in a lucrative industry for bust products and services. I trace some of the relationships between breast fashions, a trend toward the surface expression of identity, and the spread of a global Euroamerican beauty ideology. Together with slimness, smooth, hairless skin is a requirement for acceptable beauty, and chapter 4, "Body Fashion and Beauty Etiquette," surveys body hair worries and repulsions, including hair removal industries. Many new beauty practices among young Japanese men and women are not obvious or exterior, but are hidden from the public gaze. Chapter 5, "Male Beauty Work," surveys some contemporary body modification practices, consumer products, and media engaged in creating male physical identities. While previous generations of heterosexual Japanese men were evaluated primarily on the basis of character, social standing, earning capacity, lineage, and other social criteria, young men are increasingly concerned with their status as objects of aesthetic appraisal. In some cases, men's esute resembles similar phenomena for women, while elsewhere it is targeted specifically to males. These new types of men's beauty work may be linked to a variety of social issues, including sexual selection resulting from social and demographic transformations. In chapter 6, "The Well-Behaved Appetite," I examine a few of the weight-loss items currently flooding the shelves of drugstores. I see much of the dieting effort as a socially sanctioned activity tied to social relations and not simply an individual's autonomous behavior.

Advertising in Japan has often been treated as a uniform enterprise that is said to exhibit unique tendencies. Analysts generally suggest that it is more impressionistic or atmospheric than elsewhere, has less content, or does not use a "hard-sell" approach. Chapter 7, "The Language of Esute," looks at the variation, creativity, and strategies used for persuasion in advertising related to goods or services for body and beauty work. The chapter examines how contemporary use of English in such Japanese media is a deliberately orchestrated innovation valued as a linguistic commodity. The advertisements show that the use of English is not a simple process of imitation and borrowing but rather an imaginative exploitation of an already fully domesticated linguistic resource. In chapter 8, "Esute Power," I discuss some of the spinoff industries and ideas generated by the concept of esute, including esute tourism and esute in sex-for-sale services. The chapter links new body practices that involve radical body transformation to a new attitude among young people about the malleability of the body. These new body practices reflect the idea that it is possible to transform the self.

Japanese media and the beauty industry together have created a thriving beauty culture, and they supply the motivations and justifications for it as necessary. They have redefined beauty as obtainable through scientific management and hard work, and they supply consumers with exact models and recipes for creating the particular type of appearance they desire. In the following chapters, I look at foci for beauty work, some of their historical underpinnings, and how they fit into the way contemporary gender is socially constructed. Women and men are increasingly pulled into consumption of beauty products and services in order to refashion all aspects of their bodies as a means of obtaining confidence. I have tried hard to find flickers of empowerment in the beauty economies I have investigated, and to some extent I do find areas of resistance to mainstream culture. But for the most part, the modern conception of beauty is seen through the idioms of advertising and media, which are motivated only by greed and profit. The body has become a focus for capitalist expansion, and contemporary Japanese are urged to seek new bodies around which to frame their personalities. The conditions for new forms of beauty culture I have found have been created partly from egalitarian access to global culture, but the outcome has been that women, and to a lesser extent young men, are no longer judged primarily on their character but on their appearance as well. In earlier decades, clothes and hairstyles were sufficient to announce one's modernity, but today it is breasts, penises, faces, and other parts of the body around which calculations about gender and class are made.

# CHAPTER I

# Changing Beauty Ideology

An advertisement for something called Super Bust Rich in the January 1994 issue of the women's magazine *Can Cam* caught my attention. The ad for the tablets, priced at $150, promised, "For the person who worries about their bust, big news!" A Japanese model wearing a flowered pink bikini was accompanied by testimony from a twenty-two-year-old consumer: "My breasts were small, so during high school I had a complex. But this spring I had confidence and was able to get a cool boyfriend." Here was a product for something that I had always thought was not a "body problem" for Japanese women.

There are societies that do not value women chiefly on the basis of their appearance, I was once fond of telling my students. Just look at Japan, where women are primarily judged by their cheerful personalities, lineage, and good manners, not by their eye shape or bra size. Based on knowledge of others' scholarship as well as my own experience living and working in Japan in the late 1970s and early 1980s, I felt confident about making such an assertion. I insisted that Japan was free of wretched implant foolishness and widespread anorexia. In her reflections on growing up in Japan, Mori noted the difference between American women's obsession with their bodies and Japanese women's relative lack of concern: "I care about my health, but I don't dwell on the shapes and sizes of various parts of my body, the way many American women seem to. My attitude toward the body is more pragmatic, I realized, because I grew up in Japan" (1999: 109–10). Mori's words supported what I once thought was true about Japanese body attitudes, but media images from the mid-1990s did not mesh with this idea at all. I wanted to make sense of the apparent shift away from an emphasis on women as social actors, as wives, mothers, and daughters, toward sexualized female bodies and beautified body surfaces. The Super Bust Rich ad suggested that one's breast size did have an impact on the ability to get a boyfriend and, more importantly, to gain confidence.

In this chapter, I survey changes in beauty and body styles and suggest how they might be symbolic of shifting values and attitudes. I do not think that products and services for crafted beauty are only marketing outcomes. Super Bust Rich and other new products are part of a beauty system that is tightly connected to developments in the coding and definition of gender. While older styles denoted a woman's degree of commitment to modernity or tradition, such as the prewar "radio roll" *(rajio-maki)* hairstyle, recent styles more readily express a displacement of identity onto the body surface. In addition, it will be clear that there is not only one form of femininity reproduction. Changes in postwar Japanese society have allowed the creation of multiple styles that may be used to define generational, class, regional, or subcultural identities. (I use the term *subcultural* to mean a segment of the population with its own values, expectations, and lifestyle preferences.) Some contemporary concepts of female beauty have deep and enduring roots, while others are radically divergent from past ideals. Finally, the circulation of global beauty imaging results in adoption of various mixed forms that may draw inspiration from diverse cultures or historical eras. Everything about the body and fashion is subject to mash up and recontextualization. Although this type of hybrid beauty reflects domestically creolized innovation, critics often wrongly interpret it as an attempt to mimic Euroamerican appearance.

## Beauty Transformations

Over a century ago, Darwin (1859) observed that people in different parts of the world define human physical beauty according to local criteria. There is wide variation in traits considered to be aesthetically meaningful, often tied to a group's economic or political ideology (Shilling 1993; Ortner and Whitehead 1981). One theory proposed to explain the diversity in beauty perception is that a social group most values the predominant features that it is exposed to, the so-called imprinting theory of sexual attraction (Diamond 1992). Western media often report that, based on studies by psychologists (often based on survey response from their undergraduate students), some concepts of beauty, such as a female "hourglass" shape, are imprinted biologically. Yet cross-cultural research on concepts of beauty, mainly limited to heterosexual females, has uncovered no universal standards for beauty other than cleanliness and clear, unblemished skin. Even within one social group, standards of beauty vary over time, even between two generations.

Some of the most interesting changes in Japan's beauty ideology date from the Heian era (794–1185). Our knowledge of aristocratic standards of beauty derives from literary descriptions in diaries and novels, and visual representations in paintings. A court lady ideally had a pale, round, plump face with elongated eyes. The eyebrows were plucked and repainted somewhat above their original positions. Gleaming white teeth were thought to be horribly ghoul-like, so they were darkened. Positive assessment of chubbiness was also common, as in descriptors like "well-rounded and plump" *(tsubutsubu to fuetaru)* and "plump person" *(fukuraku naru hito)* (Morris 1964: 202). Perhaps most importantly, a woman's hair should be long, straight, and lustrous, reaching at least to the ground.

We know much about the beauty norms of the Edo period (1603–1867), as documented in "portraits of beautiful women" *(bijin-ga)*. These usually depict courtesans with long, thin faces, fair skin, small lips, blackened teeth, thickset necks, and rounded shoulders (Hamanaka and Newland 2000; Hickey 1998).[1] Later artistic representations of beauties often showed petite women with round faces, straight eyes with flat eyelids, and small receding chins. In 1908, young women competed in Japan's first official beauty contest, an event sponsored by the *Chicago Tribune*'s world beauty hunt and accomplished via photographic submission. A panel of thirty artists and intellectuals appraised the photos of two hundred Japanese contestants and selected the winning photo of a sixteen-year-old woman named Suehiro Hiroko, which was subsequently published in the *Chicago Tribune* (*Nishi Nihon Shimbun* 1995). Miss Suehiro had a round, pale face, a small mouth, and narrow eyes. Some Japanese scholars cite these facial features as expressions of the values of submissiveness, gentleness, and modesty (Nakamura 1980; Shirakabe 1990).

Today few of these facial attributes are promoted by the media or desired by young women. It is tempting to assume that facial features sought in contemporary Japan, such as a larger eye shape and a thinner nose bridge, stem from postwar Americanization and that one of the primary "imports" during this time was a hegemonic white American concept of beauty (C. Hall 1995; Kaw 1993; Kawazoe 2004; Kowner and Ogawa

FIGURE I.
Painting by
Hashiguchi Goyō:
*Keishō no onna*
(Woman applying
makeup), 1918.
Honolulu
Academy of Arts,
Bequest of the
Estate of Leslie B.
Andrews, 1990
(20,716).

1993). Yet modifications to existing beauty ideology were already well under-
der way during the Meiji era (1868–1912) due to Japan's increased contact
with Europe and the West. By the early part of the twentieth century, por-
traiture indicates that among urban elites, features once thought to be
unfeminine and harsh, such as a long or well-projected nose and a prominent chin, were now considered attractive. For example, a beauty of 1922
from the cover of a magazine for high school girls named *Reijōkai* (Society of young ladies) shows a thin, pale girl with huge eyes and soft, sloping shoulders (Fraser, Heller, and Chwast 1996: 109). An enduring theme
in paintings of beauties was women applying makeup, a genre continued
in the work of Hashiguchi Goyō (1880–1921). An example of modified
traditional femininity is seen in his woodblock print *Woman Applying
Makeup* (1918, figure 1), which shows a woman at her toilette. Her white

skin and drooping shoulders are old-fashioned, but her hair is a modernized version of an older style.

One prewar trendsetter for female appearance was the Modern Girl, or *modan gāru* (usually clipped to *moga*), new working women who were avid consumers of the latest fashions (Sato 2003). The *moga* used makeup to create big Betty Boop eyes with crescent eyebrows (Inoue 1998; Tsuda 1985: 62). She also had a small mouth, short permed hair, sloping shoulders, and pale skin. Seidensticker (1983: 257) once described the Taishō (1912–1926) beauty as languorous, wan, and consumptive. A typical *moga* is found in Kobayakawa Kiyoshi's 1936 woodblock print *A Bit Tipsy* (Inoue 1998: 94). In this print, he depicts a high-class café waitress with a fleshy body, pale skin, round face, and large eyes. Yet the appearance of the Modern Girl did not produce a simple contrast with the traditional woman, but rather created a continuum of style options: "Between these compelling opposites of radical modernity and reactionary tradition is a rich and passionate middle ground, where the styles and values of the *moga* and the good wife/wise mother mingle" (Brown 2001: 19).

Influence from Western fashion was seen in makeup and hairstyles more broadly than in clothing styles. In the 1930s, even women who still wore kimonos usually had adopted modern cosmetics and hairstyles. Beauty how-to books of the era provided instruction on how to achieve a modern appearance, which was not always a straightforward imitation of Euroamerican style. For example, in drawings found in one manual (Tsuda 1985), a reader is shown how the new Japanese woman's eye makeup differs from that of a Western woman (figure 2). The contrast tells us that use of borrowed makeup did not necessarily result in a simple emulation of non-Japanese styles.

In addition to the face and hair, the nape of the neck had been singled out for commentary and eroticization for at least two centuries. The nape is emphasized by the kimono, and not surprisingly, nape appreciation decreased somewhat after the 1920s, as fewer women wore them. Despite this change, the nape is still considered an erotic part of a woman's body. Audrey Hepburn's nape once drew considerable erotic attention and was often featured in print media during the 1960s. According to a poll conducted by *Fine Boys* magazine (1998), it follows the bust, legs, lips, and pupils of the eyes as the parts of the body thought to possess the most "sex appeal." The nape continues to be a focus of beauty work for many women.

A new discourse of female body aesthetics arose during the prewar

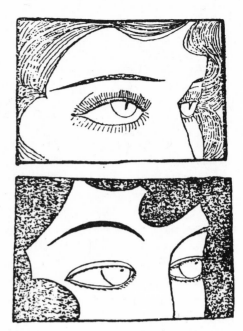

FIGURE 2. A 1924
beauty manual contrasts
Japanese- (bottom) and
Western-style (top) makeup.

period, a discourse tied to the promotion of a healthy and fertile female body required for reproductive fitness (Frühstück 2003). Robertson (2001) has linked this new aesthetic to ideas relating to selective breeding for racial improvement (eugenics) and to nationalistic ideology. The fit bodies of contestants in the first Miss Nippon beauty contest, held in 1931, were judged on the basis of their robustness and putative racial purity.

A classically beautiful type of early postwar woman was actress Tanaka Kinuyo, described as a bit zaftig and petite, with a moon-shaped face, narrow eyes, and a small, cherry-like mouth (Buruma 1984). Ochiai (1997), who has tracked imaging of women in Japanese print media, finds worship of the Euroamerican standard of beauty in the early postwar era. She notes a distinct split between depictions of healthy, cute, wholesome Japanese women on the one hand, and sensual and sexy white women on the other.[2] Until the 1960s, images of Japanese women mainly illustrated reified versions of the professional housewife ideal or modest young women and "troops of preparatory housewives" (Ochiai 1997: 165). When female sexuality was represented, it was deflected onto foreign models and actresses, so "Japanese women had to camouflage themselves as white

FIGURE 3. The cute aesthetic, displayed by porn idol Kogure Chie. From the June 1990 cover of the adult video magazine *Apple Tsūshin*.

to become sexy" (Ochiai 1997: 157). It is only during the era of high cuteness in the late 1970s and 1980s that we see a distancing from the Euroamerican standard of beauty.

Compared to the sophisticated girls of the 1920s and 1930s and the voluptuous womanly icons of the immediate postwar era (see Izbicki 1997), the ideal cute type of the 1970s seems that much more cloying and nonthreatening. Some scholars have linked the popularity of the cute style to a Lolita complex, in which images of young girls, or women pretending to be young girls, are a focal point of adult comics, pornography, and other media. For example, the cover of an adult video magazine features porn actress Kogure Chie dressed in a wholesome country-girl frock (figure 3). This change in beauty ideology was manifested in the demand for a new type of mainstream female celebrity as well. Popular singers were young women who portrayed innocence and nonthreatening cuteness. Stars such as Yamaguchi Momoe and Matsuda Seiko epitomized the desired qualities of the undeveloped girl. These mincing pixies clad in hair ribbons and frilly pastel pinafores were exemplary of endearing youth, purity, and cuteness (Kinsella 1995). A variant of the cute idol was the beautiful young maiden *(bishōjo),* a perky, well-mannered, and well-dressed young woman (Schilling 1992: 210). Media star Miyazawa Rie was once considered a premier maiden. Later, her representation in the media, where she was dubbed the "Heisei Venus," took on other, naughtier connotations after a scandal over her nude appearance in a photography book. Yamazaki Kōichi (1993: 132) noted that in 1990 the top-ranked female idols were not sexy, but rather reflected the "cool older-sister" type.

Fossilized imprints of the cute aesthetic are still around, but in the 1990s a new beauty ideology arose, which promoted a more mature-looking female body. Many Lolita pupae became "body-conscious girls" *(bodii-kon gyaru),* young women who worked hard at creating a sexy and fit body. This new body type corresponded to the "aerobics boom," which Nomura (1990) dates to around 1983. Prior to the fitness boom, thinness was not highly valued, and adjectives such as *pocha pocha* (chubby) and *fukuyoku* (plump) were meant as compliments. Spielvogel's (2003) study of the Japanese aerobics club includes many descriptions of instructors who strut around, gleefully displaying their youthful and trim figures in risqué leotards. In his book on Japan's new breed, Greenfeld (1994: 124) describes the body-conscious look as "a hybrid of Japanese comic book siren and Raquel Welch circa One Million BC" that is intended to intimidate men through a combination of style, sass, and sexual showiness. In one interview, a young woman named Keiko told him, "I dress the way I do because I like the power it gives me" (Greenfeld 1994: 126). The body-conscious girl's focus on the breasts in particular signifies a repudiation of the previous pedophilic ideal.

Since the early 1990s, there has been an expansion in the beauty types available to women as models for emulation. In addition to the cute imp style and the body-conscious style, there are more innovative looks that younger women are creating and emulating. Different parts of the body are subject to shifting concerns not shared by all members of Japanese society. People from different class, regional, and generational backgrounds also have variant ideas. My focus in the next section is on the various meanings found among young urban women, including rejection of ideals of ethnic purity and homogeneity and the marking of generational difference.

## New Beauty Ideals and the Media's "Cool" Girls

In late 1999, some Japanese high school girls had a new fad: key chains decorated with dead animal parts safely encased in plastic: little pieces of things like frogs and crickets, or mice in clear resin bubbles. After decades of pastel Hello Kitty and sappy cuteness, I found this new fad perversely refreshing. Meanwhile, social critics continued to fret over this and other fashion trends, seeing them as faults to be added to eight-inch platform shoes, body piercing, tattooing, and over-tanned skin. My feelings about some of these trends are ambivalent. I celebrate the new diversity of female fashion and beauty types as a corrective to the uniform cuteness and docility manifested by earlier icons, yet I am also disturbed by the exponential increase in the nature and amount of beauty work an average girl or woman needs to do to accomplish these looks.

The displacement of identity onto the body surface and the concurrent increase in consumer products necessary for the attainment of these new body styles have overshadowed attributes formerly considered essential to the construction of female selves, particularly family status, abilities, and character. The images found in magazines and in beauty industry promotional materials are not just depictions of archetypal fashions and styles, nor are they simply advertising maneuvers. They also provide a visible representation of values and meanings circulating in youth culture, which are pilfered, recreated, and reintroduced to a wider audience by the media. Being modern, traditional, international, and Japanese may be simultaneously imprinted onto the body. Although some of the styles that evolved since the 1990s threatened to disturb racial classifications, these youth styles are usually not connected to radical politics, but rather are self-expressions of resistance and rebellion. I would like to illustrate a little of the diversity in these beauty ideals and to suggest that while the media industries are drawing on the angry mood of female subcultures for much of their contemporary beauty imaging, young women themselves are both accommodating to and resisting the images fed back to them.

Beginning with the basic template of a thin body with largish breasts and smooth, hairless skin—core elements of the beauty system to be explored in later chapters—women are provided with additional models of beauty that index a variety of aesthetic criteria. These different beauty types correspond to numerous micromarkets, offering such diverse beauty services as tanning or face bleaching, gray-streaked hair *(messhu)* or nutbrown tresses *(chapatsu)*. Many of these styles are traceable to subcultures or to singers and other media stars. Once the innovation occurs, advertisers and media appropriate it, repackage it, and relay it back to the larger culture (Hall 1977; Hebdige 1979; Kilbourne 1999).

Okinawan-born techno/dance pop music star Amuro Namie represents one of the most popular types women have emulated, particularly in 1996–97, when she was the spokesmodel for the Takano Yuri Beauty Clinic. At that time, her long, light brown hair, makeup, slim body, and saucy outfits invoked a bar-hostess aesthetic rather than an unbaked teenager. Some observers even described Amuro as one of the new "hidden uglies" *(busu kakushi)*, women who do not represent traditional beauty ideals but who are able to transform themselves into icons solely through fashion and cosmetics. Regardless of what critics made of her, young women copied her looks and her sassy attitude.[3] Amuro is credited for initiating the "small face" fad *(mikuro kei)*, which resulted in a new market for bogus face-slimming creams, packs, masks, and other goods. For example, the aesthetic salon Esute de Mirōdo offered a Face Slim course (a treatment that supposedly makes a round face look more angular) of twelve treatments for $840. According to the manager of another aesthetic salon, "The reason for the small face trend is Amuro" (*Yomiuri Shimbun* 1997a). The brick-sized soles of Amuro's shoes took hold, with sales of the retro style generating around $100 million in the late 1990s. Early versions of these platform shoes, boots, and sandals stood around four inches high, but by 1999 women wearing eight- or ten-inch heels could be seen advancing down the streets of Shibuya. Although simply called long boots or sandals by young women, the media dubbed these "Oiran shoes" after the high-ranking courtesans of the feudal period, called Oiran, who wore tall lacquered footwear for special promenades. Mega-platforms have been blamed for accidents, injuries, and even the death of a woman in 1999. In that instance, the victim fell and fractured her skull because she had just purchased the shoes and was not accustomed to wearing them.

According to media representation, platform shoes are an aberrant, stupid, and dangerous fad (Sims 1999). I remember feminist debates about these same shoes in my own youth: the analogy to hobbling, the inability to run. Yet, from a sociological viewpoint, wearing such shoes also denotes a level of social trust that is not so different from usual operating assumptions—a compact that one will not need to run. Walking around Tokyo and riding the subways, I also recognized another, possibly unconscious, appeal: the sense of power that comes with increased height. On more than one occasion, I saw a platform-shod girl smirking down at the bald pate of a chubby salaryman, barely controlling her contempt. In interviews, one woman revealed, "You can't imagine how great it feels

FIGURE 4. *Kogyaru* style in 2000.
Reproduced with permission
of *Men's Egg* magazine.

to see the world from this height," while another said, "In the commuter train, the level of my eyes is higher than middle-aged men, who are so arrogant in the office" (Sims 1999).

The media took the big shoes, Amuro look-alikes, and other beauty trends and subsumed them all under a generalized, usually derogatory, category. The classification was the *kogyaru* (clipped from *kōkōsei gyaru*, high school girls), usually rendered as Kogal in English.[4] What started out as a subcultural trend soon emerged into the consumer arena via the media. First, average-looking amateurs began modeling for "street" magazines such as *Egg* or *Fine Surf & Street Magazine*. After that, marketers and media began to use the image of the Kogal (figure 4) as a type identifiable by her miniskirt, bleached hair, loose socks (knee-length socks worn hanging around the ankles), and big shoes.[5]

The media creates metalinguistic labels, which are in turn adopted or recycled by consumers, contributing to the widespread recognition of diverse fashion types. The Kogal, condensed to a caricature, became an important grouping in the fashion taxonomy, as well as a potent marketing category. Up until at least 2000, such women continued to be targeted in advertising as a specific category of consumer, as in an ad for a depilatory cream in which a drawing depicts a "typical" Kogal with platform shoes, dyed hair, and her arm draped over her head, exposing a smooth underarm area.

The media use of designations such as *kogyaru* transforms the possible insurrectionary potential of some of the new girl subcultures into a uniform group of mindless bad-girl consumers. It also serves as a vehicle for mainstream outrage at the economic and cultural power of youth, especially the subcultural compositions of young women. Paraphrasing Stuart Hall (1977), Dick Hebdige (1979: 85) says, "A credible image of social cohesion can be maintained through the appropriation and redefinition of cultures of resistance." We may also formulate Hall's (1977) idea this way: the media "records" girls' resistance, but then "recuperates" it through labeling and redefinition.

The Kogal style taken to an extreme gave birth to the *ganguro* (black face) style. Foreign pundits often make the mistake of seeing this style as an attempt to emulate African American looks, which is an entirely different named subcultural style (B-Girl).[6] *Ganguro,* with their screw-you makeup, are not trying to look black, American, or like anything ever seen before. One method to discredit and contain the power of girl culture is through this and other derogatory labeling, such as calling those who exhibit the new styles "mountain witch" *(yamamba)* or "ogress daughters" *(yamamba-musume)* because of their striking appearance, most notably their extreme hair colors and the contrast between these, their tanned skin, and the use of white or pale makeup around the eyes and on the lips.

There is not just one official beauty standard, of course, even in the Kogal subculture. I would like to mention a few other icons of girl culture. One of these subtypes is the faux-Hawai'ian surfer girl. Surfer girls sport deep tans, set off with white frost or opal lipstick and tropical clothing, such as the pareo or sarong. These can easily be found in shops such as G-Girls Surf or Cocolulu in Tokyo's trendy shopping areas. A feature article in *Fine Surf & Street Magazine* (1999b), entitled "This Summer I'm Gonna Be Miss Surf!," illustrated the season's coolest bathing suits, platform sandals, aloha shirts, and koa seed necklaces.

An attribute of the surfer girl that sets her apart from other types is her gleaming smile and upbeat, cheery countenance. Unlike the cute aesthetic of the past, in which women demurely covered their mouths when smiling or laughing, Miss Surf grins openly, sometimes with a little confidence boost from enamel bleaching, porcelain veneers, resin bonding, and new teeth-whitening products (technologies also popular in the United States). According to some scholars, baring one's teeth is a threat display, so covering or de-emphasis of the teeth is a submissive signal. Covering the mouth while smiling or giggling is etiquette dating to the Edo period (Casal 1966) and, like teeth blackening, might be related to a desire to subdue a woman's animalistic or aggressive potential.[7] Miss Surf and other young women who fearlessly smile are therefore challenging a long tradition of enshrouding the female mouth. Recent focus on the teeth has created a new industry in teeth-related beauty products and services, such as "dental aesthetics" (dentā esute), which usually refers to nothing more glamorous than teeth whitening. One illustration is the success of Apagard-M, a toothpaste produced by the Sangi company that whitens and repairs teeth through calcification. In March 1995, Sangi sold $40 million worth of the toothpaste, and by 1996 sales had grown to $100 million (Look Japan 1998).

Today's desired teeth are not only white, they are straight and uniform. Writing on images of women in magazines during a period when the un-baked pixie ideal was in full swing, Clammer (1995: 202) noted that there were "many with crooked teeth." Although the overlapping front teeth of idol singers such as Matsuda Seiko were once considered endearing and sweet, for Miss Surf and other young women today, they are a source of embarrassment. Beginning in the mid-1980s, there was a growth in the demand for orthodontia and dental cosmetic services, mainly among young women (Across 1992). Once the teeth are white and straight, they may still be the subject of additional beauty work. At the Japan Aesthetic Dentistry Salon, one may get treatments such as Quick Ceramics, Smile Cosmetics, and finally, Teeth Piercing, in which small gems are implanted.

Overlapping with surfer types are other deeply tanned girls. Some of these urbanites perform a sort of Kogal drag with touches of 1970s retro-chic. Styles such as these express creativity and divergence from mainstream culture, and are guaranteed to distress the over-thirty crowd. The beauty work needed to create the new styles may be expensive and time-consuming. When I asked a woman about her messhu-style (gray-streaked) hair, she explained that it required at least seven hours of work. In order to keep the deep tan, frequent visits to a tanning salon are essential.[8] At

Club The Sun Lounge or Tanning UV Zone, a thirty-minute tanning session runs between $8 and $17. In place of a visit to a tanning salon, one could use a self-tanning cream or lotion, or spend $3 for the single-use Tan Towel, a self-tanning product you wipe on the body.

Trendy styles often blend ethnic appropriations, including incorporation of Native American, Southeast Asian, or South Asian attire. For example, Yoshida Asami, of the pop music group True Kiss Destination, once appeared in a Mexican serape draped sarong-style, with suede platform boots, feathered earrings, and a tall eagle feather tucked into the back of her hair. The China fad in 1997 and the "Vietnam taste" fad of 1998 featured silk jackets and hair arranged in chignons. Tama-chan of the pop music band Hysteric Blue represents the "stateless" *(mukokuseki)* global hippie version. She often wears paisley print skirts or dresses and peasant blouses, sometimes referred to as the "folklore look." With her bleached hair and giant shoes, she resembles a suprahistorical and slightly jaded flower child. In her study of Japan's teenage culture, Merry White (1993) notes that some of these mixed retro and ethnic styles were already endorsed in the early 1990s. During the mid-1990s, forms of body art like tattoos, *mehndi* (traditional henna body painting from India and the Middle East), body piercing, and nail art made inroads into Japanese youth fashion (*Asahi Shimbun* 1997a). Their popularity suggests the transnational nature of many youth styles. It is important to keep in mind, however, that beauty trends in Japan are not "failed versions" of Euroamerican styles but rather express a separately developed aesthetic, which may nevertheless draw inspiration from outside Japan. In her analysis of recent magazine images of women, Emiko Ochiai makes the keen observation that "they do not pretend to be white women anymore. They seem to be slipping out of any nationality" (1997: 164).

Kogals, surfers, and other subcultural types created a space for women to play with a new aesthetic of the noncute or the cute infused with an ironic twist. A fallout of the Kogal blitz was that it promoted a diluted "Gal" style that has become mainstream. The term *Gal* is still used in teen media such as *Cawaii* magazine, where we find "Gal style" used for hip, trendy girlhood. The Kogal also generated an anti-Kogal fashion backlash: New Traditional *(nyūtora)*, Conservative *(konsaba)*, and Older Sister Style *(onēkei)* brought back frilly blouses and longer skirts. Instead of a deep tan, some women sought pale skin. Unlike fashion trends in the past, these new backlash styles have not made other styles obsolete but are simply offered as more options. They also constitute a form of distancing from trendsetters such as the *ganguro,* who are often from working-class back-

FIGURE 5.
B-Girl style
in 1999. From
*Hip-Hop Style
Bible* magazine.

grounds and not from the world of trading companies, women's volun-
teer organizations, and tennis dates. The conservative styles adopted by
such young people may therefore suggest enduring aspiration for middle-
class adulthood.

Tanned skin, big shoes, and processed hair are also hallmarks of a
separate African American vogue, sometimes called B-Girl style. Young
women commandeer not only the surface representation of "black" style
but ways of moving and standing as well. Two Japanese high school B-
Girls reflect this new mode in figure 5.

Hitoe, a former member of the girl group Speed (now disbanded) who
has changed her look many times over the years, was heavily into B-Girl
style in 1999. She openly admired and emulated American artists such as
Brandy, and told an interviewer she adopted this look when she saw the
American girl group TLC in their promotional video for the 1994 album
*Crazysexycool*. Hitoe told the journalist that when she saw TLC's video,
she said to herself, "I want to be like that!" (*Bounce* 1999: 120). Hitoe's

identification with this style defies the negative images of blacks otherwise projected by the Japanese media (see Russell 1998). In her attack on white American appropriation of black style and culture, as seen in media representations of Madonna, Hooks (1995: 321) says that "authentic black women can never 'publicly work' the image of ourselves as innocent females daring to be bad. Mainstream culture always reads the black female body as a sign of sexual experience." Hitoe and other female Japanese can also imitate these sexy poses and self-confident attitudes in ways denied the actual black woman. Japanese appropriation of "black style" is also narrowly limited to specific representations. Hitoe is not copying the style of the Baptist choir singer or the working mother, but rather that of hip and wealthy superstars found in films and on MTV. Japanese female culture makers exhibit a playful attitude toward racialized categories. For example, pop singer Hamasaki Ayumi skillfully confounds racial categories in 1999 CD cover jackets for her album *Appears* and her single *Loveppears,* in which she presents a "white" Ayumi and a "black" Ayumi.

Embodied in many of the new girl prototypes is a rejection of cultural proscriptions about proper female affect and presentation of self. The media provides images of models, pop music stars, and everyday girls who confront the camera with less than bashful poses and facial expressions. On music television programs, one can see irretrievably immodest celebrities, such as Hamasaki Ayumi or Hitoe, sometimes refuse to smile, giggle, or laugh when male interviewers ask patently stupid questions or make sexist allusions.[9] In place of cheerful perkiness and a demure sidelong glance, we find slouching audacity and petulant stares. The soft, sloping shoulders of the Taishō beauty have been replaced with jutting shoulders and space filled with angled elbows and hips. What I see in this and other styles is a cover for the open display of an aggressive, independent attitude.[10] The insurrectionary poses that would normally be categorized as rude, whorish, or low-class take on new meanings of hipness when aligned with subcultural fashion and makeup styles.[11]

Media saturation with faux-Hawai'ians, dark B-Girls, and Indian maidens are also, perhaps covertly, metastatements that challenge mainstream rhetoric about Japan's supposed racial purity and homogeneity. These disturbers of the cultural peace are upending tidy categories of race and gender. At the same time, this racial and temporal hybridity, in which styles from different places, ethnic groups, and eras are seamlessly appropriated, is symbolic of Japanese affluence. A young woman may select from any style she wants, and any makeup, hairstyle, or beauty technology she wants is available to her, an aspect of the beauty industry also seen in the treatments offered by aesthetic salons.

## Facing the Past?

Running counter to the tanning craze is a preference for pale skin, called the *bihaku būmu* (beautiful white boom). Dermal consciousness is ancient in Japan, and traditional beauty standards from centuries ago emphasized pale, translucent skin.[12] Shiseido discusses the Japaneseness of "white skin" in its skin-lightening product pamphlets, claiming that the whiteness of Japanese skin is different from "Caucasian whiteness," and that it is not simply the unique color but the quality of Japanese skin that is notable. "No matter where they are, everyone says that as for Japanese skin, it's somehow different from the skin of those in any other country."[13] From the Heian period (794–1185) on, women and men whitened their faces with a variety of substances: a powder made from rice, a liquid made from the seeds of the jalap plant, or white lead mixed with some type of starchy substance (Casal 1966). White makeup *(oshiroi)* is still used for weddings, in the theater, and by performing geisha.[14]

Historically, not all women were able to pursue this ideal, since the desire or ability to display pale skin was limited by one's class status. Bones of Edo-period samurai women show levels of lead contamination threefold greater than that of the bones of women from farming and fishing communities (Nakashima and Matsushita 2004). According to Ashikari (2003), the gendering of the white face occurred during the Meiji period, and subsequently the middle-class woman's whitened face came to signify native tradition and Japaneseness. Although some women in the past sought whiter skin by praying to Konsei, the Shinto god of childbirth and marriage, these days women rely on Japan's cosmetics industry, the second largest in the world after the United States, to help them achieve the complexions they want. The Japanese cosmetic market has been dominated by a small number of manufacturers: Kose, Shiseido, Kaō, Kanebo, Pola, and the French company L'Oréal. None controls more than a fifth of the market (Datamonitor 2003), and many smaller companies are able to sell niche items.

The extreme form of *bihaku* hyperpigmentation is represented by Suzuki Sonoko, founder of the successful beauty company Tokino (renamed Sonoko after her death in 2000). Suzuki had great success selling diet books, weight-loss foods, and cosmetics via mail order catalogs. She opened her first retail shop in Ginza in 1998, earning $100 million in 1999. On the first floor, decorated with Greek statues of goddesses and blue and gold draperies, one can buy her skin-lightening cosmetics. The mask, cleanser, lotion, creams, and makeup required for the lightening process are priced around $500 for the total treatment package. On the upper floors are a restaurant, cafeteria, and take-out counters for low-fat, low-salt food products.

A longing for pale skin preceded the Sonoko media blitz, however. American companies had sold skin-bleaching cosmetics for years, but those products, such as DermaFade and Porcelane, contain a bleaching agent (hydroquinone) that actually kills the skin's pigment cells, so they are banned in Japan. In 1985, Shiseido created a product that uses arbutin, which lightens skin by inhibiting the enzymes that trigger melanin production. Called Shiseido UV Whitess Essence EX, it is the leader in a $2 billion skin-whitening product category in Japan (Russell 1995). Other top-selling whitening cosmetics are Kaō Sofina Medicated Whitening Cream (considered cheap at $55, half the price of the Shiseido version), Kose Bihaku Whital Skin Care, MD Rezept II Whitening Essence, Confia Fresh Gel White, Hollywood Cosmetics Cesilla Facewhite Lotion and Extra White Lotion, and Takano Yuri's Whitening C Esthe. The American and European cosmetics companies have now created their own arbutin-based whitening formulations, which are sold only in Asia. The notion that dark skin is a "problem" that requires "fixing" makes products with names like Pond's Double White, Helena Rubinstein Future White, and Estee Lauder Advanced Night Repair Whitening Recovery Complex unsuitable for the American market.[15] Many salons also offer *bihaku* treatments, such as Estedamu Salon's Super Whitening course, which uses an agent said to "trap" the melanin, and the double chemical peeling offered at the Seishin Medical Esthe Clinic. Another clinic offers full-body whitening treatments for brides, using application of vitamins and natural ingredients, such as mulberry root.

The *bihaku* look is often accompanied by a return to conservative suits, dresses, and pearls. Although the media claim that *bihaku* is a universal fad, on my visit to Sonoko's Ginza shop I saw mainly women over twenty-two, Office Ladies (*ōeru* or OL, female clerks), and young homemakers. When female readers of a youth magazine were asked in a poll about their skin color, a little more than half the respondents, 61.4 percent, said they have a light complexion (*Ranking Dai Suki!* 1999b). The rest had different levels of either naturally or artificially darker complexions (cocoa brown, 32.9 percent; fairly dark, 3.7 percent; very dark or *ganguro*, 0.7

percent; other brown shades, 1.4 percent). The media commentariat interprets this white look as the outcome of concern over the ozone layer and skin damage from ultraviolet rays, even though one way women are getting whiter skin is by visiting clinics or salons for harsh laser treatments or chemical peels. My view is that *bihaku* beauty gentrification reflects a "rummaging in patriarchy's memory" (White 1992: 404). It is a rejection of the unwholesome connotations of subcultural styles, particularly those represented by the darkly tanned *ganguro* and B-Girls, and a return to more conventional beauty norms. Because white, translucent skin has been imagined as a specifically Japanese ideal of femininity, for Office Ladies and good girls from the middle class, the *bihaku* mode is a type of restorative of traditional values. *Bihaku* allows the greatest gender and class contrast with the leathery skin of the laborer, with his "laborer sunburn" *(rōdōyake)*. These conventional norms are also deeply nationalistic, so the return to pale skin is a return to old-fashioned Japaneseness, a type of beauty nationalism. Among subcultural girls and working-class Japanese, by contrast, the extreme white face was often spoofed, and Suzuki's chalky face and bright red lips were once featured in tongue-in-cheek goods, dolls, key chains, and stationery sold in trendy culture shops and street stalls.

Before leaving the face, I should also mention the eyebrow, which is again the focus of intense beauty work. Eyebrow plucking and shaping, or sometimes complete depilation followed by painting in a substitute, is beauty work both men and women practiced from at least the Heian era. Now the perfect Taishō crescent has been replaced with a menu of possible eyebrow types, each with its own "meaning." When I visited Shiseido's Cosmetic Garden, a makeup emporium and tryout showroom in Omotesandō, a beauty consultant gave me information on eyebrow shapes, tools, and techniques. She even provided me with a sheet listing some of the new eyebrow types: the Elegant Shape, the Up-to-Date Shape, the Youthful Shape, and the Gentle Shape. This seems to me to be a particularly forthright way to code and catechize cultural meaning.[16] One can also buy eyebrow templates representing the eyebrow shapes of celebrities to use as a guide when drawing in one's own eyebrows. New jazzed-up eyebrow maintenance products are also sold, such as the $55 Pink Free Eyebrow Make, which comes with five different attachments for brushing, cutting, and shaping the eyebrow. Some critics have noted that the new styles in eyebrow fashion often transform a face from a soft, gentle visage to one that is more harsh (*Tokyo Shimbun* 1996). Others see the trend in more positive ways. Archaic vocabulary for beauty types related to the eyebrow has recently been resuscitated. There's "moth eyebrow" (*gabi*), an antique term for a beauty with arched eyebrows, one whose eyebrows are as delicate as a moth's antenna, and "willow brow" (*ryūbi*) to describe those with brows as lovely as the leaves of a willow.

Given the availability of so many beauty products and services, the question of whether or not new beauty styles merely represent commercial indoctrination seems obvious, yet there is a complex interplay between capitalist social compulsion and individual resistance. At the same time as women are asked to submit to prevailing beauty images through consumption of products like Opera Eye Putti, an eyelid adhesive that adds a temporary fold to the eyelid, and Dr. Make Body Refining Lotion, a lotion for getting rid of cellulite, they are also given a technology for personal expression that can challenge mainstream gender norms. As Bordo (1993) and other scholars have noted, images are often dismissed as nothing more than "fashion," without asking what the "fashion" is projecting or its role in the creation of meaning. During the 1970s, round faces, scant makeup, and childish clothing were a visual code for purity and innocence. What message, then, is delivered by artificial tans, gray-streaked hair, and high platform boots? Some view these new fashions as sending the wrong cultural message—a lack of morals and perhaps an interest in amateur prostitution. We might also construe these new looks as part of women's struggle to emancipate themselves from their status as nothing more than good wife/wise mother marriage fodder and future breeders for salaryman consorts.

Representations of new beauty types have powerful currency because, similar to the British punk rockers described by Hebdige (1979) and the punk girls in the United States interviewed by Leblanc (2000), they symbolize a rejection of homogeneity, conformity, and mainstream values. These new technologies of beauty provide a space for jettisoning expected behavior and gendered norms. The images I see involve representations of women not as social beings, such as mothers, wives, and daughters, but as people with intentionally formed and decorated surfaces. These surfaces express forbidden content: an impertinent panache, independence, adult sexuality, and self-confidence. The social, political, and economic changes in post-bubble Japan have allowed many young women to challenge or play with mainstream models of desirable femininity. For young women who know they will never get into Tokyo University or become a sales director at Mitsubishi Motors, these beauty styles represent at least one avenue in their lives where they have complete control. Japan's girl-culture beauty rebellion is contained within a sociocultural context that affords little real social power. Even so, they are subverting gender norms, if only within the restricted level of the symbolic. Their images provide a type of *yantra* (a Hindu device for harnessing the mind, Eck 1996: 109): they grab the eye and focus the mind. Although Kogals and B-Girls are only a trendsetting minority, refracted through media models in ways intended to tame them, they are important because they certify coolness combined with resistance and its possibility for "ordinary" girls.

While the immature models cherished in the 1980s perfectly embodied the cultural ideals of naïveté and docility, today's menu of diverse beauty types include many who exhibit a rejection of these qualities. Visual representations of women who have had obvious encounters with hair dyes, depilatory creams, eyelid adhesives, and the newest version of the Miracle Bra encode layered ideas about gender, ethnicity, and sexuality. The outward expression of self-confidence and adult sexuality seen in faux-Hawai'ians, cheeky urbanites, and sophisticated hedonists is a radical departure from the ineffectual cuteness and immature innocence of the past, reflecting changes in women's social roles, aspirations, and experiences.

Douglas (1994) has suggested that the American media and beauty industries have succeeded in reframing a message of personal liberation as equivalent to individual bodily narcissism. Improvement, achievement, and success are expressed not in behavior or deed but through the acquisition of sculpted thighs and seamless faces. I now see the same thing in Japan, where youth identity has been displaced onto consumer-dependent beauty work, and where liberation as narcissism and its incorporation into the beauty system constitute another method for controlling the potentially disruptive features of women's economic power and the influence of female subcultures. This notion of beauty as control over the domain of the body is seen in Shiseido's campaign of the late 1990s, which used images of "individualized" beauty and featured the slogan "I'm really something." However, as Wolf (1992) drives home, beauty industries deflect female demographic and economic power away from social issues onto self-directed beauty work. While this allows a modicum of autonomy or serves as a minor ritual of rebellion, it does little to effect changes in gender relations or power structures.

# CHAPTER 2

# Aesthetic Salons

I arrived a bit early for my late afternoon appointment. Miss Ota, a chic young woman I had met on a prior visit, stood behind the counter in the reception area. She checked to see if one of the "counseling rooms" was available, and then asked me to wait in there. A second woman came in and asked that I complete three forms that were already waiting on the glass table. One was a registration form, another a chart asking for health background, and the last a survey of eating habits, lifestyle, exercise, and makeup: how often I used cosmetics, what brands I purchased, and where I bought them. Miss Ota returned to set up a video for me to look at and left again. I watched a short film touting something called "Oriental body aesthetics science" *(orientaru esute kagaku)*. There were clips of a male "doctor" in a white lab coat discussing health and weight control. After viewing this, I was asked to leave my shoes in a cabinet next to the check-in counter and was given pink terry slippers with the name of the salon written on them. I was led to a narrow locker area with a plastic draw-curtain and given a locker to use and a white terry robe to wear. In this fashion, I allowed my body to go forth to an unknown beauty worker's hands in the precincts of a type of Japanese business enterprise called the esute (aesthetic) salon.

Although beauty is an abstract idea that changes over time, businesses like the aesthetic salon are grounded locales that ostensibly provide services and products intended to produce actual beauty on the body of the customer. This chapter will examine how beauty is formulated and sold by the aesthetic salon, one of the most successful beauty industries. What type of treatments do beauty merchants offer in the salon as a new mode of consumption? Is the salon similar to or different from the beauty parlor or the Euroamerican spa?

In this chapter I suggest that while the aesthetic salon industry shares in a transnational beauty system in which beauty ideology, treatments, technologies, and, to put it bluntly, spurious gimmicks circulate across borders, these salons are also specifically Japanese settings that produce their own concepts of body and beauty. In some cases, salon treatments reflect the homogenization and normalization of Euroamerican beauty norms, yet even imported beauty regimes are altered and endowed with local meanings. At other times, salon treatments reflect long-standing Japanese beauty concerns. For example, one of the most popular services provided by salons is body hair removal, beauty work that has been prevalent in Japan for many centuries. Salons also offer numerous services derived from existing treatments found in traditional East Asian and South Asian medicine, thereby linking beauty to issues of health and ethnicity. The aesthetic salon is, therefore, a location where the interplay between globalization and the processes of localization occurs in fascinating ways.

Attention to the aesthetic salon is crucial because the salon differs from beauty programs of the past by offering new methods for mechanizing and commercializing body reform. Salons attempt to rationally maximize beauty gain through scientific management, an approach that appeals to the Japanese regard for empiricism. The salon delivers forensic documentation of beauty: the body is divided into individual parts or elements that are minutely scrutinized and traced. Precision measurements gauge the state of beauty's progress, even against eyewitness accounts of the ineffectiveness of the treatments. The aesthetic salon has been successful in the face of economic malaise and media tracking of consumer fraud because it sells the possibility of change, of ugliness defeated by technology. The salon is at the forefront of creating anxieties and fantasies of beauty attainment through consumption available to women of all ages.

## The New Beauty Merchants

The esute salon is not at all the same as a beauty parlor. Although there is some overlap with the contemporary Euroamerican spa industry, some features of the esute salon are unique to this type of commercial enterprise. Salons are a huge part of Japan's beauty culture. It is estimated that aesthetic salons are a $4 billion industry, with an average annual sales revenue of $350,000 per salon.[1] Like pachinko parlors, the aesthetic salon occupies a place on the border between legitimate business and shady operation, as do home loan services and English-language schools. Given this slipperiness, it is difficult to determine exactly how many salons there actually are in Japan.[2] Estimates range from approximately 15,000 in 1994 (Keizai Yakumu Torihiki Tekiseika Kenkyūkai 1994) to 13,000 in 2003 (Société Centrale d'Echanges Techniques Internationaux 2004). This seeming decline stems from the lack of government regulation and the fact that new salons are constantly opening while others close down. The average length of time for a salon to stay in business is 9.1 years, and 40 percent are less than five years old. In 2000, the salon chain Esute de Mirōdo went bankrupt, and 30 of its 108 shops were taken over by other salon chains, including Fuji Beauty and Takano Yuri Beauty Clinic (InterNet Bankruptcy Library 2000). Even so, salons are a lucrative industry, and demand for salon treatments stays strong in the face of a poor economic climate. Despite the recession and regardless of how effective or fraudulent salon treatments may be, this market is still growing at around 3 percent per year.

The majority of salons (70 percent) are privately owned, while the remainder are part of salon chains that are national (more than one hundred salons) or regional (five to one hundred salons). Many of my visits to aesthetic salons were to the large national chain shops Slim Beauty House, Takano Yuri Beauty Clinic, and Socie (table 1). In 2004, Takano Yuri Beauty Clinic was one of the most successful aesthetic salons, earning a total of $4 billion.

The aesthetic salon in Japan is somewhat different from the Euroamerican spa industry, which has roots in the domain of leisure instead of self-improvement. The word *spa* derives from the village of Spa in Belgium, home of mineral baths famous for a combination of health and relaxation. In the United States, Ojo Caliente hot springs in New Mexico was established as a spa location in 1880. By 1970 the Euroamerican idea of a spa came to include beauty farms for the wealthy, who visited them for periods of weight loss and recuperation in luxury accommodations. Some of the first spa treatments were offered on cruise ships, which hired their own aestheticians as a pampering service for passengers. Few of today's spas are based on natural hot springs, yet they almost always provide water-based therapies with facilities such as Jacuzzi, saunas, and pools. A spa visit still suggests leisure, involving resting periods between massage or facial treatments.[3]

In contrast, esute salons rarely have honest spa facilities, and even the

TABLE I. National Chain Salons

|  | Year Established | Shops | Employees | Annual Sales |
| --- | --- | --- | --- | --- |
| Tokyo Beauty Center | 1976 | 417 | 2,400 | ¥41.7 billion ($398 million) |
| Socie | 1971 | 74 | n/a* | ¥21.5 billion ($205 million) |
| Takano Yuri Beauty Clinic | 1979 | 120 | 1,050 | ¥16 billion ($152 million) |
| Slim Beauty House | 1987 | 102 | 900 | ¥10.2billion ($97 million) |

*Not available.

NOTE: This is not a complete list of the national chain salons, which compose approximately 16 percent of the aesthetic salon market.

SOURCE: Company web sites: Tokyo Beauty Center, www.tbc.co.jp/profile/gaiyo.html; Socie, www.socie.co.jp/; Takano Yuri Beauty Clinic, www.takanoyuri.com/i?i=2&p=2; Slim Beauty House, www.slim.co.jp/company/index.html.

showers are often makeshift affairs. Water therapy (balneotherapy or *onsen-ryōhō* in Japanese) is seldom part of an aesthetic salon's menu. Nor do esute salons normally offer services such as hair coloring and styling, which are part of a separate hair-styling salon industry. Two other primary services offered at the Euroamerican spa, pedicures and manicures, were not offered at any esute salons before the late 1990s. Some esute salons began catering to specific style markets by opening up nail salons or offering limited manicure treatments. For example, in 1999, a major esute salon opened a separate nail salon in Shibuya to cater to young Kogals and other subcultural types. Occasionally foreign critics of the Japanese beauty industry confound the cosmetic surgery clinic and the esute salon (Gilman 1999: 103). While both offer electrolysis, an aesthetic salon cannot perform surgery.

The spa and the esute salon promise different experiences. Euroamerican spas market themselves as primarily for relaxation, rejuvenation, and a refueling of the spirit. Advertisements suggest, "Designed to beautify and pamper you" (Deerfield Spa), "Leave your worries behind and let us nurture and heal your body, mind and spirit" (Skin Care Institute, Denver), and "Whether you stay for a week or a weekend, our friendly staff is here to indulge you" (Topnotch Spa).[4] The main purpose of the esute salon is not to pamper the client but to correct her body "defects." If she does not already know what her deficiencies are, the salon will point them out and offer treatments and products to fix them.

TABLE 2. Services Provided by Aesthetic Salons

|  | Percentage of Salons | Average Cost per Session | Average Time per Session |
|---|---|---|---|
| Facial care | 98.1 | $45 | 52 minutes |
| Hair removal | 56.7 | n/a* | n/a* |
| Body care | 64.5 | 60 | 50 minutes |
| Slimming | 52.4 | 90 | 60 minutes |

*Not available.

SOURCE: Société Centrale d'Echanges Techniques Internationaux (2004). Based on an estimated 13,000 salons.

So what services do esute salons provide? Each esute salon has its own lexicon of treatment types, all of them in flux as the promotional staff devise new ways to repackage and market services. Most salons offer a menu of treatments that can be grouped into three distinct categories: "facials," work that smoothes, shapes, and clears up the face; "hair removal treatments," which can entail just about any method one can imagine to rid the body of hair; and various types of "body treatments" to assist in weight loss and body-reshaping (see table 2). Salons typically offer an elaborated menu of treatments in each of these categories, and compete with one another in devising novel body experiences to sell. For example, in 2004, Tokyo Beauty Center launched a campaign for "teens and mama" discounts and "mother-daughter pair esute." All branches of the Slim Beauty House salon chain offer a minimum of eleven facial courses, twenty-two body treatment courses, and nine hair removal courses, in addition to other specialized services, such as bridal esute. This last category, bridal esute, is part of a brilliant commercial ploy in which existing services are repackaged and sold as body or face tune-ups for marriage. Bridal esute usually consists of a bundle of treatments offered over a specified period of time. Packages run from $760 for Esute de Mirōdo's Margaret Body Course of ten treatments (figure 6), to Takano Yuri Beauty Clinic's $2,400 Diamond Course. Socie de Esute salon urges customers to plan for that special day by relying on their unique bridal esute technology, which may cost $1,200 for the one-month Proportion Making Course, or $900 for a three-month Body Treatment Course. Women who might otherwise feel hesitant about experimenting with esute may justify this expenditure on the self, which could otherwise be seen as hedonistic or selfish, as necessary preparation for a very important institutionalized and reified social event.

FIGURE 6.
Aesthetic salon
advertisement
for bridal esute.

Although many women told me they found the facials given at esute salons pleasantly relaxing and good for the skin, most said other treatments, aside from electrolysis, generated no results. Everyone expressed the view that salon treatments are overpriced. A few people also mentioned short-term body damage, such as welts, swollen tissue, or numbness in various areas, resulting from treatments. These comments are often reported in the mainstream media, yet women (and men) are keeping the salon industry afloat, even during the decades of economic recession. It appears that rather than attracting huge numbers of customers, the salons rely on high-pressure sales and expensive treatments to stay in business.

Getting a solid sense of how many and what types of women have visited aesthetic salons is virtually impossible. Different surveys and reports have provided rather different demographic profiles. Some say the primary consumers are Office Ladies in their twenties, others that it is women in their thirties or forties. For example, a survey of 858 women, conducted by a professional association of aestheticians, asked, "Have you ever been to an esute salon?" The majority (52 percent) answered yes; of that total, 67 percent were women aged forty to forty-four (Kyōdō Kōkoku Kikaku Kyoku LIPS 1989: 119). According to the Kokumin Seikatsu Center (1992), the majority of women who visited esute salons in 1992 were between twenty and thirty years old (65.8 percent). In 1991, a different consultant group interviewed seven hundred women, of which all knew what an esute salon was but fewer than 10 percent had actually visited one (*Mainichi Shimbun* 1991). A later survey of one hundred women between twenty and thirty years old found that half had patronized salons (Japan Soap and Detergent Association 2004). It is also clear that women of different age groups are interested in different treatments. All age groups pay for facials, whereas other procedures, such as electrolysis, are most often given to younger women.

The esute salons target a variety of micromarkets with slightly different ideas about beauty, and tailor their advertisements and promotional materials accordingly. One market consists of the upscale *ojōsama*, or well-bred miss, who models herself after people like Crown Princess Masako. Before it closed, Esute de Mirōdo salon went after this segment of the population, with treatments focused on achieving good skin and tidy bodies (figure 6). Most of the large salon chains, such as Socie and TakanoYuri Beauty Clinic, however, appeal to the aspiring classes of clerical workers, the yearning Office Lady consumer. These customers have a different model of beauty in mind when they go to a salon for a treatment, often striving to look sexy, like J-Pop stars Hamasaki Ayumi or Aikawa Nanase. Despite differences in the type of women they try to attract as customers, all the salons promote bodies that are ultra-thin and hairless.

## The Science of Beauty

Salons sell beauty as a commodity that consumers can acquire by participating in their treatment programs or "courses." The model of beauty they purvey emphasizes aspects of both new and old notions of what is aesthetically pleasing. A crucial attribute in contemporary beauty ideology is slimness. One of the esute salon's primary routines is to document

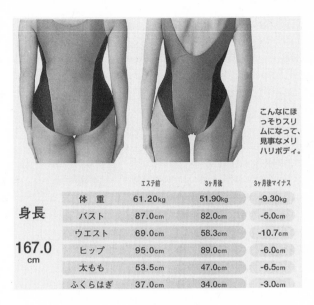

こんなにほっそりスリムになって、見事なメリハリボディ。

| | | エステ前 | 3ヶ月後 | 3ヶ月後マイナス |
|---|---|---|---|---|
| | 体　重 | 61.20kg | 51.90kg | -9.30kg |
| | バスト | 87.0cm | 82.0cm | -5.0cm |
| | ウエスト | 69.0cm | 58.3cm | -10.7cm |
| | ヒップ | 95.0cm | 89.0cm | -6.0cm |
| | 太もも | 53.5cm | 47.0cm | -6.5cm |
| | ふくらはぎ | 37.0cm | 34.0cm | -3.0cm |

身長

**167.0**
cm

FIGURE 7. Visual anthropometry: Takano Yuri Beauty Clinic brochure entitled "Cinderella Book," 1996.

the body's progress from possibly plump to extraordinarily thin. The process begins by taking the subject's height, weight, and body-part measurements and writing these down in a "medical" chart. As Balsamo (1996) notes, often individual body parts are targeted as sites for fixing, and salon advertisements offer up a visual anthropometry in which each segment of the body is scrutinized. A vital supplement to gauging beauty is knowing the exact amount of change that has occurred during a treatment. For instance, Takano Yuri Beauty Clinic singles out the bust, waist, hips, thighs, and calves as separate areas that are tracked and evaluated (figure 7).

Before-and-after measurements and photos detail and celebrate changes in body measurements and weight loss. (We might also note that in figure 7 the bathing suits are not identical, and that the "after" one is cut to show more skin and emphasize the waist.) The esute salon's understanding of beauty is specific and measurable, and therefore suggests scientific management. A pleasing appearance as presented to the naked eye has no meaning unless it is confirmed by "correct" weight and size as entered on the chart. Science is harnessed to aesthetics: if so many kilograms have been lost, it must mean that the woman has achieved "beauty." Some forms of beauty Taylorism are quite sophisticated, with a microcomputer that determines the individual's caloric limits based on height, weight, and age.[5]

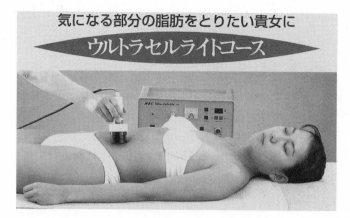

FIGURE 8. Beauty technology: Esute de Mirōdo aesthetic
salon booklet, 1999.

In the scientific beauty process, the body is fragmented, its parts iso-
lated and then redefined as inherently flawed or pathological. Attention
to specific body measurements really took off after 1954, when fashion
model Itō Kinuko took third place in the Miss Universe Beauty Pageant.
Her physique expressed the concept of "a beauty with a well-balanced
figure" *(hattō shin bijin)*. Although the term referred to an ideal proportion in which the length of the head equals one-eighth of the height, the
measurements were those of contemporary beauty pageants (bust, waist,
and hips). Whereas physical beauty had once been viewed as mainly a matter of the face, the new consciousness about body "proportion" began to
shift attention downward.

The steps invoked in fragmentation are also part of scientific management. The segmentation of the female body into parts for discussion
has roots in pornographic idioms of representing the body. As in the
United States (Douglas 1994: 79), the prevalence of pornography in Japan
has resulted in adoption of its conventions and imaging in other media.
The "scientific" analysis of the female body as an object of measurement
and review dates from the 1980s. For instance, in a regular feature in an
adult video review magazine, entitled "Laboratory Analysis of Woman's
Body," a naked actress has her measurements taken by a male "scientist"
wearing a white lab coat. Using calipers and other anthropometric instruments, the scientist takes measurements of every imaginable part of her
body, including the depth of her vagina and the length of her clitoris. All
the information is presented in photographs and formal graphs (*Apple
Tsūshin* 1990).

Visual materials are an important means by which salons socialize women to see and admire certain body styles. Salon brochures and advertising materials are lavishly illustrated with close-up full-color shots of selected body sections and models who have supposedly benefited from their treatments. One salon sponsors a baroque Esthetique Cinderella Contest in which the woman who loses the most weight in the shortest period of time becomes the Grand Prix winner. At her crowning, where she wears an official magenta swimsuit with matching high-heeled shoes, she is adorned with a faux-diamond tiara and presented with a lavish bouquet. One outcome of the salon business is the transformation of the concept of beauty from a subjective idea into a standardized notion of "beautifulness" that is quantifiable.[6] Whereas something like appreciation of the nape of the neck was nebulous—any neck is fine as long as no moles dot it—these days not just any waist will do, but only one 61.5 centimeters or smaller, like the Cinderella Grand Prix winner's. The concept of beauty becoming available through the power and prestige of science and technology defines much of the esute domain.

## On the Edge of Legitimacy

Because the salon business is so unregulated, there is wide variation in the legitimacy and nature of individual salons. Some of the salons I visited have gone out of business, others have changed their names. In some cases an esute salon might be an adjunct and feeder business to even more lucrative businesses, such as cosmetic surgery clinics and cosmetic product firms. For example, Avant began as a cosmetics firm in 1972 and entered the lucrative esute salon industry in 1996, when it opened a shop in Ginza. I saw an advertisement for an esute salon named Sapho Ladies Healthy Dock and, given the name selection, wondered if perhaps it was a specialty lesbian esute salon. Curious, I went there but was greeted a bit rudely and realized that it was a very exclusive place reserved for wealthy matrons. Standing in the reception area with my ratty canvas knapsack, I clearly did not fit in, and not just because I was a foreigner. The prices for treatments were higher than those at most other salons. I asked about the salon's name and was told it is a Greek name and hence denotes "beauty." When I had asked enough questions to become a pest, they let me know that the salon is actually a "side-business" to the cosmetic surgery clinic located in the same building.

The problem of consumer fraud continues to plague much of the esute salon industry. This is because, much like the American diet industry, it is selling a dream central to the business of gender construction. Most surveys uncover spurious and questionable practices. Customers are promised giveaways that never materialize, manipulated into signing expensive long-term contracts with frequent-visit coupon enticements, or duped with bait and switch tactics. One woman complained that instead of the expected facial, she was pressured to buy cosmetics (*Shizuoka Shimbun* 1997). During a one-month period in October 1989, the "esute 911" consumer hotline received 182 complaint calls (*Nihon Keizai Shimbun* 1990).

The majority of complaints (59 percent) were about electrolysis treatments. For example, in one case a woman reported that salon workers told her she needed to do a special body-hair consultation before getting electrolysis. After the "test" she was told that her body hair was fatter or thicker than a "normal" person's, so instead of the advertised $4,200 hair removal course she would need a course that cost $5,900 (*Yomiuri Shimbun* 1989). One salon chain was ordered to pay twenty-five million yen to a woman who ended up with a hernia because her treatments were so rough (*Mainichi Daily News Interactive* 2002). In another case, a woman was arrested for running a bogus esute salon from the back of a restaurant (*Mainichi Daily News Interactive* 2003a). She had earned twenty-seven million yen by luring in potential customers for "mole" divination and removal. Although laser equipment is supposed to be used solely by specially trained technicians, some salons allow any staff to use them for hair removal treatments. The number of salons sanctioned for this is low, however. In one case, a salon owner and four of his employees were arrested for breaking the relevant Medical Practitioners Law only because of a reported injury (*Mainichi Daily News Interactive* 2003b). According to the police, the owner told his staff anybody could operate the lasers without fear of punishment. In 2002, the Japanese government began taking steps toward regulating the aesthetic salon industry, appointing a study group to make recommendations on an authorization system and on the training of aestheticians (Ministry of Economy, Trade and Industry 2004).

One of the most troubling aspects of the aesthetic salon industry is the training for those who provide beauty services. The focus of training appears to be on good sales technique rather than beauty technology. Although most salons portray their aestheticians as having received special technical training, in interviews I received ambiguous, evasive, and sometimes contradictory information about the nature of this training. In some cases, distinctions are made among the employees of salons, who may be categorized as counselors, dieticians, and aestheticians, each with different duties and uniforms. Promotional materials often claim that salon employees are graduates of special esute schools or training courses. Unlike hairstylists, for whom there are rigorous national certification procedures, there is no national testing of qualifications for aestheticians. By contrast, in order to obtain a license as a beautician, one must pass a national examination given by the Ministry of Health, Labor and Welfare. Most beauticians have some formal training from a trade school and have participated in some type of internship.

Trade schools like the Hollywood Fashion and Beauty College offer legitimate two-year programs to become an aesthetician. These schools offer courses and specialized training for careers as a cosmetician, beautician, fashion model, bridal beautician (which includes learning how to put a kimono on customers, an important service described by Goldstein-Gidoni 1997), salon owner, nailist, makeup artist, colorist, stylist, and aesthetician. The aesthetician's program focuses on facials, massage, and aromatherapy. Students live in dorms and attend classes daily. (The school also offers less rigorous night courses and correspondence courses.) Students get hands-on training at the Hollywood Beauty Salon. Of the several students I spoke to who were studying there in 1999, all of them were happy with the school's program and optimistic about future job prospects.

Much of the course content at Hollywood Fashion and Beauty College and other beauty schools, such as Shiseido Biyō Gakuen, is similar to that offered by any two-year women's college (McVeigh 1997). There is always instruction in language and social etiquette. In a few cases, students may train for jobs as aestheticians at the high school level. An example is the Total Esthetique Course offered at a vocational high school in Miyazaki.[7] Students study language, science, math, history, and art, and take courses on esute theory, esute practice, makeup application, business etiquette, and aerobics as part of their training for the beauty industry. In addition to full-scale programs such as these, there are also short-term courses and workshops available for learning esute and other beauty lifestyle techniques. For example, the Herbal Life College offers classes on aromatherapy, ayurveda, herb candle crafting, and home therapy.

Many graduates of legitimate beauty schools go on to work at esute salons, but for most salons, the company does its own in-house training once the person is hired. The majority of aestheticians who provide services at the big chain esute salons are trained by the company itself. All the salons use inflated titles for their version of new recruit training. For example, Socie aestheticians are said to be graduates of the International

Beauty Academy, while employees at the Takano Yuri Beauty Clinic all have attended the Japan Aesthetic Academy Institute. Neither is a certified trade school or, indeed, an actual school. I was interested in the way that the Takano Yuri Beauty Clinic promotes its Aesthetic Academy as the training center for all its aestheticians, and tried to find this academy. The address listed was the same as the head office of the company, where I was told that the academy "is not a school." New employees of the chain are given a three-month training program, much of it at the head office. They spend two weeks learning about etiquette, language, and manners, as well as basic body treatments. The rest of the training is spent as an apprentice at a salon. After working for six months, they are given instruction on giving facials. If they want to specialize in giving electrolysis, they need additional training and have to pass a test.

According to promotional materials provided by Slim Beauty House, esute salons generally have six different "professional jobs" at each site: receptionist (answers the telephone, schedules appointments, and "reassures customers"), counselor (confers with the customer to determine which treatments are most appropriate), dietician (recommends which foods and diets are best for "getting a beautiful body"), facial technician (does facials), hair removal technician (does the various depilation procedures), and bodywork technician (does all the remaining body treatments). Perhaps they should have added laundress to this list, because each time I visited the Slim Beauty House in Kanazawa, I saw all the women working there doing laundry in the back of the salon. I was told that there were six women working at that branch and that all of them did all the salon duties and treatments. I asked one of my aestheticians specific questions about training. She was evasive but in the end did admit that she had received no special training. In fact, she had joined the company the week before and had been given only a one-day introductory session. Many of the aestheticians at this salon had no real knowledge of beauty science, were unable to answer many of my questions about the beauty treatments, and seemed bored and indifferent to the concerns of their customers.

In addition to problems with poor training of aestheticians and resultant bodily harm from mangled electrolysis treatments, the Japan Consumer Protection Center receives complaints about the terms of salon contracts, described as complicated and sometimes fraudulent (Keizai Yakumu Torihiki Tekiseika Kenkyūkai 1994; Tanaka 1991). Clients who are unsatisfied with the services they received may be given compensation in unwanted cosmetics and other products, but rarely will they get out of paying the full amount specified in their contracts. Another disturbing finding is that the majority of customers paid for treatments with credit (84.2 percent) instead of funds on hand (Kokumin Seikatsu Center 1992). Partly this is because many women who visit esute salons for the first time do so with a special discount coupon and really cannot afford these treatments.

A colleague told me about her experience with esute salon fraud. Her daughter became a frequent customer of an esute salon following an initial trial visit. Many salons bring in new customers with discount tickets, frequent visit coupons, and one-day trial "experience" packages. This young woman did not realize that the price of services on later visits would be twenty times higher, and ended up signing contracts valued at $42,000. My colleague consulted a consumer advisor, who helped to negotiate with the salon and was eventually able to cancel the contract.[8] As a professor at a university, she had the clout and aggressiveness needed to challenge the salon. Many women, however, are too embarrassed or intimidated to do anything about such scams. Stories such as this are common, and this was the government motivation for instituting a cooling-off period before esute contracts are signed.

At Socie, I tried to get information about training from one of the aestheticians, "Maeda," but she was coyly evasive. Maeda was in her fifties, had short hair, and wore heavy makeup. Maeda's voice (which sounded to be the product of tobacco- and whiskey-cured vocal cords) and the businesslike way she dealt with my body reminded me of a *mama-san,* or hostess at a small bar. From what I was able to learn from her, she was from Tokyo, had studied esute techniques at a "school" there, and had been working in the salon business for five years. I never got over the feeling that Maeda had been reassigned from a "soapland" brothel to her current job. The "back" treatment areas are more likely to be populated with women from businesses (such as prostitution) where they are accustomed to handling the bodies of strangers. By contrast, the people who worked in the "front" areas of Socie, such as receptionists and managers, were young and fashionable.

The suspect nature of these purveyors of beauty does not mean that individual aestheticians are uniformly crooked. In many cases, they seemed to know, and care, quite a bit about the beauty business. Salon employees are almost always women, including managers and senior sales staff. The salon business is one of the few occupational niches in which Japanese women may be found in managerial positions and achieve positions of authority. The same is true in Euroamerican beauty culture as well, where women entrepreneurs pioneered several beauty-related businesses and franchise operations (Peiss 1998). Like Elizabeth Arden, Helena Rubinstein, and Madam C. J. Walker, an African-American entrepreneur who became a millionaire in the 1800s selling hair-care products, a few Japanese women have achieved incredible successes in the beauty industry. One such person is Suzuki Sonoko, who reinvigorated the white face ideal. The cosmetics and food company she established in 1974 earned around nine billion yen in 2000.

Another success story is Takano Yuri, who was drawn into the beauty business as a result of problems with acne. In 1972, she read about French skin treatments and created her own product based on what she learned. She began selling the first face creams in 1973, and in 1977 opened a beauty clinic. In 1979, Takano branched out into hair removal treatments, and her business had evolved by the 1980s into the aesthetic salon category. She has frequently been a leader in salon trends, introducing the Israeli Dead Sea Salt fad in 1990, the Romiromi treatment from Polynesia in 1994, and the Egyptian craze in 1996. In 1995, Takano invited Dr. Sudha Ashokan to visit Japan, where she gave instruction on ayurvedic treatments to body stylists at several of the salons. The Takano Yuri Beauty Clinic and other salons actively keep abreast of spa industry innovations and constantly offer new and unusual treatments to entice new customers into their precincts. Once inside, the client is subjected to the latest trends in beauty culture.

## The Esute Salon Experience

Whereas spas in the United States strive for an understated New Age elegance offset with soft earth tones, peaceful woods, and plenty of greenery, the Japanese esute salon typically exudes an aura of unabashed luxury. In many salons, for example, a mythological era of luxury and beauty is exemplified by what might be called French Antique. As a general rule, "Frenchness" has symbolic associations with beauty and elegance. (Esute? *Mais oui,* it is French!)[9] Since the first Japanese beauty school was opened by a French woman between 1910 and 1930 (Seidensticker 1990: 93), perhaps this is a long-standing association. As a motif that defines space — Gottdiener (1997) calls this a "themed milieu" — French Antique is not concerned with historical verisimilitude but rather aims for a mood of both intimacy and luxury.[10]

In the same way that my health-care services are located in a basic brick and glass building optimistically named a pavilion, many esute salons are found in compacted urban spaces bearing evocative or fanciful names such as Aesthetics of Milord (Esute de Mirōdo), Sapho Ladies Healthy Dock, and Na Nio Paliza.[11] Because the majority of salons are located in modern glass and steel office buildings, drastic reworking of interior space is needed to achieve French Antique. This requires use of decoratively flocked wallpaper and elaborate draperies featuring swags and jabots, even when there are no windows to cover. Reception areas contain furniture of the intimate sitting room, such as French Provincial wing chairs covered in flowery chintz, where Mademoiselle (or Madam) may sit gracefully to wait for her treatment. The favored color schemes are shades of rose, pink, or peach with flourishes of gold and cream. There are often display cabinets that contain not Fabergé eggs but rather lighted collections of Enchanté Aqua Concentrate High Cellular cream, lotion, cleanser, astringent, and mask. The pinks and pastels may extend to the treatment areas as well, where towels, robes, and even frilly toilet paper roll dispensers continue the motif.

Because the presence of modern salon apparatus, such as the GX-99 Vibratory Endermatherapie System used for cellulite reduction and body contouring, would seriously compromise the French Antique atmosphere, these are discretely tucked away in separate treatment rooms located in the back. If the front of the salon is devoted to luxury and a delicate femininity, the treatment rooms are where science and technology, albeit in more cramped surroundings, are called on to do their duty.

Receptionists and managers may dress in sleek trendy fashions, but like the physician's clothing worn by quack surgeons in medieval Europe, the aestheticians who work on the body wear the uniform of the health-care professional or laboratory technician. Thus all wear nurselike uniforms or else the serviceable lab coat. The lab coats and nurses' attire also serve to depersonalize the individual doing the treatment. This just is not any person touching your breasts, but a trained professional! Pink or white nurse uniforms define the aesthetician as a beauty expert, a technician to whom one may safely entrust one's body. This function has been explored by Blumhagen (1979) in his analysis of the physician's white coat in American health settings. He notes how the coat transforms a taboo activity into a socially admissible one. The use of health-care uniforms allows disrobing in front of a stranger, turning a violation or form of impropriety into a normal, routine act.

In addition to borrowing the clothing of the medical specialist, there are other ways in which the beauty treatment adapts to the conventions of the medical encounter. The salon experience is constructed to resemble the treatment of the body in health-care contexts, including the preparation of a medical chart and the manipulation of frames and boundaries designed to demarcate the esute domain. The actual space of the salon contributes to this conversion, through use of doors clearly marked "Treatment Room" or set off with curtains from other salon areas. The consumer allows a stranger to do things to her body that perhaps no other human is allowed to do. In order for this to happen, the interaction needs to be framed in such a way that the *body* rather the person becomes the client of beauty. Young (1997) beautifully describes the process within the medical encounter through which the body is transformed from a social subject into a medical object. This same dislodgement of the social self from the body occurs in the salon through examination and measurement of the body parts, during which "the body is materialized even as the self is banished" (Young 1997: 1). Within the esute salon, the body becomes an object with parts that are measured, arranged, massaged, and worked on. In consenting to a beauty treatment, a woman is, as Young put it, absenting herself from her social personae, divesting herself of clothes along with the social self.

In the world of esute, the formerly slippery and subjective concept of beauty has been redefined as being specific, concrete, and measurable, and therefore subject to the applications of science and technology. In a capitalist market that has provided us with micro CD players, the cellular phone, and the Hello Kitty car (cute and styled just for them), young women willingly turn to a proposed "science" of beauty that is not only possible but desirable and perhaps even necessary. In the space of the salon, beauty is no longer amorphous but rather predictable and controllable by the woman and her beauty specialists. Beauty methods clothed in the guise of science and technology are used for almost any type of body work. Slimming treatments in particular involve electro-muscle stimulation using strapped-on electrode patches connected to machines that emit some type of ultrawave or microcurrent. These ineffective "EMS" (Electrical Muscle Stimulation) machines are also popular in the Euroamerican spa business, and are not to be confused with the legitimate transcutaneous electrical nerve simulator (TENS) machines used by physical therapists, which provoke muscle contraction to reduce pain. Another contributing reason for the popularity of machinery to replace hands-on massage is that it eliminates the need for extensive or long-term training of salon employees.[12] The ultimate in scientific emulation is perhaps the esute machine named the Beauty Dome, promoted by the Takano Yuri Beauty

Clinic. It is supposed to foster weight loss through vibration that loosens up the fat tissue. It looks exactly like a magnetic resonance imaging (MRI) scanner.

Salons all follow a similar process when funneling guests through their programs. After making telephone appointments, guests are given counseling sessions, selected treatment regimes, and finally home-care advisory sessions. Salons do not like people to walk in off the street for a treatment without having made a prior appointment over the telephone. One reason is that they like to stagger appointments to make sure clients do not compare prices and opinions on the efficacy of their treatments. Esute salons contract in advance for expensive long-term treatments such as bridal esute or electrolysis.

When she presents herself for a treatment, a customer is given an initial sales talk under the guise of a "counseling session," such as the one I described above. The counseling session takes place in a room set aside for filling out forms and perhaps viewing a promotional video. These sessions can take up to an hour. In one case, I was asked to provide financial and work information, sign a form releasing the salon from responsibility for any resulting serious medical problems, and fill out a questionnaire about my body. All the salons ask similar questions, including bank account numbers, savings balances, and credit card information. The detailed questions on these surveys reveal their function as a marketing tool. The questionnaires ask what brands and types of cosmetics are used, where these are purchased, and how many times a day makeup is applied. They also ask how much money is spent at hair parlors, whether the guest has ever been to another esute salon, and to identify any past illnesses or allergies. Some forms ask whether the client has a "chilling disposition" (*hieshō*), an aspect of folk health classification described by Ohnuki-Tierney (1984). All salons require that guests self-identify "problems" in their appearance through questions like "What is the primary worry about your body?" Slim Beauty House assumes that a woman is worried about her weight and skips directly to questions like "How much weight do you want to lose?" and "What kind of diet are you on?" The actual treatment is cushioned between visits to a locker room. After being led to a treatment room, the customer is meticulously weighed and measured, and this information is entered on the "medical chart."

In addition to the counseling sessions, sales pressure can occur at any point in the salon experience, as I discovered when I received a treatment at Slim Beauty House. My aesthetician, "Miho," led me to a cot in a partitioned area and asked me to take off my robe and lie down face up. I lay on a dark blue mat covered with plastic. Miho wrapped the plastic around me, and the blue mat was then fastened over it with Velcro. This was the electrically heated BioSlim Thermal Blanket "Sauna." I was covered with towels and told to rest a bit while the "sauna" worked. I lay there swaddled and sweating for about ten minutes before Miho returned with my chart and asked if I would make an appointment for the next treatment. I said I would think about it. Miho departed but was soon replaced by the salon manager, who also carried my chart. She stared at me intently and asked how long I would be in Japan. I told her only a few more weeks. She said that was plenty of time to come in for another and better treatment.[13] I said I would think about it. She departed but returned a few minutes later. Still sweating and wrapped in the BioSlim Thermal Blanket, I was grilled some more. She asked which part of my body I most wanted to slim down. I told her that I was not particularly worried about losing weight. Surely I desired a slimmer and smoother body, she suggested. Not especially, I said. She looked at me with disgust, referred to my weight as officially entered on the chart, and pointed out that it was too much. But I feel fine, I told her. This made her even more unhappy. The fact that a woman had no burning desire to change her body was inexplicable to her, as it was to every person I met in the esute business. Prior to this research, I had assumed that a middle-aged woman would be exempt from this sort of pressure, but all women are fair game, and Slim Beauty House even features a fifty-nine-year-old Cinderella woman in its weight reduction contest.

After changing and before leaving the salon, customers may be given a home-care advisory session, which is really another sales talk. Indeed, after seeing the extensive array of suggested body-care products and their prices, I began to suspect that many of the salons are owned by cosmetic companies who see the esute treatments mainly as a way to bring in potential buyers of cosmetics and other salon merchandise. An example of this is the Carita aesthetic salon, which is owned by makeup giant Shiseido. Takano Yuri Beauty Clinic sells a home-use hair removal set for $1,550 and a home body-care package for $1,945. The esute salons also do brisk catalog sales of noncosmetic items, such as foundation undergarments, home cupping sets, diet teas and elixirs, gas pills, purses, clothing, and jewelry.

Before I visited the aesthetic salons, I expected they would be similar to a place I frequented in Osaka in the 1980s, "Ladies Sauna." Ladies Sauna was essentially a dressed-up public bath. For a set entry fee, customers were given clean, fresh towels, a locker, and access to three different saunas and eight or so different baths. I remember that one of the saunas contained a large color television. Showers were equipped with complimentary shampoo, disposable toothbrushes, toothpaste, body soap, and hair conditioner. In the daintily appointed vanity areas, management provided hair dryers, lotions, and astringents. There was also a noodle bar where one could order a cold beer and buckwheat noodles. For an extra fee, massages and facials could be scheduled. In a softly lit lounge area furnished with plush chairs and recliners, customers could rest or sleep after their baths and saunas. Women in the "water business," such as bar hostesses and sex workers who dropped in to freshen up between jobs, were a large share of the clientele at Ladies Sauna. It was a very relaxing and enjoyable social place, and women often went there in pairs or with groups of friends. Clark (1994: 136) notes that such places are newer forms of the public bath and similarly provide a communal place for social interaction and recreation.

I expected the salons would also be an arena for sociability, a leisure venue with pretty spa areas in which to relax and visit with friends. Instead, I never saw customers in pairs or groups, and although there was occasionally friendly banter with aestheticians, the regimented salon programs did not foster interaction between clients.[14] Even while waiting in the reception area, I rarely had an opportunity to chat with other customers. In many instances, women sat waiting for their appointments with their heads lowered, never looking up. I wondered about this until I realized that many salons ask that you arrive without any makeup on. The focus of the aesthetic salon visit is the individual self and self-absorption in one's own bodywork, not relaxation with friends. It seems that the leisure and social aspects of the public bath or sauna have leaked over into the fitness club category (see Spielvogel 2003), while the salon is a place dedicated to the serious work of creating beauty. The primary reasons most women visit esute salons are to lose weight, get skin-care treatments, or for electrolysis. In contrast, according to a survey reported by Benson and Elliott (1999), the treatment that generates the most income in the American spa industry is massage.

As journalist Jenkins (1998) writes in several essays on physical culture, one challenge in visiting a spa or salon is figuring out the etiquette involved in negotiating the space and proper conduct within it. In my case, I had no problem dealing with the deployment of robe and slippers but did run into difficulties elsewhere. Esute salons provide complimentary panties to their guests when they arrive. The gratis undies ensure that the nether regions are covered with something clean and that items from outside are not brought into the treatment space. Salons routinely treat the lower parts of the body differently than the upper half. For example, most salons have discrete price structures for hair removal, and all of them treat hair removal from the "bikini line," or crotch area, as a separate and special treatment. This distinction between the upper and lower body halves reflects concepts of pollution and purity in which the upper is cleaner than the lower, which is, in the Japanese spiritual universe, unimaginably dirty (Ohnuki-Tierney 1984: 57).

The first time I went for a salon treatment and opened the package of tiny disposable undies, I was sure they would never make it over my un-Cinderella-like thighs. I peeked out of the locker room and suggested this possibility. There ensued a squabble in which the aesthetician insisted they would be fine while I countered with embarrassed doubt. When observing other guests at these salons, I noticed that they too were hesitant and nervous about comportment of their bodies through locker rooms, showers, and treatment areas. Once, while in a narrow dressing area after a shower, I opened some folding doors less than a foot from where I was standing, curious about where they led. Behind them was another customer lying on a massage table with towels draped over her. I apologized and withdrew. Salons try to herd people through their visits in ways that will minimize this sort of mishap by relying on schedules and timers, but the tight space and most visitors' lack of familiarity in navigating it inevitably lead to a certain amount of discomfort.

Some aspects of the salon experience are pleasurable, of course. One association of women writers (Kyōdō Kōkoku Kikaku Kyoku LIPS 1989: 116) coined the term *esutekusutashii,* a combination of esute and ecstasy, to describe the good feeling derived from getting a salon treatment. During a visit to Socie, I was directed to an actual sauna, albeit only a small one-person pine box. The salon manager knocked on the door while I was inside and handed me a tray. On it was an ice-cold hand towel and a civilized glass of chilled plum juice. But my enjoyment of these was short-lived, as she told me that another customer would be entering the shower area and sauna soon and therefore I should prepare to decamp to the reception area. Next to the sauna was the makeshift shower box, a space not at all conducive to a pleasurable experience. It was plainly tacky, with no soap and a defective shower nozzle that kept falling off.

Tanaka (1991) believes that the main function of the salon is to impart a sense of superiority derived from the opulent surroundings, and to provide a feeling of relaxation and indulgence. Although these aspects of the salon should not be overlooked, and interior design is an essential attribute of the experience being sold, as already discussed, the primary function is the correction of bodily defects, often accompanied by a good dose of pain to alleviate the pleasure. After all, as they say, "Good medicine tastes bitter" *(Ryōyaku wa kuchi ni nigashi)*. For instance, one aspect of any facial is to show you the flaws in your skin and how the beauty work provided by the salon will address them. At Esute de Mirōdo, my aesthetician, "Junko," taught me about my skin using a machine that looked exactly like the setup my dentist uses to document the condition of my gums. This was a micro laser camera attached by cable to a computer that greatly magnifies any object and displays it big as life on a monitor. This is sold as the Beauty Scope Electronic Hair and Skin Magnifier in spa industry catalogs.[15] Junko ran the Beauty Scope camera lens over the surface of my skin, pausing to point out where the wrinkles were particularly deep. Looking at my skin on the monitor was like viewing the San Andreas Fault from the air, or else the crust of a desiccated planet. When talking about my skin with Junko, it was like discussing a piece of material, a hide that was separate from me, thus showing how the salon treatment, exactly like the medical examination, dislodges the self from the body so that the body can be handled as an object (Young 1997: 29). The Beauty Scope was used again at the end of my facial to pinpoint improvement and note where problems remained that could, of course, be managed with continued visits and some take-home products. Another busy machine used in the facial involved a sort of suction hose that drew grease out of my pores. At the end of the facial, Junko proudly showed me a small glass pipette that reportedly contained all the nasty oil she had extracted from my skin. I think the intent here is to so horrify the customer by this evidence of the perfidy of her face that she will return for future treatments to prevent a relapse.

## "Authentic" Asian Aesthetic Treatments

In addition to using technological apparatus like the Beauty Scope to legitimize their offerings, salons also sell treatments that are presented as age-old beauty work that connects the client to her history. Scholars of Japan have often reflected on the nostalgia for an earlier age expressed in post-1970s cultural domains such as towns or neighborhoods (Robertson 1991; Bestor 1989), the travel industry (Ivy 1988), and the wedding industry (Edwards 1989; Goldstein-Gidoni 1997). The internalization of an exotic self-image, a type of auto-orientalism (Tobin 1992), is worked

FIGURE 9. "Oriental" cupping treatment at Slim Beauty
House aesthetic salon. Reproduced with permission of the
Slim Beauty House Co., Ltd.

out in the esute business as well. The salon treatments pointedly imbue
the beauty work with an Asian-indexed cultural identity. Asian esute is
part of a broader trend in appreciation of or interest in Asian cultures
other than Japan, the so-called Asia boom. Within the Japanese beauty
world, 1993 was the year Korean *akasari* "dirt scrub" was a big hit, followed by South Asian aesthetics *(Indo esute)* in 1994, and Bali and Thai
esute in 2002.

One Asian-inspired esute salon offering is the "cupping" treatment.
Cupping (figure 9), a form of acupoint stimulation without needles, was
borrowed from a menu of long-standing Chinese acupuncture treatments.[16] It is related to the principles of moxibustion, the burning of a
grain-size cone of mugwort on the skin over the acupoints. Within the
Chinese-derived medical system, called *kanpō* in Japan, cupping has long
been used for muscle pain, headaches, insomnia, and blood stagnation,
and to move energy, or *ki,* to blocked areas of the body. Esute salons market cupping as a "natural" treatment to improve blood circulation,
which promotes both beautiful skin and weight loss. Originally, a lit candle or a burning piece of cotton dipped in alcohol was held inside a bam-
boo cup. The flame exhausted the oxygen inside, creating a vacuum that
drew the skin up inside it.[17] In the esute salon, aestheticians use cups
made of break-resistant plastic and prefer a suction pump connected to
the cup through an air-release locking system. The cup is placed on the
body and air is sucked out with a squeeze trigger handle, which is then
lifted off, leaving the cup with the flesh bubbled up inside it. The cups
are left on for fifteen to thirty minutes, and when they are removed puffy

bruises are left on the skin. Although this does not seem like the best way to create beauty, the marks disappear and the presumed weight loss remains.

I decided to try a cupping treatment at Slim Beauty House, where cupping is described as authentic "Oriental body aesthetics" *(orientaru esute).* The salon's treatment room was similar to a hospital clinic, with individual cots separated by white curtains hung from a frame that is suspended from the ceiling. After a shower and an automated massage in one stall, I was led to a space set aside for cupping. I lay on my stomach while the aesthetician, "Yuko," draped a towel over my backside, tucked it into the panties, and pulled them down slightly. She then attached twenty-one cups to my back and legs. (When I received a different cupping treatment on another occasion, the aesthetician noticed that my feet and toes were cold, so she also put cups on the soles of my feet. She said it might feel uncomfortable but would be good for me.) The cups are supposed to be placed over acupoints *(tsubo),* but they seemed to be applied haphazardly. Yuko covered the cups with a few towels, handed me a buzzer, and told me to summon her if any of the cups fell off. She set a timer for fifteen minutes and left. I could hear other treatments going on in adjacent stalls, as well as four aestheticians whispering to one another outside the curtained stalls while waiting for their customers' treatment times to end. The aesthetician massaging the person in the stall next to me repeatedly bumped my arm through the curtain. One of my cups kept falling off, and Yuko seemed irritated when she had to come reattach it, as if I were interrupting her gossip session with co-workers. When my time was up, Yuko removed all the cups and put towels over me. She then took a large, square electro-vibrator massage unit and "ironed" the puffed-up skin orbs, some of them one inch high, back into place. Prior to the cupping treatment, I had been told not to eat a heavy meal before the treatment or do exercise afterward. I was also told that the marks from the cupping, which looked like giant hickeys, might last three or more days, which they did.

An esute treatment related to cupping and also borrowed from the *kanpō* inventory is *mimi tsubo,* electro-stimulation of acupoints on the earlobe (it is called "auricular therapy" outside Japan). *Mimi tsubo* is done with a hand-held needle probe connected by cable to an electro-acupuncture device with knobs and levers for adjusting a biphasic pulse and microcurrent frequency. During my *mimi tsubo* treatment, I was handed a silver metal grounding pole connected to the unit. As the aesthetician worked, the unit emitted a sound like a Geiger counter. I held the pole in my right hand when she

TABLE 3. The Five Elements System

|  | Wood | Fire | Earth | Metal | Water |
|---|---|---|---|---|---|
| Color | Blue/green | Red | Yellow | White | Black |
| Direction | East | South | Center | West | North |
| Organ | Spleen | Lungs | Heart | Liver | Kidneys |
| Taste | Sour | Bitter | Sweet | Pungent | Salty |
| Tissue | Tendons | Blood vessels | Muscles | Skin | Bone |
| Odor | Goatish | Burning | Fragrant | Rank | Rotting |

SOURCE: Williams (1996).

did the right ear, and in my left hand when she did the left ear. She pricked the ears in several places, supposedly for different functions, such as appetite suppression, muscle relaxation, and increased blood flow. I felt exactly the same after the treatment as I had before it.

Another treatment that works to reaffirm an Asian cultural identity is the Ying Yang Five Elements Treatment *(in'yōgogyō toriitomento)*.[18] According to the Slim Beauty House brochure, this is a treatment "gentle on your body [and] derived from 4,000 years of history." The Five Elements system originated from Chinese Taoist doctrine, in which the elements Wood, Fire, Earth, Metal, and Water metaphorically represent the dynamic processes of the natural world in balance. Each element is associated with different colors, directions, body organs, odors, and other phenomena (table 3).

When I had the Five Elements Treatment, the aesthetician first massaged my back, legs, feet, and arms with an unscented "pure" vitamin C oil. Afterward she brought in a cart with the products for the "hard treatment." There were five large plastic containers full of colored lotion, each with a large Chinese character for the element written on it. The aesthetician said that I should select two lotions based on my "beauty objective." Since I did not have one, she suggested the Fire Element for overall general beauty. This lotion was red and had eucalyptus in it. It reminded me of Tiger Balm or BenGay. She massaged it onto the front of my body, asked me to turn over, and then applied the second element lotion. I asked for the lotion corresponding to the Metal Element, which was white and had a sweet scent. Following this application, I was mummified: wrapped in plastic, towels, and finally the trusty BioSlim Thermal Blanket. The idea is to sweat out all the impurities to restore balance. The aesthetician set the timer for twenty minutes and left me to stew.

Throughout the treatment, I asked questions about the meaning of the Five Elements. For example, instead of the color black usually associated with the Water Element, the salon's lotion was dark maroon. The aesthetician could not explain why or say much else about the significance or pattern of interrelationships among the Five Elements. Traditional correspondences not congruent with notions of beauty or elegance are ignored or changed, such as the odor correspondences. The scent associated with the Metal Element is "rank," for Wood it is "goatish," while for Water it is "rotting." Needless to say, none of the salon lotions adapted this aspect of the cosmology, at least not intentionally. As Handler and Linnekin (1984: 280) have noted, in a different context, "The invention of tradition is selective; only certain items are chosen to represent traditional national culture, and other aspects of the past are ignored or forgotten."

In 1995, a new esute fad began appearing in all the salons that was characterized as South Asian aesthetics based on the ancient medico-philosophical system from India called ayurveda. One could buy treatments like Shirodhara, which involves a continuous flow of oil onto the forehead. As the oil drips onto the brow, it is said to induce a meditative state. Another popular treatment, Abhyanga, involves two aestheticians who simultaneously massage warm sesame oil and herbs into the entire body to promote relaxation and encourage skin rejuvenation. However, in the appropriation and repackaging of ayurveda, some aspects of the system, such as medicated enemas, cleansing laxatives, therapeutic vomiting, and nasal purging, are completely pushed aside. None of those ayurveda treatments are available at the esute salons. In a fashion similar to the way New Age proponents sample bits of other cultures without adapting the total precepts of those systems (Torgovnich 1996), esute salons are interested in the "traditional" only when it is able to signify the exotic or natural without compromising local sensibilities. I am not suggesting that there had once been a pristine version of Taoist or ayurvedic doctrine, which is being bastardized by Japan's beauty merchants; rather it is not the doctrines themselves that matter, but only that they are Asian and related to the surface of the body. Only the malleable and exotic aspects of these systems are transposed into the realm of beauty practice.

The various treatments described above appeal to outside, established forms of authority to suggest a respectability or efficacy in the offered service. Something as mundane as spreading lotion on the body is transformed into a link with ancestral rites of beauty and spirituality. Yet at other times it is not stodgy grandmother esute that is being sold, nor is it quite what one would find in a local *kanpō* clinic. "Authentic" Asian beauty methods from a remote, ancient history are not simply posited as a blunt return to the past and a Luddite refutation of modern technology and science. Instead, the two are occasionally manipulated and recombined to create something uniquely reflective of a modern woman's sensibility, knowledge, and command of both.[19]

## Transnational and Creolized Forms of Beauty

Beauty treatments and ideas actively journey around the world as part of a global body transformation enterprise. For example, a "beauty boutique" in Paris named Queen of Sheba offers *épilation à l'orientale,* in which sugar, lemon juice, and orange-blossom water are cooked until gummy, then spread over the body for hair removal. At the Neiman Marcus Beauty Salon in Palo Alto, a hair removal technique is sold under the name "threading." This is characterized as a South Asian and Middle Eastern technique in which unwanted hairs are removed by twisting a folded piece of thread along the hairs and lifting them out with a swift tug.

Beauty culture fads and technologies are dispersed through the world partly through industry and association trade shows and conferences. The world's aestheticians, massage therapists, aromatherapists, reflexologists, holistic practitioners, cosmetologists, dermatologists, and plastic surgeons meet at places like the Esthétique Spa International in Montréal and the International Esthetics, Cosmetics and Spa Conferences. Professional associations, such as the American Society of Esthetic Medicine, provide members with lists of resources, certificates proving membership, lapel pins for uniforms, workshops, management advice, and insurance plans covering accidental death or dismemberment. Another group, the Aesthetics' International Association, hosts annual Aesthetics World Expos in Puerto Rico, Beverly Hills, Toronto, and New York at which members may enroll in classes and troll display booths. Many Japanese salons participate in these world expos or are members of international associations where they learn about new services. It was most likely at one of these events that ayurveda was "discovered" as a mother lode for new treatment ideas.

Gimmicky ideas are part of this global movement of trends and practices. I had difficulty figuring out the lineage of a treatment sold in Japan as *romiromi,* a rhythmic rocking massage using elbows and palms, until I saw an American spa industry advertisement for it that unblushingly described "Lomi Lomi" as the "ancient healing massage of Hawai'i" as taught by "Aunty Machado." It actually has its origin in a Maori massage technique, named *romiromi*, used to beautify men and women by kneading the muscles with the fingers, but now it has acquired a pan-Polynesian identity, or even a purely "Hawai'ian" one. In one sense, Japan's salons and the Euroamerican spas are comembers of an "ethnoscape" (or perhaps a "beautyscape"?) of which Appadurai (1991: 194) states, "It is this fertile ground of deterritorialization, in which money, commodities, and persons unendingly chase each other around the world."

The esute salon delivers beauty from around the world and from any time in history right to a woman's own town, to the office building on her own busy intersection. Although she might consume esute as part of foreign travel, a woman no longer needs to go overseas to find the world's most cherished beauty secrets. Takano Yuri's brochure tells us she offers "from England, herbs and body packs, cupping from China, oil massage from Hawai'i, electrolysis science from America, ayurvedic esute from India, Red Sea esute from Israel, Egyptian herb wraps from Egypt, and mineral Fango packs from Italy." Access to a variety of global beauty practices also positions Japanese women in a world where self-attention and self-absorption in the physical body is "normal," what all women do, and therefore not selfish, immodest, or disgusting. Importing or creating globalist practices legitimizes paid beauty work. The message is: women in other places spend money and time on this type of bodywork, so a Japanese woman should also have this right. Global beauty practices also cultivate ideas about cultural prerogative and birthright. World esute becomes a "shortcut to the exotic experience" (Root 1996: 42). There is a certain degree of esute connoisseurship involved on the part of the consumer, who may select from any number of exotic or novel experiences. For instance, if one is in the mood for a Middle Eastern–inspired treatment, Slim Beauty House offers a weight reduction program called Egyptian Slimming, while Takano Yuri Beauty Clinic sells a $520 Egyptian Body Making home esute set, which is composed of a lotion that accompanies a set of white mummy bandages for self-wrapping.

Although expressed in different ways, many scholars and critics see globalized forms of practice and consumption as a type of cultural imperialism (Tomlinson 1991) in which consumers are induced to buy products that have no meaning or role in their "native" culture. Yet there is also acknowledgment that, instead of passive absorption, individuals in the local setting proactively select and adapt what they want (D. Miller 1995; Howes 1996). Many researchers point out that the exchange of goods and ideas is not simply determined by capitalist strategies. The same is true for new forms of esute. Individual consumers play a role through overseas purchase of beauty goods, access to new images through the Internet, and exchange networks of bootleg goods. Japanese women traveling overseas, for example, became aware of trends like aromatherapy and then requested similar services when they returned home. The result is that there are now esute salons that provide nothing but aromatherapy treatments, such as the Aromabēru salon in Tokyo. There can be no disputing that American media culture has oozed out into unimagined crevices of the social world, influencing many aspects of beauty ideology (such as hypermammary fixation). Yet it is also a mistake to see everything as simply emulation of the West, a "'mimicry' that our own Western narcissism so often demands and derides" (Treat 1996: 8).

Many beauty industries have always had a mixed Euro-Japanese genesis. As part of her argument that there is a new global marketing of uniform images and beauty ideals, Chapkis (1986: 39) quotes an *Advertising Age* article that claims the cosmetics firm Shiseido only recently began presenting an "international thrust" to its advertising as well as an image that hints at its Asian origins. However, Shiseido was international and self-exoticizing from its inception. In 1872, Fukuhara Yushin, the son of a *kanpō* medical practitioner, opened the first Western-style pharmacy, named Fukuhara Shiseido (Gumpert 2000; Koren 1990). Fukuhara's son, Shinzo, went to Columbia University to study pharmacology, after which he spent time in 1913 traveling around Europe studying cosmetics, fashion, and art. When he returned to help run the shop in Tokyo, he began emphasizing toiletries and carried the first line of Western-style cosmetics. In 1917, he hired a design director, Yabe Sue, to assist in the creation of a genuine brand name. A fan of artist Aubrey Beardsley, Yabe incorporated art nouveau imagery to advertise Shiseido as modern and European-inspired while at the same time retaining its image of being guided by *kanpō* philosophy. In 1979, Shiseido hired French photographer and makeup artist Serge Lutens to refurbish its image (Shisedō Hanatsubaki 1979). Lutens used imagery from the Silk Road boom and from Roland Barthes's *Empire of Signs* to reinvest Shiseido with an exotic Asian lineage.

In the process of borrowing or inventing novel spa treatments, Japanese salons have elaborated some while rejecting others outright. The Fango treatment, an application of mineral-rich mud to the body as a pack, is found everywhere, while a popular spa treatment described as "enzyme masks of aloe vera, Japanese green tea, and lavender" has been less successful as a salon treatment.[20] For centuries Japanese used a homemade facial scrub made with rice, but rice-based products have been less successful outside Japan because they are much less exotic than seaweed or algae. In turn, there are international spa services that do not travel well to Japan. I never saw any treatment that resembled the European "Vichy shower," wherein a guest lies on a mat and is showered by directed water jets, or "crystal cleansing." A spa vogue that is unlikely to be found in an esute salon, despite its fictive Japanese-inspired name, is *watsu,* or "water shiatsu," New Age aquatic bodywork in a pool in which the client lets the practitioner twirl her around. The reverse is true as well, resulting in cases where Japanese salon innovations are not transportable elsewhere. One example is the "radon sauna," offered at the Takano Yuri Beauty Clinic when I visited in 1997 but now missing from its menu of treatments.[21] The radon was supposed to enlarge blood vessels and stimulate circulation. On the other hand, a Japanese invention, the electric towel heater mass-produced for serving up warm hand towels *(oshibori)* in restaurants, has been earnestly adopted by the Euroamerican spa industry for facial treatments and is now considered a basic piece of spa equipment.

Salons, spas, and related beauty industries might be thought of as diverse business types subsumed under a universal form of beauty consumption, to paraphrase Wilk's (1995) description of beauty pageants. Of that form of beauty consumption, he adds: "The beauty pageant presents that basic paradox of globalization in an especially clear form: in each place the pageant is made into a local institution, embedded in specific social relationships, invested in a particular historical context" (110). In other words, there is a basic matrix of global beauty culture that may nonetheless be idiosyncratically altered in local settings. There is the internationally ubiquitous GX-99 Vibratory Endermatherapie System, to be sure, but this in no way means that esute salons are completely dependent on the outside market to come up with new gimmicks. There is a flow of goods back and forth across national borders. Most electrolysis machines are imported to Japan from the United States, but other machines, such as the electro-acupuncture device and cupping sets, are exported from Japan to other countries. For a short time an esute salon was selling "Astrology Treatments," in which individuals were given a custom treatment based on their Western astrological signs. But customers never took to this idea and it soon vanished from salon menus. The salon business is a cultural domain characterized by a "ferocious eclecticism" (Torgovnich 1996: 173), in which internationally shared creations are modified or combined with independently arrived at innovations.

Young women are sold the idea that they are not able to gain self-confidence on their own without the assistance of the beauty industry.

They are also pressured to buy beauty while they are young, when it will be maximally useful. At one particular salon that I repeatedly visited, I always spoke with salon manager Ota, who, although polite and cheerful, left no doubt in my mind that she was a calculating businessperson who was shrewdly estimating exactly how much profit she might extract from me. Once I waited in the reception area after my treatment so I could ask some more questions. Another client, a pretty young woman in her twenties, sat near me on an adjacent loveseat while Ota squatted next to her. There was a calculator displaying the price of a treatment set before them, and the customer kept repeating how expensive it all seemed: "But isn't it a little expensive for a bank worker like me?" Ota's voice went way up the pitch scale and assumed a rhinophonic quality as she replied, "But you're still young, right?" They both examined her legs (she was wearing a miniskirt), noting both good and bad points. Between giggles, Ota kept insisting, "But you're still young, right?" *(Demo, mada wakain deshō?)*. The esute salon business is fascinating because its practically overt bogusness is pushed aside by consumers, who must block out indications of fraud in order to accept the dream of beauty. The salon business sells anxiety and desire about appearance, and the idea that the body is something that can be assuaged only with esute products and services.

# CHAPTER 3

# Mammary Mania

---

Browsing through a Japanese women's magazine, I found an advertisement for a product called Angel Wing (figure 10). The copy announced, "I stopped being an A cup the day I got a present from an angel." The item being sold for $220 was a set of battery-powered pink bust pads modeled on the body of a nude Japanese woman. Supposedly, any woman is able to increase her breast size in only a month if she uses the Angel Wing for less than an hour each day.

There are three notable things about this advertisement. First, breasts without a few modest stars or some text covering the nipples would normally not have been found in women's print media a decade ago. Second, advertisements for such bust products appeared only occasionally before 1990. During the mid-1980s, goods and services for breast augmentation were rarely seen in the pages of young women's magazines.[1] Third, when such advertisements did appear, the eroticization of the breast was safely displaced onto a foreign woman's nude body (Clammer 1995; Creighton 1997). Yet, since at least 1992, we find an astonishing proliferation of bogus gadgets like Angel Wing hawked in almost all magazines geared toward women, including those aimed at high school girls.

In this chapter I examine the shift to a new model of female beauty that incorporates an Americanesque view that a "full balcony," to borrow from the Italian, is an essential attribute of womanhood. In addition to extreme thinness and smooth hairlessness, homogenization of beauty imaging has led to consideration of the size and shape of the breasts as an important index of female attractiveness. American hypermammary fixa-

FIGURE 10. Angel Wing "bust-up" product advertisement.

tion is old hat, continuing from earlier decades into the new millennium, but enthusiasm for large breasts is of new vintage in Japan. Particularly in women's magazines and the aesthetic salon industry, we see aggressive competition for new customers who want to transform their figures into a top-heavy shape. I look at some of the changes in breast fashions and symbolism that have occurred in Japan, and examine how a new focus on the breast as an aspect of female beauty is reflected in a lucrative industry for bust products and services. The chic breast is a body region that may be fashioned with the help of numerous new technologies, products, and services. Capitalist industries fuel anxiety and desire to install these new breasts, but at the same time, bust enhancement practices ironically allow for an assertive type of individual self-expression that runs counter to social norms about proper female self-presentation. As noted earlier, this last point is contentious in feminist research. Whether or not breast trends are fabricated by corporations in order to foster consumption, they reflect much more than "just fashion."

My focus on the breast is not intended to exoticize or eroticize Japan or Japanese women, or to serve as yet another exposé of the bizarre (what, after all, could top the fact that *millions* of American women have had plastic baggies of gel sewn into their chests?). Rather I aim to show linkages between breast fashions, a trend toward the surface expression of identity, and the spread of a global Euroamerican beauty ideology. During my stay in Japan in the late 1970s, I was impressed by what I saw as a generally nonjudgmental attitude about female breasts. In the public bath, co-workers, friends, and even strangers might occasionally comment on someone's chest, but overall the breasts lacked the intense focus of anxiety I saw among American women. They were not considered critical attributes of womanhood, beauty, or sexuality. However, the radical change in breast consciousness I encountered in later years led me to consider this topic. What happened to transform the aesthetically preferred planiform body shape into one with a pronged front?

## Biology, Breasts, and Culture

Despite cross-cultural data to the contrary, many writers believe that some concepts of female attractiveness are universal and are therefore intimately grounded in biology and evolution (Cowley 1996). Campbell (1970: 263–64) asserted that "well-rounded buttocks and breasts have always been attractive to men." Popular science writer Morris (1994: 122–23) believed that female hominid breasts evolved as "buttock mimics" to attract males and therefore are an inherently sexual form of display. In addition to serving as rationalizations for a researcher's own erotic preferences, such theories fail to explain or even address the issue of why there are differences in breast size or shape in different regions of the world, within a population, and over the course of an individual woman's lifetime, or to address other possible symbolic meanings.

Hamilton (1984) provides in-depth discussion of the androcentrism reflected in such evolutionary theories. American breast fetishism appears in other forms of "science," such as the ethnocentric diagnosis of small breasts as a "disease" by the American Society of Plastic and Reconstructive Surgeons in 1982, and the pages of *National Geographic,* where ethnographic representation of exotic peoples often means the display of a set of breasts (Lutz and Collins 1993: 75). Mellican (1995) shows how a claim of scientific objectivity often filters out critical social and cultural information, in this case how beauty ideals generated the perceived necessity of breast implants.

Concentrated breast obsession in the United States is actually not that old. Both Hollander (1993) and Yalom (1997) have illustrated transformations that occurred in the visual representation of female breasts in Europe and the United States, and note that today's intense obsession dates to the post-1940 era. According to Wolf (1992: 209), "The mega-mammaries that men pant over in *Bust Out!*" were once considered abhorrent, and "it wasn't until the mid-nineteenth century, when women cinched in their waists with corsets, that commodious breasts became alluring." In 1956, Horace Miner published an article spoofing anthropological writing that enumerated aspects of American behavior in the guise of a tribe called the Nacirema. Along with other body rituals and beliefs, Miner mentioned the odd concern with female breasts exhibited by this group: "Still other rites are used to make women's breasts larger if they are small, and smaller if they are large. General dissatisfaction with breast shape is symbolized in the fact that the ideal form is virtually outside the range of human variation. A few women afflicted with almost inhuman hypermammary development are so idolized that they make a handsome living by simply going from village to village and permitting the natives to stare at them for a fee" (Miner 1956: 506).

The rites that Miner alluded to included padded bras, bust creams, and exercises heavily promoted during the 1940s and afterward. Although the British created something called the Lemon Cup Bust Improver in 1890 (which contained a coiled spring in each horsehair-padded cup), it was not until the elaboration of the breast as an erotic fetish that Americans got truly creative with these contraptions. In 1948, the same year that Frederick's of Hollywood came out with their push-up bra, 4,500,000 sets of bra padding (colloquially named "falsies") were sold. The following year, Maidenform introduced the heavily stitched and pointed chansonette or "bullet" bra (*Self* 1995). Not long after, in 1953, Hugh Hefner began publishing *Playboy* magazine, the main intent of which was to display photos of women with abnormally massive bosoms.[2]

Sociobiologists conceive of breasts as adaptive "strategic instruments of persuasion" to keep males tied to dependent females and babies (Low 1979). Both Gallup (1982) and Short (1976) postulate that permanent breast enlargement in humans developed as a method for enhancing the postpartum pair bond and increasing the likelihood of aid-giving by males. The core of such ideas is not only that breasts are universally sexual, but that they evolved in the context of female competition for the attention of powerful and resource-controlling males. It is striking to see the degree to which an erotic aesthetic of twentieth-century American men has affected theories of directional selection in human evolution. As noted by Mascia-Lees et al. (1986) and others, many of these androcentric notions derive from the assumption that female hominid ancestors were universally "dependent" rather than active food gatherers or competitive foragers (Hrdy 1986), which is an alternative view. Our understanding of the nature of foraging economies based on ethnographic study does not support the notion of female dependence.

It is, of course, easy to develop scenarios to explain human breasts that do not rely on male academics' sexual responses in the guise of concepts such as "sexual selection," "differential parental investment," and "female dependency." Writers strangely ignore obvious explanations, such as those related to nursing and the storage of milk or fat, or Morgan's (1972) novel idea that breasts were something for babies to cling to, enabling the mother to engage in foraging activities. Even when breasts are viewed as perhaps having something to do with increased fat reserves to support infants, male researchers still link this to men rather than babies, claiming that the breasts are "signals" to males of the woman's ability to produce a large quantity of milk, thus offering a payoff for male parental investment (Cant 1981; Low et al. 1987). Yet there is no basis for a claim that breast size is in any way correlated with lactation success (Anderson 1988). Biodeterministic theories such as these actually mimic the American male scholar's own folk theory and obsession with the breast. As Washburn (1978: 416) warned us some years ago, it is a mistake to view one's own culture as synonymous with human nature. To judge from the nature of "scholarly" attention to the breasts, as Steinbeck (1947: 5) once put it, "a visitor of another species might judge . . . that the seat of procreation lay in the mammaries."

## Breast Commodification and Symbolism

Japan's new bust-consciousness began as another dimension of the "body-conscious" look, and may in fact represent a rebellion against the cult of cuteness and ineffectual innocence still endorsed by many Japanese men (see figure 3 in chapter 1, of porn actress Kogure Chie, which illustrates the durability of the cute aesthetic). In the 1970s, the media was flooded with images of childish-looking women who visually coded the desired traits of docility, naïveté, and powerlessness. An indication of this change of attitude is that since 1996 Japan has been home to the Nyūbo Bunka Kenkyūkai (Breast Culture Study Association), a group of academics, artists, and enthusiasts. Marketers of breast products exploit the sense of independence and power available to women through body transformation. One advertisement for a breast enhancement service says, "Goodbye to the old me—at the Bust Clinic I'll get confidence!" Another company sells a breast augmentation massage unit together with magical lotions with the message "The breast is a woman's self assertion . . . The most important thing is not size but that they point upward," thereby linking breast style to a self-presentation of youthful assertiveness and forcefulness.

The change in breast symbolism, in which adult sexuality and self-confidence are indexed through the commodified breast, is not only the result of savvy advertising; it also indicates a change in the cultural model of femininity. This is a definite shift away from the past, in which the cute and submissive girl was first of all evaluated as a future occupant of the wife/ mother social category. The breast no longer denotes just maternity and motherhood; it has also become a visual cipher for the independent, sexualized self. The commodified and eroticized breast supplements or supplants the original maternal ur-breast.

From anthropological research, we learn that breasts are not necessarily a part of erotic communication and may have no role in heterosexual activity in some societies (Davenport 1976). "In the great majority of cases the bare bosom is not inconsistent with ideals of feminine modesty" (Ford and Beach 1951: 47). For instance, among the Polynesian Mangaia, female breasts are not considered sexually arousing. In the case of Japan, folklore, mythology, art, and popular culture indicate that, at least prior to the Pacific War, the breast had a subsidiary role in sexual fantasy and practice, in which the focus has predominantly been on the genitals (Levy 1971; Bornoff 1991). Screech (1999: 100) also supports this view, noting that while depictions of nipples on both men and women in erotic prints, or *shunga,* are considered erotic, the breasts are not: "In *shunga,* male and female bodies appear virtually identical other than the genitals; even female breasts are downplayed and rarely appear as sites of sexual interest." One indication of this is that no extravagant lexicon of euphemisms for breasts exists in Japanese as it does in American English, yet the lexicon for female genitalia is greatly developed. For example, Constantine's (1994) compendium of Japanese slang contains around 260 terms for the vagina, including technical words, mob argot, euphemisms, puns, historic expressions, regional and occupational descriptors, Buddhist terms, poetic phraseology, and English-inspired neologisms. There are only six terms given for breasts, however.

The breasts are perceived as having a feeding function more than a sexual role in the majority of cultures. This may be indicated by the fact that few traditional societies require their concealment by clothing. The dissociation of nudity, breasts, and sexuality is especially true of prewar Japan, where mothers in the countryside customarily breast-fed infants in public. Richie describes vivid scenes of life in Japan in the early part of the twentieth century. He writes: "By summer many were unclothed. There

were no more laws against going naked and so people naturally did . . .
Bare breasts in the suburbs were not uncommon" (2001: 28). During the
Occupation period, etiquette books for Japanese cautioned that foreigners do not like to see women nursing in public and advised that one should
learn to refrain from doing it. The custom of public and mixed-sex bathing
also illuminates how nakedness within certain contexts (bathing, physical labor, breast-feeding) deflected or downplayed any sexual meaning of
the breasts in Japan (Lebra 1976, 1984; Clark 1994; Downs 1990). According to Nomura (1990), decontextualized nudity was not considered erotic
before contact with the West, and it was only as the habit of wearing more
clothes spread that the concealed body became an object of desire. Western criticism led Japanese authorities to begin imposing regulations in 1872
stipulating that people could not continue to walk around semi-naked or
wearing only Japanese-style underwear in public. A brief insurrection
against the new rules included the slogan "Allow nakedness!" among its
demands (Garon 1997).

Prior to the twentieth century, the female breast signified motherhood
before anything else, and celebrations of mothers' breasts appear in Japanese plays, poems, songs, nursery rhymes, and folklore. Lebra (1976: 59)
notes that "in Japan, women's breasts have been adored more as a symbol of maternal nurturance than of sex." Early references are found in the
*Man'yōshū* (Collection of ten thousand leaves) and in provincial reports
from the Nara period ( AD 710–784), where a mother or parent is sometimes called *tarachi* or *tarachine*.[3] This expression may have derived from
*tabishi* (full), or perhaps it already meant "drooping breasts," as it did when
it later came to be used by poets. Scholars have noted the emotionally intense nature of the breast in Japan not only as a nutritional source but in
connection with play and a symbolic connection to the mother. Contact
with mothers' breasts may be considered a type of "skinship," the intimate skin-to-skin contact found in bathing and considered essential to
healthy relationships (Clark 1994). The closeness and security associated
with breast-feeding was enhanced through traditional sleeping patterns,
in which many children co-slept with their mothers for five or more years
(Caudill and Plath 1966). Wagatsuma and Hara (1974) take this idea a dubious step farther when they suggest that the widespread acceptance of
alcohol indicates that it may function as a substitute for the maternal breast
and help men sleep.

Allison (1996) became aware of this maternal breast while watching a
television program for children. She was charmed yet surprised by the
naked, rounded, and full cartoon breasts she saw floating on the television screen. In her analysis, she suggests that the gaiety and fleshiness of

bouncing "permissible" motherly breasts serve to de-emphasize the genitals. This contrasts with the female breast in American culture, where it is exclusively sexual and display of maternal breasts is never part of public space and may even be illegal in some states or when children reach a certain age.[4] Eroticization of the breasts results in their becoming less permissible in a breast-feeding role. Whereas 70 to 80 percent of women in Japan breast-fed in 1955, less than half do now (Jolivet 1997). Some Japanese writers attribute a shortened breast-feeding period to the new consciousness of breasts as primarily sexual (Asami 1997).

## The Fashioned Breast

The shift from maternal to sexual breast meanings was accompanied by changes in clothing styles. In the past, the wearing of the kimono influenced ideals of female attractiveness, creating a focus on parts of the female anatomy other than the breasts. The kimono gives the female form a columnar look that de-emphasizes the breasts and waist and draws attention to the neck, hips, and ankles. As Cherry (1987: 21) notes, "Traditionally, a Japanese woman's appeal was said to reside in an anatomical part that most other nations ignore: the nape *(unaji)* of the neck. More than breasts, buttocks, or legs, the nape exuded sensuality." Although mostly thought of as a prewar preference, nape appreciation was still popular enough in the mid-1980s that Cherry found a women's magazine article on nape beauties *(unaji bijin)* accompanied by photos of celebrity napes.

The body shape thought best suited to the kimono is slender with a willow-shaped waist. Large breasts are said to disrupt the flow of a kimono's lines. A derogatory term for a woman whose large breasts alter the desired pillar-shape is "pigeon's chest" *(hatomune desshiri)*. Prewar posture also de-emphasized the chest. Writing on deportment for well-bred Japanese girls and women, a nineteenth-century writer said, "The head and shoulders should be carried slightly forward, and the body should also be bent forward slightly at the waist, to secure the most womanly and aristocratic carriage" (Bacon 1891: 50–51). A requisite undergarment worn beneath the kimono can also "correct" bodily defects, such as overly large breasts, so that the figure approaches the ideal tube shape. The body is molded into a proper cylinder with the aid of V-shaped bust pads and bust-suppressing sashes.[5]

Goldstein-Gidoni (1999) describes in detail the use of gauze and padding to correct the body in the process of kimono dressing. The bust

FIGURE 11.
The chest-flattening kimono
undersash *(datemaki)*.

is subdued with an undergarment called a *datemaki,* which is wrapped
around the body from the chest to the waist (figure 11).[6] The breasts are
further depressed with another outer sash. Dalby (1983: 290) notes that
there is a subtle correlation between the placement of the final sash, or
*obi,* and one's social status: An *obi* tied somewhat low over the breasts denotes a more mature woman, while an *obi* tied high up over the bust line
indicates a virginal and innocent unmarried woman. A modern geisha ties
her sash lowest of all, and also displays more of the erotic nape. Twenty-
five years ago Dalby fretted, with accurate foresight, that "cultural notions of ideal beauty seem to influence actual physical characteristics, however; as Western notions of long-legged, big-bosomed glamor have
affected postwar Japan, amazingly, such physical types seem to have blos-
somed. The cultivation of this new type of figure does not bode well for
the kimono" (Dalby 1983: 286).

Although napes still make an appearance on male lists of "favorite female body parts," the breast repeatedly emerges at the top of the list, as
in a 1999 magazine poll (*Ranking Dai Suki!* 1999d). The most frequent
answers men gave to the question "Which part of a woman's body do

you like most?" were, in descending order, the breasts, legs, eyes, face, buttocks, hair, arms, lips, nape, and hands.

One reason for Japan's new fascination with "milk mountains" is the globalization of media. Through the agency of transnational television, film, magazines, and especially pornography, Japanese became infected by an American-derived erotic fetishization and commodification of the breast. Haiken (1997: 203–204) observes that the American male presence in Vietnam during the 1960s, with its *Playboy* visual culture, inaugurated new standards of beauty that led to increased incidence of women seeking breast augmentation. In a similar vein, it was only during Japan's Occupation period that public viewing of unclothed female bodies, with a corresponding focus on the breasts, became common forms of entertainment. This is when the American idea of a "strip show" was first introduced and popularized (Seidensticker 1990). The postwar emphasis on breasts was one aspect of a general "flesh boom" *(nikutai būmu)* that celebrated physicality and sexuality. The popularity of Tamuro Tajirō's 1947 novella *Flesh Gate,* which immortalized the *panpan* girl, an Occupation-era sex worker, reflects the interest in a new type of carnality. In her article on postwar depiction of the female body in film, Izbicki (1997) notes that some critics explicitly connect the popularity of 1950s actress Kyō Machiko, who was described as buxom, with fleshy thighs and a small waist, to an American influence. In her analysis of women's magazines, Ochiai (1997) points out that the earliest photograph of a Japanese woman in a bikini was found in a 1968 issue of the magazine *Josei Jishin* (Ladies' Own).

The ideal of a voluptuous body was later replaced by another ideal—the innocent, prepubescent look of the girl next door. The quest for girlishness over womanhood meant the rejection of a mature woman's body as an object of desire and an increase in the "Lolita complex" among middle-aged males. During the 1970s, I remember women friends claiming that large breasts were "embarrassing" because they visibly marked a woman as having moved beyond the virginal state of the untouched girl. Shiokawa (1999) has traced alterations in the representation of female breasts in the *manga* (comics) world. During the 1960s to 1970s, comic artists were reluctant to emphasize mature attributes, and the breasts of both prepubescent and grown-up heroines were barely hinted at. A change began to occur by the mid-1980s, when more buxom female characters emerged.[7]

As the forms and availability of pornography grew, so did certain restrictions. Because censorship laws banned the depiction of pubic hair, Allison (1996) thinks, as do I, that the deflection away from the genitals resulted in an increased eroticization of other body parts, such as breasts and buttocks. Yet the new body ideal is not a simple return to the mature

FIGURE 12. Sex/breasts for sale: signboard on Tokyo street. Photo by author.

and shapely look of someone like Kyō Machiko. Instead, a large chest is combined with an ultraslim, smooth, and youthful-looking form to create a body that is impossible to achieve without the assistance of the beauty industry. This model, together with the new association between breasts and sex, was presented in a startlingly frank manner on a street near the Yushima subway station, where I found a signboard (figure 12) for a sex service called "raw body aesthetics" *(nama esute)*. The sign featured a drawing of a *manga*-style prostitute with unrealistic bombé breasts that she is pushing up for inspection.

The first Japanese women to experiment with surgical breast enlargement were mainly postwar *panpan* girls and entertainers who needed to respond to the tastes of the Occupationnaire. The compulsion to change breast size and shape has now extended to other sectors of Japanese society, and is sought through both medical and nonmedical methods. Celebrities and sex workers are likely to resort to surgical intervention, while other Japanese women seek out nonsurgical techniques. An example of the acceptability of surgically enhanced breasts among public professional women is the Kanō "sisters" (the relationship is tenuous), Kyoko and Mika. Although they are described as "beauty and life consultants" and produce a stream of books, photo albums, videos, DVDs, CDs, calendars, and videos, they are mainly personages famous for being famous, the Hilton sisters of Japan. Breasts no longer symbolize status as a wet nurse for a salaryman, but rather market value as a sexual commodity.

## Medical Forms of Breast Augmentation

The history of breast augmentation, particularly the story of how silicone ended up in the mammaries, has by now been retold in numerous popular and scholarly reports (Kosover 1972; Larned 1977; Schalk 1988; Swartz 1995; Byrne 1996a, 1996b; Haiken 1997). The breast implant foundational narrative goes something like this: Postwar streetwalkers in Japan had liquid silicone injected directly into their breasts in order to cater to the erotic tastes of American Occupation servicemen. The practice spread to the United States, where it was adopted by exotic dancers in California and Nevada. According to Byrne, "Long before electronic gadgets and Toyotas, silicone injections became one of the first successful exports to America" (1996a: 41).

The story picks up odd flourishes, like Byrne's (1996a: 41–42) claim that immediately after the Pacific War, transformer coolant "disappeared" off the docks of Yokohama Harbor and was used in breast injections. There is a strange slant to the chronicle that necessitates a conception of Japan as a backward culture without a bona fide science of cosmetic surgery. One way this is accomplished is to insinuate that Japanese doctors, not quite up to the strictures of Western medicine, filled their syringes with unsterile industrial-grade silicone, or that it was weirdly "adulterated" with things like cottonseed, croton, peanut, sesame, or olive oil, even though European and American doctors also diluted silicone with other substances. While the story of breast augmentation in Japan is distressing, it differs little from Euroamerican medical history. Since at least 1896, Japanese doctors have been ploddingly documenting medical experiments and case studies in a scientific fashion, including their efforts at breast augmentation, and dutifully publishing findings in professional journals.

In any case, the historical picture is not at all linear and shows a considerable back-and-forth influence between Japan and other nations. A foreign substance, paraffin, was first injected into breasts in the 1890s in Vienna by Robert Gersuny (Goldwyn 1980). Following Gersuny's reports describing breast injections, he and other doctors experimented with injections of various paraffin mixtures, vegetable oils, lanolin, beeswax, and Vaseline. With paraffin, the resulting breasts were often deformed or discolored, and the practice soon ended in Europe but later resurfaced in Japan. It is not known when, exactly, it arrived, but documented cases date from 1952 (Mutou 1980). Until 1960, the most commonly injected substances were members of the paraffin group. One, called Organogen, was a mix of Vaseline and Arabian gum, and the other, Bioplax or Bioplaxm, included Vaseline and lanolin in its formula (Maeda 1956).

Complications from these paraffin-based injections were reported in the Japanese medical literature soon after, so by 1960 most doctors had switched to silicone-based substances for breast injections. The first was dimethylpolysiloxane or DMPS, sold in Japan in 1956 as a medical fluid called Elicon.[8] DMPS was eventually combined with different oils to create a formula that would retard the migration of the silicone, and one became known in the United States as the "Sakurai formula" after a Japanese physician (Kagan 1963). In 1958, Sakurai began using Dow Corning 200 Fluid, or dimethylpolysiloxane, diluted with 1 percent animal and vegetable fatty acids. The solution was sterilized before it was injected. Beginning around 1958, various sponge-type prosthesis techniques were also attempted.

By 1958 women in Japan were already seeking help at hospital clinics for complications from the injected paraffin or silicone (Akiyama 1958). Motou (1980) refers to a number of studies that document medical problems resulting from breast injections.[9] Most common was the formation of lumps. Other difficulties included connective tissue disease, migrating globules, scar tissue formations, gangrene, pneumonia, infections, blood clots, immune dysfunction, cancer, and death.[10] Problems resulting from breast injections can take as long as thirty years to develop, and starting in the mid-1980s increasing numbers of surviving middle-aged women suffering from the toxic effects of the postwar injection boom began seeking treatment. For instance, a fifty-five-year-old woman who had had breast injections nineteen years earlier eventually suffered from stromal sarcomas that required mastectomies (Miyata, Okano, and Kuratomi 1997). Japanese doctors occasionally treat these recent cases as an opportunity to "earn as you learn" while they perfect a new procedure, an immediate reaugmentation of the breasts using adipose tissue from the lower abdomen (Aoki, Mitsuhashi, and Hyakusoku 1997).

Some historians assumed that the hypodermic syringe method of breast augmentation died out, but this is not the case. Despite the serious medical consequences, Japanese doctors continued to inject silicone into their patients' breasts. Writing in 1989, some plastic surgeons conceded, "We must regrettably admit, however, that the injection of foreign material has not been completely discarded; there is no legal control and some aesthetic plastic surgeons are not members of JSAPS [the Japan Society of Aesthetic Plastic Surgeons]. In fact, all too often there are new patients with postoperative disorders of augmentation mammaplasty" (Ohtake et al. 1989: 67). Two studies (Ohtake et al. 1989; Yayoi 1982) indicate that the injection method actually escalated from 1956 to 1965. Although the silicone bag implant was legally introduced in Japan in 1972, the injection method continued to peak until 1976. Silicone injections were given by some clinics as late as the 1980s, and even though silicone was banned in 1992, the practice appears to continue illegally at some clinics. In 1994, doctors at a hospital in Okinawa treated a thirty-nine-year-old housewife who had recently been given silicone breast injections. The gel had already migrated to her lungs (Matsuba et al. 1994).

In 1959, a duo of Houston doctors came up with the idea of encasing the silicone in a pack, and in 1962, they implanted the first prototype into the breasts of a woman named Timmie Jean Lindsey. Silicone bag implants were approved for sale in the United States in 1963 but were not legally imported to Japan until 1979. Even so, it seems that many Japanese doctors were already using them, because the American prefilled bags proved to be too large for Japanese chests. As a result, in 1965, some Japanese doctors began using an inflatable bag, which was first inserted into the chest before being filled with silicone (Mutou 1980). Yet during the thirteen-year period before silicone implants were banned, only around twenty thousand Japanese women had breast implants, 80 percent of them for cosmetic reasons (*Daily Yomiuri* 1992). This is much less than the American frenzy, where implants in one year alone exceed this number.

The American FDA moratorium on sales of silicone moved the Japanese government to ban the importation of silicone implants in 1992. Since then, patients have been able to choose cohesive gel, hydrogel, or saline implants. Clinics will also perform an adipose tissue transfer to the breasts. Cosmetic surgery clinics push tissue transfer surgery as the most effective way to, as one outfit put it, "get slimmer and get a big bust at the same time," since fat is usually taken from the hip or thigh. They also shamelessly insist that this procedure is completely safe because it uses one's own flesh. Some clinics also inject the fat into the breast over a period of time, perhaps as long as three years, with tissue "harvested" from the abdomen, hips, and thighs. Fat transfer, or "microlipoinjection," is popular among Japanese cosmetic surgeons not only for breast augmentation but for penile enlargement as well. Hypodermic injection of hormones, as well as orally ingested hormones, is also a popular method for breast enhancement. As efforts to develop safer, or at least newer, breast augmentation practices continue in the United States, these inevitably diffuse to Japan as well. Currently, American doctors are considering the insertion of a spongelike material composed of a woman's own cells into her chest, which would supposedly trick the immune system into growing cells over it, thereby increasing bust size. Another product in the research stage is the trilucent implant, a soybean oil–filled bag with a silicone shell. One suggested complication is that the oil might become rancid and produce a body odor. Whether or not these innovations eventually will become popular in Japan remains to be seen.

In one study, all eighteen patients who had received silicone or paraffin breast injections between 1954 to 1966 were "homemakers" aged twenty-six to fifty-five (Kumagai et al. 1984). It could be speculated that although they were homemakers at the time of the study, they might not have been when they had the injections, since during the early postwar years breast enlargement was mainly a concern of the demimondaine. The total number of women who had injection augmentation between 1955 and 1970 is estimated to be fewer than twenty thousand (Yamazaki et al. 1977). Together with an estimated twenty thousand implant surgeries, the total of forty thousand women who have had medical breast augmentation is quite low compared to the situation in the United States. The number of American women getting breast implant surgery has increased by an incredible 593 percent since 1992. In 2002, an estimated 237,000 women had breast augmentation (American Society for Aesthetic Plastic Surgery 2004). Until around 1990, Japan's cultural milieu did not exert enough pressure on most women to worry about upper torso issues. And even now, with the new bust consciousness, invasive surgical procedures like implants are not very popular among women who are not sex workers, models, entertainers, or personages such as the Kanō sisters.

Part of the apprehension over implants could stem from a Confucian belief that the body should not be tampered with, as seen in a continuing legal and cultural debate over removal of organs and organ transplants.[11] According to Confucian ideas, the body is an inheritance from the parents and so should not be maimed or mutilated. To fundamentally alter the body is to show disrespect, and such alterations therefore demonstrate a lack of filial piety. One way to honor parents and ancestors is to preserve one's body intact. There were, at one time, strict taboos against human dissection (Kasulis 1993). There is consequently much hesitation, on the part of both doctors and patients, over cutting technologies and transplant surgeries, especially when compared to the United States. Ikegami (1989) wonders if the low rates of hysterectomies, cesarean sections, and other invasive procedures in Japan stem from the Buddhist philosophy of noninterference, and a resignation to events beyond human control. There is widespread belief that the application of some technologies, such as transplants and possibly implants, should not be used to change the "core" of Japaneseness, such as the body, as these might be seen as a threat to the moral order (Lock 1995). The body is seen as something inherited from the lineage, and alteration severs this link. A woman who had breast implant surgery said that she herself, her mother, and her grandmother all worried about whether it was a good thing to "damage the body which one has received from parents."[12]

Another persistent cultural belief that may have influenced a sense of repugnance toward some surgical techniques stems from Shinto concepts of purity and pollution. In Japan there has been a long-standing symbolic equation of the "outside" with pollution, and the "inside" with purity (Ohnuki-Tierney 1984). Implants and injectable substances are materials originating outside the body, so they have a great potential to be polluting. The appeal of fat-recycling methods may be that they alleviate pollution concerns. Even so, all medical procedures are costly and time-consuming, so the beauty industry has been quick to offer the consumer many alternative methods of breast enhancement.

## Salon Treatments and Programs for the Flat-Chested

One consequence of the aversion to implants is a burgeoning market for nonsurgical breast enhancement products and treatments. The term in Japanese for anything intended to change the breast into a larger or different shape is "bust-up" *(basuto appu).* "Bust-up" is an example of "Japan-made English," native blends that are an imaginative syncretism of both

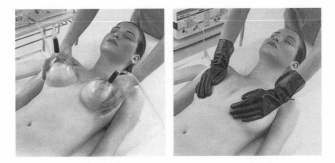

FIGURE 13. Bust-up treatment at an aesthetic salon.
Reproduced with permission of Shōgakukan Publishing
Company.

languages. The native word for breast or chest is *mune,* which has a broad
range of meaning. *Mune* can refer to the heart area, and abstractly to the
seat of the emotions. It is found in idioms that refer to strong feelings,
such as *mune ga itamu* (gut-wrenching), *mune ga ippai* (the heart is filled
with emotion), and *mune ga sawagu* (to be worried). One way to indicate that one means the erotic female breast is to use the narrowly defined
"bust." Neo-English terms for female breasts have also appeared in slang
forms created by high school students. In colloquial speech, mothers'
breasts are called *oppai* or *chichi.* Neologisms derived from these include
*non-chichi,* a combination of *chichi* and English "none," for a woman with
very small breasts. Another nondictionary label for a flat chest is a blend
of *oppai* and the English "raisin," yielding *rēzunpai,* breasts so small they
are like raisins.

Since 1992, the bust-up product and service category has provided a
boost to the Japanese beauty industry. Aesthetic salons shrewdly zeroed
in on this particular body "problem" and began offering nonsurgical techniques in the 1990s. Salons provide bust-up under the general menu of
body treatment courses, or else as a special service. Usually a bust-up treatment course at a salon involves manual massage, the application of creams
or packs, and mechanical stimulation with some type of appliance or apparatus (figure 13). Often, something like a suction cup linked by cables
to an electromassage machine is placed over the breasts as part of these
treatments. Tokyo Beauty Center's Bust Treatment Course includes a clay
mask, a pack, and a manual massage. Slim Beauty House provides a Bust
Care Course in four steps. The first procedure is called "Firming," in which

the aestheticians use an "advanced hand treatment." The second step is called "Toning," during which the client has conduit patches placed around the breasts that deliver a low-frequency electric current through cables connected to an electromassage machine. The third step is called "Larging," of which Slim Beauty House literature says nothing more than that it is "original." The last step is called "Lifting" and includes a collagen sheet pack stretched over the breasts. At the Takano Yuri Beauty Clinic, the customer is reassured that she can lose weight without decreasing her bust size if she enrolls in the Taut Bust Course, in which a greenish mud pack is applied to the chest.

For a bust-up treatment, I visited the Socie salon in 1997 for the basic Bust Care Course. When I arrived for my treatment, the manager of the salon introduced my aesthetician, who bowed formally and asked me to follow her. She was wearing something like a nurse's uniform and had a name badge that identified her as "Maeda." Maeda led me to the Treatment Room, where I was told to sit on a massage table while she took measurements. She used a tape measure to collect calculations of various sorts, such as the size of my breasts at the top and bottom and the distance from shoulder to nipple, which she then entered onto a medical chart.

I lay on the table, and Maeda covered my legs with a large warm towel and began to apply a thick brown exfoliating scrub to the top area of my chest. Salon literature identified this as an ultrarich Fango poultice, a special blend of minerals from Tuscany, first used by the Médici family two thousand years ago. The scrub was meant to extract impurities. I was directed to a shower to wash it off, and when I returned Maeda swabbed on another mud product, also, of course, from Italy. This one had many kinds of minerals and herbs in it. After spreading the thick paste over my chest, she covered me with blue plastic and several towels. My eyes were covered, the lights were dimmed, and I was left alone for around ten minutes.

After returning from a second shower, I was ready for the hardware. I lay on the table again and Maeda wheeled over a fussy electromassage machine. The machine had various knobs and meters, and two metal wands attached by cable. Maeda modestly covered my left breast with a towel, and then massaged a rich cream onto my right breast. Maeda used the proper "etiquette of touch" (Young 1997: 32), and the draped white towel turned each breast into a unique object of scrutiny separate from my person. She fiddled with the machine a bit, ostensibly to "adjust" it, and set a timer. The machine began emitting a rhythmic beeping sound.

She used three different techniques as she vigorously manipulated the two metal wands over my chest region, applying the thick cream liberally between and during each technique.

The first method was a full-on pressing or poking with the wands, which were pushed in near each other by their tips. She held one wand in each hand and pressed in with a sense of deliberation, held the wand punched into the breast for a few seconds, and then moved to another area to repeat this maneuver. She worked her way around the breast, only poking the top and undersides. Maeda adjusted the machine, and a different beep pattern started. This time, she used a rolling motion with the sides of the wands and pressed over the nipple area as well. After a third adjustment to the machine, the flesh of the breast was kneaded with the wands, a type of mixing motion. After completing the first breast, she began the entire process again on the left breast. I had no sensation of electric current at all when the right breast was worked on, but did feel a slight tingle on the left and for the first time was actually concerned that this magic machine might in fact be doing something. While Maeda worked, I repeatedly made efforts to look closely at both the machine and the wands. I would peek out from under the towel, or move my head to displace it, but each time Maeda firmly replaced the towel over my eyes, instructing me to "relax."

After the treatment was completed, Maeda measured me once more. She entered the findings onto my chart and announced that my bust had increased by 1.5 centimeters. I asked if I might get a copy of this chart, and later the salon manager did mail it to me. This chart (figure 14) is one of many artifacts that reflect the aesthetic salon idea of measurable beauty. As a written document, the chart is intended to verify that an increase in bust size took place. Although I might have been swollen from all the massage and manipulation, my bust size did not, in fact, change at all.

Many other bust-up programs follow a similar format, in which measurement is critical in determining "progress" toward an ideal or correct breast shape. For instance, one enterprising salon, Erufurāju, promotes itself as "the bust specialty shop" and offers advice based on computerized data. A "Check Your Bust" scale gives codified measurements and a formula for determining a proper bust-to-body ratio. According to the salon, an ideal bust size for a twenty-year-old is presented as a definitive measure: one multiplies their height in centimeters by the standardized number 0.515 in order to obtain the "correct measurement" for the top of the breast.

Another form of bust-up service is available through a consortium of

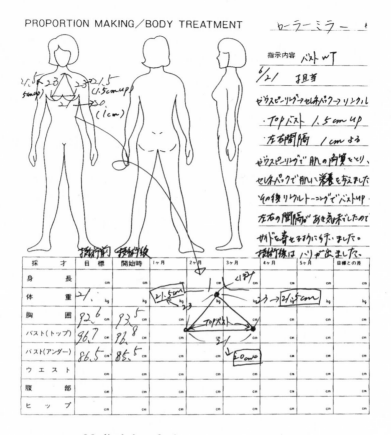

FIGURE 14. Medical chart for bust-up treatment from Socie de Esute aesthetic salon.

salons that furnish special "bust clinics," such as the JBCA Bust Clinic. This clinic is offered by a group of at least eighteen salons, including Esute Studio Moga, Esute Erimon, Club Esute Y, and Japan Total Beauty. An advertisement for the JBCA Bust Clinic reviews the various reasons one might want to visit the clinic. One reason for seeking bust-up would be to develop a better breast shape. Accompanying text explains that, for example, if one were going on a big date in a racy dress, it would be unavoidable to "compare oneself with others and to lose confidence." The recommended treatment is mud packs. Another reason for a visit to the salon would be that the breasts are too small, resulting in "unfavorable comparison with friends." The remedy for this problem is using suction massage cups. According to the text, "When you have this treatment you

won't be embarrassed in front of your friends. You'll get a fabulous bust."
It is interesting to note that it is the monitoring gaze of other women
that is featured rather than a potential male surveyor. Lastly, attending
the bust clinic is recommended for those who have given birth, the idea
being that birthing somehow distorts the breasts.

The graphic representations of salon bust-up treatments in brochures
and advertisements often show a nude pair of breasts with two unidentified
hands, presumably those of an aesthetician, firmly cupping or stroking
them. Getting massages and other types of body work from strangers is
very close to getting paid sex. Many of the carefully designed interactions
and conventions seen in both American spas and Japanese esute salons
have similar functions: to render the services more wholesome and natural, masking the fact that they involve strangers touching nonpublic parts
of your body. As Jenkins (1998: 143) says, "In my experience, it's much
harder to get someone you love to rub your feet and cut your toenails
than it is to get him to perform oral sex. And almost no one will squeeze
your pimples no matter how much they love you." Bust-up mud packs,
delicately placed towels and sheets, and scientific apparatus cannot quite
disguise the fact that essentially what one is paying for is a very vigorous
breast massage.[13]

## Products for a Mammoriented World

Unlike the Kanō sisters, the majority of Japanese women have reserva-
tions about seeking either surgical measures or aesthetic salon-assisted
breast augmentation. Yet their anxiety and fears concerning breast ade-
quacy, fueled by late capitalist logic, leave them susceptible to unscrupu-
lous marketing of strategies that can be attempted in privacy. Surgical
measures are dangerous and aesthetic salon treatments are expensive and
time-consuming, not to mention potentially embarrassing, so for the less
affluent or brave, beauty products for breast enhancement that can be purchased for use at home are an intriguing alternative.

By looking at the methods used to sell home bust-up products, we can
track changes in the conceptualization of breast. Starting in the mid-1990s,
marketing of bust-up products becomes linked to ideas of self-confidence
and identity. In earlier decades breast anxiety hinged on concerns for ad-
equacy as a mother and attractive wife. The earliest home bust-up devices
were described as products that would elevate motherhood and wifely
sexuality. A 1960s version is Nippon Medical Supply Corporation's Bus-

teen, a "massaging and milking apparatus." The company's product flyer also expresses the antique idea that bust size is retarded during adolescence because of "overwork of the brain" from education and stress.[14] Women contaminated by the educational system could therefore recuperate their desirable femininity through use of the product.

Contemporary ladies' bust technology is often prissily scientific, using technological gadgets that have lots of knobs and levers and cables but are molded in dainty pinks, aquas, and lilacs. These pastel units with their patina of scientific legitimization are reassuringly modern. Techno-products try to appeal to consumers by offering convenience, such as the New Bust Gurami, a small portable unit with sets of cables and pads that are inserted into a bra top. One advertisement claims that after it is switched on, it efficiently goes to work with a pulse wave that makes the most of its unique mechanism. Products such as New Bust Gurami can set a woman back as much as $250, so for those on a budget there are numerous low-end bust-up goods available at drugstores.[15]

Other home-care bust-up products take the form of topical creams, mud packs, and powders, which are spread over the breasts. Presumably, bust-enhancing ingredients work directly through the skin. Bust-up products easily articulate as many identities, statuses, and attitudes as other cosmetic products. Through a combination of name, text, and container design, manufacturers can suggest either high-end elegance (consider Lait Buste) or no-nonsense pragmatism (with products like G-Cup Gel and Miracle B Cream). For instance, one may purchase a cheap tube of Best Bust Up Gel, for "Up esute!" (see figure 30 in chapter 7), or the more up-scale Institut Esthederm Paris Bio-Action Treatment Cream for Breasts, an international product also sold outside Japan. For the class-conscious, there are designer bust-up products, such as Ethpital Modela Bust Care by Shu Uemura. Even the lingerie company Wacoal has entered the bust-up product market with its Wacaol Dear Body B-Gel. A routine framing idiom used in bust-up product design is a French or Parisian identity (*mais oui,* French), especially indicated through the use of a romanized name with plenty of diacritics.[16]

Some of the products are differentiated by specific actions they ostensibly will take. A woman can discipline her breasts with Phytobuste Botanical Intensive Bust Control, which contains herb extracts and essential oils. Or else she might battle the ravages of time with Crème Fermenté du Buste with Anti-Aging Factor. To mold the breasts, she should use Elancyl Firming Bust Gel for Shaping and Tightening. Even having large breasts is not sufficient. A product named Perlage claims to "correct" droopy, unperky, or unbalanced breasts. One massages the Perlage cream, which is said to be from Italy and contains mint and other herb extracts, onto the breasts after a bath. Another treatment, Rudo, comes in either an after-bath cream or pill form. According to Rudo advertisements, ingredients include precious animal placentas, supposedly quite effective for bust-up, perhaps operating as a form of sympathetic magic. Other products also boast this unique ingredient. Labusty claims that the 1995 Miss Japan used their elixir, and that it contains not only placenta extract but collagen, ginseng, and Chinese herbs as well. Bust-up products are also sold as herbal medicines and orally ingested potions or tablets. One of Japan's newest vending-machine bottled drinks is Love Body, an herb tea with an ingredient said to boost breast size (Stevenson 2002). Bust Queen claims to be based on a formula transmitted through the "Indonesian Royal Family for women's cosmetic health." Indonesia, home of many beautiful women, seems to provide the special ingredients one needs for an opulent chest. Another product in pill form, Bust Plantes, claims to be made with "Indonesian herbs."

Competing equally with a French or high-tech identity are products sold as if they were a type of *kanpō* remedy. There is a widespread belief that *kanpō* drugs are safer to use than Western medicines because they do not use artificial substances but are instead composed primarily of "herbs." Yet the Chinese semantic category sometimes translated as "herbs" often includes root, mineral, and animal matter. Recipes might include cicada husks, oyster shells, barks, tiger eyeballs, tapir skins, and rhino horn. When sold for bust-up purposes, the *kanpō* substances are rarely identified other than as "Chinese herbs." The coding of a bust-up product as *kanpō* is often achieved through the use of archaic Chinese script, old-fashioned color schemes, and packaging that mimics that found in *kanpō* apothecaries. One product sold as *kanpō*-like is Powder Up Bust, which is applied to the breasts daily at bath time. According to product literature, it is different from Western medicine, which acts only on specific problems, while it seeks to restore a person's total body balance. In one advertisement, a testimony from a Mrs. Hayada claims, "After giving birth I was completely deflated; there was a period of celibacy." Mrs. Hayada had two children, and then used Powder Up Bust and massage as a type of "preventive medicine," and eventually "recovered" her breasts—"Just like before I got married!" Here, the necessity for Mt. Fuji–style breasts is linked to normal heterosexual married life.

The idea that breasts should never sag but must conform to a youthful shape for the duration of a woman's life does not have a long history in Japan. Notions about suitable breast shape are also of recent vintage.

## Good Breasts and Bad Breasts

In populations in which the breasts are thought to be an aspect of female beauty, there are nevertheless differences in what their preferred form should be. Among the Siriono, large yet firm breasts with nipples that face outward are considered attractive, whereas the Azande prefer long and pendulous mammaries, and the Masai like to see breasts that are upright and hemispherical (Ford and Beach 1951). Much of the bust-up industry triggers a consumer's anxiety that she might not measure up, not just in terms of size but according to other breast fashion criteria as well. There has thus been a borrowing of American breast fixation coupled with the notion that there is a standardized or ideal breast shape. Dr. Ikeda tells readers of a young women's magazine that "the objective for a beautiful bust is not only that they are bigger, but that they face upwards" (*Seventeen* 2001c). In another article specifying what constitutes a "bad body," the consultant, a Dr. Yamada, states that a bad body is apparent when "the bust is small but the hips are big. Looking from the side, there's no thickness, and the chest is narrow" (*Can Cam Beauty* 1996).

The idea of measuring breasts in cup sizes is an American invention dating only from the 1930s, when the Warner lingerie company began offering its A B C Alphabet Bras in lettered sizing. Prior to that, because camisoles and waists were generally worn, it was acceptable that the breasts be much lower. It is with the assistance of bras that breasts are refashioned to present uplift and cleavage (Ewing 1971). The dominant breast motif in Japan replicates this mode of highly placed and evenly round breasts. The "fantasy of pneumatic boobs" (Greer 1970: 24) has therefore created a notion that breasts that are not grapefruit-perfect are "bad." In one Japanese bust-up advertisement, a twenty-five-year-old Office Lady laments, "The shape of my breasts is bad. It's clear they are unbalanced." We find the same worries about breasts surfacing elsewhere, such as in a magazine article that polled fifty women about bust apprehensions (*Can Cam Beauty* 1997a). The respondents had five particularized worries: that their breasts were small, faced outward, drooped, were too fat underneath, or were different sizes.

The concept of breasts as either "good" or "bad" is explicitly conveyed in materials produced by a home correspondence bust-up course. Students

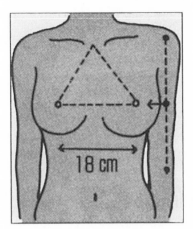

FIGURE 15. The breasts positioned
correctly. From a bust-up product
advertisement.

in Nihon Health Academy's breast program receive four textbooks, a
guidebook, two thirty-minute videos, a biorhythm chart, measuring apparatus, forms and envelopes for transferring payment, and a certificate of
membership. The program is "for people who have breasts that are too
small, hang down, or are big but have a bad shape. American exercise methods are combined with *kanpō* know-how." One also gets a form modeled
on a typical medical chart, the Pure Beauty Bust Making Training Chart.
Again we see the idea that an ideal or correct bust exists as a template for
treatment goals. Through the use of self-massage exercises, preparatory calisthenics, and bust exercises tailored for the individual, Nihon Health Academy teaches students in the home course how to achieve "good" breasts.
According to their literature, students know they have succeeded when a
perfect triangle can be formed between the nipples of both breasts and the
center of the collarbone (figure 15). They also state that "when the bust
and hips are the same size, or better yet, when the hips are smaller, that is
the ideal. If the waist is around 72 percent of the bust size, this is average.
But if it's 65 percent, then that's a really beautiful body."

The breasts are not just measured and charted but "scientifically" cat-
aloged into types. One doctor presents readers of his book with a detailed
taxonomy of breast types (Asami 1997: 27). According to his schema,
breasts fall into six basic divisions: disk, cone, hemisphere, pyramid,
drooping, and flat. Only a few of these natural breast shapes are considered aesthetically acceptable. Nipple color, discussed in a later chapter, is
another aspect of the good breast.

Of course, not to be forgotten is the role of undergarments in upholstering the front of the body: as the Japanese lingerie company Wacoal tells us, "A nice body before anything starts with underwear." Wacoal has introduced a new line of bras, including the Make Up Bra, the Good Up Bra, and the Magical Top Bra. Wacoal was originally an outfit named Wako Shoji that sold accessories (Ribeiro 1987). When a bra pad became the company's first big success, they switched their focus to lingerie. During the 1920s, there were numerous "improvements in underwear" campaigns that attempted to socialize Japanese women into the habit of wearing Western-style underwear (Garon 1997: 133). But after so many women went back to wearing a kimono for the cold winter during lean wartime years, Wacoal had to convince consumers to return to wearing Western-style lingerie, especially the harnessing bra. Wacoal also developed a Silhouette Analysis System, which measures a woman's proportions with the goal of providing "ideal" measurements for each stage of life. In 1986, Wacoal created the high-tech Sofee Bra Kokochi E, which contained a nickel-titanium alloy with a shape memory function. When the bra comes into contact with body heat, it returns to its original shape. Of course, other manufacturers have been equally successful at marketing bras for propping up the bosom, including the Angel Bra, the Get Up Bra, and the Melon Boobs Bra. Bras that were a huge success in the American market in the 1990s, such as the Wonderbra, do a thriving business in Japan as well. Magazine articles that provide instruction in the science of bra administration for maximum advantage are regular features in most women's magazines (*Can Cam* 1999; Ray 1997a).

## Breast Accountability

Although alternative explanations for Japan's new bust consciousness may contribute to our understanding of this trend, the important role of mass media culture in creating and spreading a uniform gender ideal should also be kept in mind. These breast worries wonderfully illustrate themes proposed by Bordo (1993), who specifies two ways mass culture presents a culturally constructed and sanctioned form of female beauty. First, the media images *homogenize,* or smooth out any deviation from a heterosexual ideal. Second, the media images *normalize* by portraying the dominant models against which individuals must continually evaluate themselves. For example, respondents in a magazine article on breast worries were asked to name famous people they think have an "ideal" bust (*Can*

*Cam Beauty* 1997a: 59). The list included the actresses, models, and celebrities Iijima Naoko, Fujiwara Norika, Naomi Campbell, Hinagata Akiko, and Umemiya Anna. Number 2 on the list, Fujiwara Norika, was born in 1974 and was a *Can Cam* fashion model before she became a popular actress. Her publicized measurements led to descriptions of her in the press as having a healthy and "intense" body. With the sheer ubiquity of their images in all forms of media, women who look like Fujiwara and Iijima eventually take on the status of "normal."

For presentation of breasts in the latest style, a certain amount of beauty work is necessary. Since beauty has been retooled as something that may be accomplished through consumption, inability to achieve the fashionable breast is the individual's fault. It displays her lack of discipline, willpower, money, and good aesthetic sense. The result is a generalized sense of worry about whether or not one is doing the right things to create or keep a trendy bustline. Women's anxiety about what they should or ought to do is exploited by advertising. One bust-up product admonishes us that "a voluptuous bustline is the greatest 'charm point' for a woman. But if you have small or droopy breasts, your appeal gets reduced by half." Here we learn that without proper bust augmentation, no woman can hope to be considered acceptably attractive.

Breast work and other forms of body transformation might very well be cognized by a consumer in terms of individual control and expression (and may concurrently reflect the coding of adult attributes such as maturity, sexuality, and assertiveness). Yet pressure to create the breasts that are in vogue has become yet another beauty responsibility for individual women, and the culture that has commodified and eroticized the breast is exempt from responsibility for creating unrealistic expectations. Responses to conformity in gendered body proscriptions include self-policing and "self-normalization" (Bordo 1999). Accountability for good or bad breasts is deflected onto the individual, since they are obtainable commodities she may acquire. In an advertisement for skin bleach used to change nipple hue, a consumer states that by using the product together with esute salon bust-up treatments, she was able to attain "perfect" breasts. A woman with "bad" breasts thereby becomes just another fashion failure who evidences a lack of effort and taste.

A popular topic for writers and academics is Barbie. The doll's position in American culture since her 1959 debut is feverishly contested.[17] Is she a model for female gender construction? A vehicle for subversive behavior? Is there a connection between Barbie's peculiar body proportions and the epidemic of eating disorders among American women? Regard-

FIGURE 16. Shrine votive *(ema)* for ample breast milk, Kigandō.
Photo by author.

less of what one makes of Barbie, everyone seems to agree that her enormous chest is emblematic of America's obsession with female breasts. Initially, Barbie had to be redesigned into a less buxom form in order for her to sell in Japan. Barbie was left on the shelf for almost twenty years before Mattel allowed the Takara Company, its Japan partner, to redesign her. Among other changes, she was given a somewhat smaller bust. In the first two years after modifications, sales figures rose from near zero to almost thirteen million (Pollack 1996). In earlier decades, the bust had not been the focus of female beauty, and Barbie's original shape was just too strange for Japanese tastes. One wonders if such an alteration would be as necessary were she being marketed for the first time today.[18]

The history of female breasts in Japan is noteworthy because it illustrates the power of media images, the influence of American culture, and how easily, and quickly, culturally molded behaviors and ideas become naturalized as "normal." Yet we know that American images of huge-breasted women have been in Japan for decades, so something else must be contributing to the new trend. A general focus on the accomplishment of desired bodies, including idealized breasts, may therefore reflect a certain degree of female agency and empowerment. By rejecting the ineffectual body style of the unbaked maiden, still desired by many men, women are asserting a degree of adult independence and sexual autonomy.

In conclusion, we should note that an additional method for obtaining good breasts, and an obvious display of honest effort, is to pray for them.[19] One can often find antique votive plaques *(ema)* at shrines and temples used to petition for ample breast milk to feed infants. The votives often depict milk spurting from breasts, as in an old one found in a collection at Kigandō (figure 16).

Ōkunitama Jinja, a Shinto shrine in Fuchū City, now has an underground reputation as a bust-up shrine.[20] Traditionally, this was a shrine mothers visited to pray for good breast milk. It seems to have acquired this identity due to an ancient gingko tree that supposedly had magical qualities, something to do with its white sap.[21] But recently the shrine was described in a popular guidebook as also specializing in bust-up (Shinbutsu Goriyaku Kenkyūkai 1989). When authors of a book on contemporary religious practice visited the shrine, however, they saw "no signs of such activity," and the shrine's priest, when questioned, denied any connection to bust-up (Reader and Tanabe 1998: 243–44). However, when I visited the shrine in 1999, I asked two shrine maidens/attendants *(miko)* about the guidebook entry. They said that, yes indeed, numerous women go there just to pray for "bust-up." I noticed many groups of two or three young women praying and giggling at the shrine, as well as mothers with children in tow. Although shrines and temples have long offered pragmatic services for such things as passing university entrance exams or finding a spouse, the attribution of a shrine offering bust-up help is quite new, suggesting that mammary mania is indeed a recent kind of anxiety.

# CHAPTER 4

# Body Fashion and Beauty Etiquette

I sat in my cramped housing in Japan, squinted at the microscopic hair on my arms, and wondered what the aestheticians thought as they applied creams and packs to my body. Did they go home and tell boyfriends and husbands about the "hairy foreigner"? My body is not particularly hairy, and I rarely spend much time on leg or underarm hair removal, one of the requirements for gender construction in my society. Despite this, within the context of the Japanese aesthetic salon, I felt much closer to my primate cousin *Pongidae paniscus*. Salon aestheticians were constantly suggesting that I would like the results of hair removal treatments. They repeatedly brought to my attention a part of my appearance to which I was quite oblivious: the downy fine hair on the face, called *ubuge*. Looking in a hand mirror, the *ubuge*, once invisible to me, seemed glaringly obvious. I recalled a novel by the famous Japanese writer Endo Shusaku that described a character's foreign wife—"a Western woman's skin with the downy hair growing on it" (Endo 1995: 103). I worried about this, even as I acknowledged that my newfound concern derived mainly from my study of the beauty industry and contact with pushy beauty culture saleswomen.[1]

My experience served to emphasize that the work of creating an acceptable appearance is often naturalized and found in commonly accepted everyday activities such as shaving. Hair is always culturally defined and understood, a point illustrated in a collection of essays on hair in Asia (Hiltebeitel and Miller 1998). This chapter examines a few of the ways that beauty is accomplished, from daily routines to more drastic measures.

Some of these practices are not obvious or exterior, and may entail alteration activities concealed from the public gaze.

When we speak of a sociology or anthropology of fashion, most often external clothing and physical appearance come to mind. Scholars have profitably looked at outward costume as an index of gender, class status, locality, ethnicity, and numerous subcultural identities. For example, McVeigh (2000) has analyzed the meanings of uniforms in Japan across different layers of society. In addition to this direct system of social labeling, following Butler (1990) and her notion of "styles of flesh," the body itself may be considered a part of the fashion system. For today's youth, the minutiae of the body are addressed through a variety of new means, including genital modification and facial surgery. New body styles have joined other attributes as important aspects of a person's identity, and modifications to the body are often seen by young Japanese as nothing more than elements of the fashion system. This is no different from people in other societies in high modernity who likewise see the body in terms of malleable surfaces ready to be inscribed with new meanings (Featherstone 1991). The body proposed and deployed by multinational capital rationalizes every imaginable form of consumption for the purpose of aesthetic progress. This is an important point to keep in mind so that we view the Japanese attention to changing the body as an aspect of modernity instead of a lavish emulation of foreign body styles. In other words, as I argue here and elsewhere, Japanese beauty experimentation does not always have to be read as a form of deracialization. By allowing for recognition that body and beauty transformation may have a local significance that is beyond mere imitation, we honor local cultural histories and meanings. Nevertheless, one area where this debate becomes especially heated and complex is cosmetic surgery. Particularly when it comes to eyelid surgery, a common reaction is to claim that Japanese who undergo this modification are trying to reproduce "Western" eyes. In this chapter, I ask that we think about eyelid modification and other cosmetic surgery as encompassing and expressing more than a simple desire to approximate non-Japanese appearance.

One outcome of the body in modernity is that beauty routines and reworkings have become naturalized through commercial and media exposure. In this chapter, I sketch two of the methods used to sell and justify new forms of beauty consumption: the presentation of various forms of beauty work as good etiquette, and the discourse of beauty work as the result of scientific knowledge. Science, or approximations of science, provides the rationalization for producing the tidy, socially inoffensive body transformed with cutting-edge surgery. In many cases, the capitalist body becomes a locale for the expression of social manners. Beauty therefore is not simply a personal issue but a problem of public etiquette. The body may be rescued by rationalized products and practices. Science, bona fide or otherwise, provides the antidote to body worries.

In her aptly named book *Beauty Secrets,* Chapkis writes, "Each woman is somehow made to feel an intensely private shame for her 'personal' failure. She is alone in the crowd pushing toward the cosmetics counter, the plastic surgeon, the beauty specialist" (1986: 5). Although Chapkis is describing the situation of American women, her words are applicable to people in Japan as well. Young Japanese men and women are also made to believe, through the power of media images and a new beauty ideology, that they are somehow defective and in need of constant beauty work to remove hair, lift eyelids, and abolish odors. Their desire to conform to images presented as typical sends them to drugstores, aesthetic salons, and aesthetic surgery clinics to remedy their "personal" problems. In addition to overt practices such as hair coloring, there are many less visible beauty techniques, including cosmetic circumcision, pubic hair styling, and nipple bleaching. In describing these body modification techniques, I run the risk of contributing to an English-language literature on "weird Japan" that attempts to exoticize Japanese cultural behavior. My interest in pointing out these practices, however, is to underscore how, in contrast to earlier decades, a new menu of bodywork has become culturally acceptable.

## Body Hair Worries and Repulsions

The removal of body hair from women and men is found in many cultures, and was especially common among the elite of ancient Minoa, Greece, and Egypt. Razors were used to shave chest and pubic hair in ancient India (Corson 1972), while chest hair was not a part of the Greek ideal of male beauty. An absence of body hair in Euroamerican cultures usually denotes nonaggression and sensuality. Whereas facial or body hair on men is viewed as a biological marker of masculinity in places where men are customarily hairy, it conversely indexes the wild or uncivilized among those populations with less body hair, such as China. Darwin, whom we might think of as the father of the imprinting theory of sexual attraction, noted that "the men of the beardless races take infinite pain in eradicating every hair from their face as something odious, while the men

of the bearded races feel the greatest pride in their beards" (1859: 87). Japanese writers often commented on the excessive body hair of the foreigner.
Tanizaki Jun'ichiro (1970) wrote that although Western women might
have better body shapes than Japanese women, their coarse and hairy skin
turned him off completely.

For many centuries Japanese have held hairy bodies in some disfavor.
In earlier times, hairiness was exemplary of the uncivilized barbarian, as
illustrated by the pejorative label for a white person, *ketō,* literally "hairy
Chinese." In both China (Dikötter 1998) and Japan, excessive body hair
came to symbolically represent ethnic or racial boundaries. Body hair suggests a regression from a state of civilization. The hairy body might index the outside foreigner or else the domestic "other," such as Ainu or
Okinawans. The term for "antipathy" or "prejudice" is *kegirai,* literally
"hair hatred." Hairiness, with all the whiff of the barbarian it entails, is
shunned by many of today's young men, and is strictly taboo for women.
So important is keeping hair and beards trimmed that an Osaka citizens'
group demanded that immigration authorities provide individual electric shavers to detainee foreigners who shared a communal shaver ( *Japan
Times* 2002).[2] Hair anxiety is perfectly illustrated in famed novelist Enchi
Fumiko's 1953 collection of stories, *Himojii tsukihi* (Days of hunger), in
which someone insults a woman by forcing a depilatory substance on her
in a congested train station (Enchi 1997).[3]

Twenty-five years ago it was rare to see a woman wearing skimpy
clothes like shorts or tank tops in public. Now young women wear a broad
range of different styles, many of them involving the display of bare flesh
on almost all parts of the female body, and these new fashion options have
led to heightened self-consciousness about the quality of that flesh. In
late 1999 there was a "bare leg" boom, as well as the "seasonless" clothing fad, in which camisoles or slip dresses were worn year-round. This
meant that many women who once had worn pantyhose and long sleeves
year-round walked around with more bare skin exposed. Therefore, in
order to maintain strict gender borders, there is virtually no part of the
female body on which body hair is considered acceptable. For example,
women who exhibit underarm hair are seriously resisting social norms.
When adult film star Kuroki Kaoru displayed underarm hair in her
movies, it was seen as shockingly deviant (Bornoff 1991). Allison (1998:
215) interprets this act of defiance as a displacement of interest in pubic
hair. Nonetheless, it is good to keep in mind that such behavior is also a
radical refusal to conform to female beauty norms. Many foreign observers
were surprised, considering Japanese racism, when black fashion model

Naomi Campbell served as a model in an advertising campaign for the huge aesthetic salon chain Tokyo Beauty Center. Yet Naomi's smooth, flawless skin represents the hairlessness promoted by the beauty industry, and many advertisements featuring her emphasize this aspect of her beauty. In a poll of young women asking them what they attend to most before putting on a bathing suit, the majority (57.5 percent) said "body hair" (*Ranking Dai Suki!* 1999e: 39). The body is home to around five million hair follicles, which is a lot of hair to manage. Even when most of the body is concealed by clothing, the female face must be absolutely smooth, without even the microscopic hair that covers everyone's skin, Japanese and foreigner alike.

Face shaving is ancient beauty work in Japan, and many woodblock prints from the sixteenth century onward depict women using long, thin razors to plane their faces. A shaved face and neck is also a prerequisite for brides before they are covered by the thick white makeup worn at the wedding ceremony (Goldstein-Gidoni 1997).[4] For nonbridal, everyday beauty work, women can purchase very cheap thin and dainty razors especially for face-shaving. An example is the Soft Lady facial shaver, whose label instructs readers to use the shaver before putting on foundation. It advises that women shave their faces two or three times a month to make it easier to put on makeup. There is a method to the face-shaving (figure 17). For the forehead, the surface is shaved up to around 1 to 1.5 centimeters from the hairline, leaving a margin rather than shaving right up to the edge, which is said to look unnatural. This also preserves the *momiage,* the tuft of hair under the temple. For the cheeks, shaving progresses from bottom to top. Under the nose, it sweeps downward toward the lips.

Targets for hair removal include not only the face, but also the underarms, back, arms, legs, belly button, breasts, crotch area, fingers, and toes. There is a technique here as well. For the arms and legs, the skin is prepared with a hot towel, shaved, and then cooled with a clean towel to revive the skin. Some women's magazines advise that lotions be avoided for a few days. This is beauty work that women are told to do every two weeks. When shaving the back, magazines advise women to ask a family member to help. If no one is available, then they advise deployment of two mirrors, keeping in mind that the hair on the back grows slightly downward. In addition to the unassuming razor, there are other methods for hair removal. Hairs can be plucked out individually with tweezers. Hair may be bleached to disguise it. Topical agents such as wax, honey jelly, sugar water, creams, lotions, and tapes may also be used to remove hair. Many Japanese cosmetic companies provide a full range of products

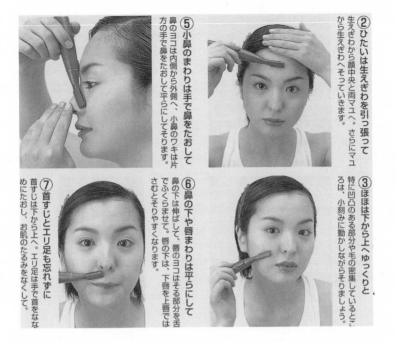

FIGURE 17. Face-shaving technique. Matsushita Electric Company catalog, 1997.

to suit every taste. Kanebo's Epilat series offers cream, tape, honey jelly, milky cream roll-on, and foam depilatories.

For the science of hair removal, women may consult any number of instruction manuals and guides. The Takano Yuri Beauty Clinic provides one entitled *Epilation Manual Book,* displaying on its cover the English words "Trouble less, negative less, heartbreak less, be happy." Another primer is published by the Matsushita Electric Company to help promote its National line of depilation gadgets. Entitled "School for Youthful Aesthetics" *(Seishun esute gakkuen),* it contains information on various forms of hair removal. Also included is a chart entitled "Speed at Which Hair Grows in One Day," where we learn that face hairs grow at a rate of 0.35 millimeters, the eyebrow at 0.18, the underarm at 0.30, the "bikini line" or crotch area at 0.20, and arms and legs at 0.20.

The crotch area is an important site for hair removal, and here we find the novel euphemisms "Venus Line," "V-line," and "V-zone," derived from "mound of Venus" *(biinasu no oka).* Also found is the borrowed "Bikini Line." As Ohnuki-Tierney noted, the lower part of the body is considered unclean; even clothing worn on the lower part of body, especially underwear, is washed separately from other clothes (1984: 30). Because the lower body region is considered dirty, salons usually have separate price structures in place. For example, at Sapho Ladies Healthy Dock, hair removal from the crotch area—euphemistically referred to as "under" *(andā)*—is differentiated from hair removal treatments elsewhere on the body.

Consumers may also purchase depilatory creams targeted at that kinky hair *(kusege no andā hea)* found in the nether regions. During the Edo period (1603–1867), professional sex workers, called Yūjo, kept their pubic hair trimmed or plucked. According to Dalby, "An experienced rake could supposedly tell the degree of a woman's sexual skill by a mere glance at how she pruned her shrubbery" (1983: 55). Similar to these fashionable prostitutes, today's young women are led to believe that crotch management is necessary beauty work. A magazine article directed at high school students demonstrates styling tips for the amount and shape of "V-line" hair. Each of the six different pubic hair styles is associated with a personality type and divination forecast. A poll of favorite under hair designs is also included (*Ranking Dai Suki!* 1999f). According to the high school girls who participated in the survey, the top three styles were the "inverted pyramid type," the "turtle-shaped scrub brush type," and the "downy angel hair type." Personality assessments are given for each of the six styles. For example, the "youthful straight line type" is said to be preferred by someone who is narcissistic: "It doesn't matter who she hooks up with, she's always No. 1." There are also new, specialized products to buy that will help create the dressy crotch. An example is Takano Yuri Beauty Clinic's Etiquette Soap especially for the "delicate" areas of the body.

Although a decent shaving device has been adequate for most women for centuries, the beauty industry has now created a need for more sophisticated hair removal products and services, in particular electrolysis, the removal of body hair by destroying roots with a needle-shaped electrode. There is no medical basis for the claim that shaving will affect the amount or coarseness of body hair, yet all the aesthetic salons audaciously assert that shaving will eventually leave even an attractive woman looking like a beast (figure 18). Advertisements for hair removal products and services are often accompanied by illustrations of the perils of ignoring this regimen. Drawings of bodies with eruptions of stubbly hair are commonly used as a rhetorical device meant to repel the consumer and goad her into action.

Tapping into a widespread fear that fat black hairs will sprout all over if left to themselves, salons market electrolysis as the main solution to

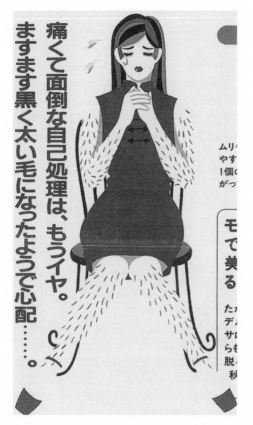

avoid endless shaving and the chafing of skin that will result. There are now two primary types of electrolysis offered by the salons: the traditional probe electrolysis and the newer laser electrolysis. The cost for electrolysis treatments is unbelievably high. Treatments take from twelve to eighteen months to complete, and denuding one body may run as high as $10,000. According to one source, 60 percent of electrolysis customers are Office Ladies aged twenty-three or twenty-four (Itoh 1997). Aesthetic salons are now targeting younger women as consumers of hair removal treatments. Tokyo Beauty Center began a campaign in 2003 targeting junior high– and high school–aged girls. It opened salon branches with new "Teen's TBC," revamped spaces for thirteen- to nineteen-year-olds. When they sign up for the treatments, they are given a "Hair Aesthetics Card."

The first account of electrolysis used for hair removal was in the United

States in 1875, when an ophthalmologist in St. Louis relied on it for a case of ingrown eyelashes. By the 1920s, electrolysis was no longer confined to the medical profession but had become a beauty treatment provided by lay electrologists. With the publication of professional journals, such as *Electrolysis Digest* (1956–86) and *International Hair Route* (1979–present), knowledge of this procedure spread widely in the United States and overseas. By the 1980s, electrolysis technology had become a global enterprise and equipment had become computerized, compact, and more efficient. Concern over AIDS in the 1980s prompted two Japanese doctors, Kobayashi Toshio and Yamada Shiro, to develop a new technique using an insulated needle. One of the first Japanese salons to offer electrolysis was Takano Yuri Beauty Clinic, which started doing treatments in 1979 after the founder, Ms. Takano, read that Elizabeth Taylor had used it. Later she studied and obtained an electrolysis license in the state of California. This license is prominently displayed on walls and proudly adorns most of the clinic's brochures and ads.

In 1984, the Ministry of Health, Labor and Welfare declared that electrolysis is a medical procedure and that use of the technique by anyone except a doctor is a violation of the government's Medical Act (*Asahi Shimbun* 1997c). The medical profession is greatly concerned about protecting such specialized knowledge and its lucrative business, so they aggressively campaign against the aesthetic salons in the media.[5] The government's edict has not slowed down the salons any, however, and this service accounts for an estimated one-third of all current salon industry business (Itoh 1997). Nonetheless, salons frequently allow untrained aestheticians to perform the treatments, with the result that many women walk away with severe burns and darkened skin patches (*Shizuoka Shimbun* 1997; *Nihon Keizai Shimbun* 1990). When describing the poor training at a men's salon, one of the workers talked about how blood spurts out everywhere when an inept aesthetician misuses the probe (Connell 2004). Many salons seem to employ at least one person with a legitimate license to do electrolysis, and this person then "trains" others at the salon branch.

Unlike medical clinics, salons cannot prescribe antibiotics to prevent infection, so this is also a continuing problem. Some salons impose their own forms of self-regulation and participate in professional organizations that provide training and monitor the industry. One such group is the Japan Association of Medical Epilation. But this group only has around 130 salon members, whereas more than six thousand nonmember salons offer electrolysis. A law took effect in 2000 that requires apprenticeship and an exam for all practicing electrolysis technicians, but many salons simply ignore it. Another self-monitoring group, the All Japan Aesthetic Industry (Zen Nihon Esuteteikku Gyōrenraku Gikai), was founded in 1985. In 1994, it had 1,565 member shops and 11,277 individual members. The Japan Aesthetic Association (Nihon Esuteteikku Gyōkai), founded in 1973, boasts 4,800 individual members (Keizai Yakumu Torihiki Tekiseika Kenkyūkai 1994).

Getting electrolysis is an involved process. At the Takano Yuri Beauty Clinic, the client must first call to schedule an appointment (no walk-ins allowed), then meet for counseling and negotiation over terms and fees. A provisional contract is signed, followed by an eight-day cooling-off period now mandated by the government due to consumer fraud. After ten days, the treatments begin. Each session lasts about fifty minutes. For the first month, the client gets a treatment twice a week. After two to six months, it is reduced to once a week, and the course is completed in about one year. Some salons keep the customer paying even after the treatments are complete. At Tokyo Beauty Center, they are urged to buy products for "Hairless After Care." One set is the HL Plus TR Lotion ($30) and the HR Plus Treatment Roller ($135). According to salon informational material, this "after-salon treatment" gadget delivers a faint microelectric current of 1100 Hz to "cool down the skin's Ph." One is supposed to use it use for five minutes once a day for about a year. At Takano Yuri Beauty Clinic, the home-use hair removal set costs $1,730.

If expensive treatments at a salon are beyond the customer's means, there are many dubious machines and gadgets sold as "home electrolysis." An example is the Soral Elimina My HR 208 Electronic Hair Remover ($192). Many of these devices are no more than elaborate household tweezers disguised as "scientific" apparatus. Most are sold with various lotions or gels. But these must be classified as nothing more than consumer fraud, since there is no evidence that anything other than electrolysis will dissolve hair down to the root and prevent outgrowth, and no evidence of permanent hair removal, as these products claim.

Unlike the bathing described by Clark (1994), most people do not find shaving or other forms of hair removal a pleasurable activity. But, similar to bathing, hair removal is a common, routinized behavior, and the presence or lack of hair carries multiple cultural meanings. In response to new beauty ideals for young men, products and treatments to control male body hair are also part of this lucrative business (as discussed in chapter 5). The Japanese beauty industry has reformulated hair removal as an aspect of etiquette. Failure to remove body hair is not only aesthetically déclassé, it is rude. A discourse in which beauty activities are framed as social manners is one way to shift this form of consumption away from individual desire, making it an acceptable form of spending. Properly pampered bodies represent good manners.

## Beauty Manners

In a magazine article, a twenty-two-year-old man confessed that he worried about whether or not he had a weird problem as he matured, and began to see hair removal as a form of etiquette or good manners for adult men (*Across* 1989). In addition to body hair, other body anxieties are exploited to sell a broad range of products and services to address the body's perceived shortcomings. In this section I survey a few products and services that illustrate how effectively the beauty industry has succeeded in reformulating body hair and body odor as social problems related to public propriety. By linking properly denuded, odorless, made-up, and adjusted bodies to notions of social etiquette, consumption activities are also positioned as necessary beauty work rather than as self-centered indulgence in upgrading one's appearance. One scholar suggests that even wearing foundation makeup in public places is a form of etiquette for mature women (Ashikari 2003).

The English word *etiquette* (itself a loan word from French) has been used in Japan for many years to mean manners, decorum, or proper speech. Etiquette was borrowed from the domain of interaction to refer to the consequence that beauty work, or lack of it, will have on others. One use is related to hair removal, with products sold as "depilation manners" *(datsumō echiketto)*. The idea here is that it is uncouth to walk around offending other people's sensibilities by your body hair. To not remove body hair is not a matter of personal inclination but rude behavior and an affront to others.

Many scholars have noted that Japanese attitudes toward cleanliness derive from symbolic notions of purity and pollution. But they usually relate practices of hygiene to either the native ethnomedical system or to Shinto religious beliefs and rarely tie them to overlapping concepts of aesthetics and beauty, forgetting that "beautiful" and "clean" are the same word *(kirei)*. Similar to the way the sanitary products industry in the United States reformulated menstruation as a hygiene problem (Brumberg 1997), the Japanese beauty industry has refashioned beauty as an interactional problem requiring good etiquette or good manners. In addition to hair removal, elimination of body odors of whatever origin

FIGURE 19. Etiquette Up tablets for beatifying body waste, sold by Takano Yuri Beauty Clinic.

is also classified as a form of etiquette. A contemporary outcome of the intertwined concepts of beauty, cleanliness, and purity is the development of a market for goods that make the user cleaner and hence more beautiful. Occasionally termed the "etiquette goods" *(echiketto guzu)* market, it originally referred to mouthwashes, breath fresheners, and breath mints, such as Gilco's Kiss Mint for Etiquette gum. Other new uses of the term are in relation to good sex manners, as when a condom company names its product the Koji Etiquette and Travel Safety Rubber.

Next to ads for the latest platform shoes and hippest makeup, women's magazines sell products designed to beautify odors that emanate from the intestinal tract. Fragrant feces and sweet-smelling farts can be produced through consumption of new smell-eliminating products that promise to make a woman pretty to the last detail. The Takano Yuri Beauty Clinic sells Etiquette Up, a remedy for those participating in its weight-loss programs, which promises to "make the inside beautiful" (figure 19). Etiquette

Lady tablets, from another company, also promise to rid the body of bad breath and eliminate feces smell. They are supposedly perfect for the "etiquette generation."

Another product, Kyrie, claims that mushroom extract will get rid of the smell of gas and feces. According to the label, "We are entering an era in which people must be responsible for their own odors." A woman who purchased one of these etiquette products told me she tried it because she was planning an overnight trip with her boyfriend and was concerned about stinking up the hotel room when she used the toilet.

Finally, the Aoyama Clinic in Tokyo offers expensive "internal body aesthetics" *(tainai esute)* that will beautify the body's pipes and plumbing through elaborate enemas and other treatments. Colon cleansing is thought to not only clean and beautify the inside but contribute to a more beautiful exterior with clearer skin and fewer blemishes. However, not all the salons that offer this service are qualified to professionally insert objects into the anus, and salon operators have been arrested in the past for performing the service illegally. A popular Tokyo salon named Grace reportedly made more than $840,000 over a three-year period by giving unauthorized "hydro colon cleansing" (*Mainichi Daily News Interactive* 2003c).

Other beautifying etiquette services include the "Etiquette Box," a one-person cabinet that, for a small per-use fee, sprays a cleansing air around the person, removing cigarette and other bad smells from the clothing. Also gaining in popularity is surgical removal of the underarm odor-producing glands. In addition to glands, body parts such as penises and nipples are also the object of aesthetic attention.

## Beautifying Genitals and Nipples

One consequence of hypervigilance about the body is that concern about potentially repellent parts has extended to areas of the body that are usually kept private. One of the primary "hidden" areas of the body, the pelvic region, is the focus of some new types of beauty work for both men and women. There are numerous cosmetic surgery clinics devoted exclusively to men, which provide specialized procedures in addition to facial surgery. One can get aromatherapy for male "power up," or impotence, as well as various types of genital surgery, such as penile implants, silicone injections, and silicone bead or pearl insertions.[6]

A new fad in upgrading a man's appearance is cosmetic circumcision, since the majority of Japanese men are not circumcised at birth. Many young men decide to have the foreskin surgically removed at male-only clinics. There are two primary removal methods, as well as different penis styles that one may select. A desire to be more appealing to women, who say that the circumcised penis is "cleaner" and "looks better," is often concealed by rhetoric about health concerns.[7] Statistics are not available on the number of adult circumcisions performed in Japan. In the rare instances when infant circumcision is performed, the parents must pay for it. Japanese who are new parents in the United States sometimes are surprised by the way hospitals treat it as a routine, unquestioned procedure (Fetters 1997). Insurance covers adult male circumcision only for a medical reason, such as disease or inflammation. Statistics are kept for insurance-covered surgeries, but these do not distinguish between circumcision and other types of penile surgery.

Although no solid numbers are available, the popularity of circumcision among young men is apparent by the number of new clinics that specialize in this procedure.[8] The average cost is $830 to $1,330. The Yamanote Clinic, which has ten branches, goes to great lengths to safeguard privacy, promising that customers will not run into other clients, that staff members are all male and so "really understand other men's worries," and that "not even one woman" will be found on the premises, in order to protect "male pride." Other cosmetic surgery clinics, such as Shibuya Aesthetic Surgery and the Ueno Clinic (which likewise has ten branches), advertise that they, too, have all male staff and clientele. Surgery clinics rely on embarrassment to inflate fees and unfairly overcharge clients. For example, one clinic claimed that expensive collagen injections were needed before the removal of the foreskin, raising the usual cost of the procedure. According to Schreiber (2002), Japanese newspapers cite the Ueno Clinic as being especially unprincipled in this regard.

Advertising for the Shinjuku Clinic claims that an uncircumcised penis is "not popular" with women, who feel it is "impure" (*fuketsu*). Other ads say that clients will turn into "cool men" (*ikemen*) and have good relations with their girlfriends if they have the operation. Male worries about this aspect of the penis may stem from international pornography, in which the circumcised foreign penis is available for emulation, but more important is the prevalence of media commentary from young women who openly discuss penile qualities. For instance, an uncircumcised penis is often derogatorily referred to by women as an "eyeless stick" (*menashibō*) or "mud turtle" (*suppon*). These new views concerning the circumcised penis contrast with historic attitudes toward circumcision as being quite bizarre. An Edo (1603–1867) scholar named Atsutane Hirata wrote, "A Dutchman's penis appears to be cut short at the end, just like a dog. Though this may sound like a joke, it is quite true, not only of Dutchmen but of Russians" (Keene 1969: 170).

A poll of young men's attitudes toward the penis was published in the girls' magazine *Seventeen* for the edification of its female readers (*Seventeen* 2001b). The boys were asked what sort of thing they would compare themselves to when they are in an aroused state "down there." Some of the items they mentioned were a mushroom, a plastic water bottle, a sausage, a cocktail wiener, and a *kokeshi* doll. These wooden dolls have neither arms nor legs, but a large head and a cylindrical body. Another poll asked the young women to name a comparable item (*Egg* 2000). Their list included a banana, a king cobra, and an overgrilled pink frankfurter. In the same magazine, young men were asked what their ideal size would be, and the resulting numbers were presented with helpful visuals of items such as hair conditioner bottles and bottled tea, which approximated the named lengths. These polls let young men know that women are interested in comparisons and evaluations, and are avid consumers of this knowledge.[9]

Recent attention to the female breast has given rise to a unique commercial product category: nipple bleaches. A Japanese folk belief holds that the more sexually active a woman is, the darker her nipples become. The color of the nipple does darken with age but in fact has no correlation with sexual activity. A special summer issue of *Can Cam* included reader questions about their breasts (*Can Cam Beauty* 1997a). One reader wondered, "Is there a relationship between nipple color and the number of times you've had sex?" The response explained that nipple hue depends on the amount of melanin in the body and, to some degree, age. Another reader asked, "Is it true that smart people don't have big nipples?" Similar anxieties are found in *Seventeen* magazine, where young girls ask questions like "Does someone who has a lot of sex get big breasts?" and wonder why their nipples are dark although they are virgins (*Seventeen* 2001c: 72). Women concerned about projecting a pure, innocent, or naïve image are eager to buy skin-lightening creams and lotions for topical use that will lighten the nipple's hue. The cream Virgin Pink, which uses the "combined action of placenta and aloe vera to slow down melanin production," is one way to address nipple worries. Virgin Pink advertisements usually feature photos of a brown nipple with the cautionary words "Before you turn this color . . ." Another product, Natural Pink Excellent, also claims to have placenta as an ingredient, as well as vitamin C. A similar product is Best Bust Pink Cream, with a partially English label that assures the buyer that using it will enable her to become a "Topless Beauty." Other products in this category are Crystal Gel and Babe Pink Bleaching Creme.

## Changing the Eyelid

In the late 1970s, I worked in Osaka and developed a strong network of female Japanese friends. I lived in an apartment in the city and had several sets of spare bedding, and friends would often flop at my place if we were out late and they had missed the last train to their distant suburban homes. In this way I came to learn about one of the beauty secrets of ordinary Japanese women: eyelid tapes and eyelid glues (figure 20). These were temporary techniques to pull the eyelid up just a little, to give the impression of a deep crease. My friends would remove the tapes before going to sleep, but since this was not the sort of thing I had lying around, like tampons or hair conditioners, they needed to carefully preserve them for reapplication with glue in the morning. The process took a long time and necessitated their getting up early. They would clean the eyelid, and then use tweezers to take up the thin, transparent tape and place it about 3 millimeters above where the eyelashes grow. The tapes were cheaper than using the glue alone—only a few hundred yen—but they "showed" more easily. If they were using only eyelid glue, it was smoothed on the eyelid, and then a small crutchlike implement was used to push back the eyelid to create the fold. The pose had to be held for ten or fifteen minutes per eye in order for the glue to set. Most of my friends refused to skip this regimen, considering it an essential part of their daily beauty routine.

The eyelid tapes and glues are one reason so many women at beach resorts refuse to go in the water. I eventually came to understand how, if one became accustomed to seeing one's face with the eyelids just so, taking the next step and having an eyelid crease surgically made permanent would save time and, over the long run, money. The surgery, colloquially called the "double-eyelid surgery," is thought to be the most commonly performed cosmetic procedure in Japan (Cullen 2002).[10] *Hitoe mabuto,* the Japanese term for the single eyelid, means that the eye has no visible fold (or pretarsal crease) above the eye opening. The double-eyelid shape is called *futae mabuto.*

Although accepted by my friends as just one of many beautification

FIGURE 20. Double-eyelid glue technique. From *Popteen* magazine, 2003.

practices, outside Japan, doing things to the eyelids is the subject of much passionate and scholarly debate. Most often a desire to change the eye shape is seen as obvious evidence of the dominance of a Euroamerican beauty ideal, in which the round eyes of the white model are the target of emulation (Kaw 1993). The crux of the critique is that Asians and Asian Americans are subjected to pressure to conform to what Kawazoe (2004) calls the "global standard of white beauty." Of course, the situation of Asians and Asian Americans in the United States better exemplifies this case, since they are living in a culture in which European facial features and body types dominate the mediascape. Recently, those who diverge from an Anglo norm of beauty have achieved some popularity, such as Jennifer Lopez, Halle Berry, Salma Hayek, and Naomi Campbell. But for a Japanese person living in Japan, the situation is more complex and multi-determined.

Japanese are not homogeneously derived from one ancestral group (Katayama 1996). One result is that, unlike the populations of China or Korea, a much larger percentage of the population naturally has a double-lidded eye. Estimates vary, but according to Mikamo (1896), the double eyelid is the more prevalent variant, found in perhaps 80 percent of Japanese. (For Pacific Asians in general, the estimate is 55 percent [Lee 2005].) Other suggested rates are more modest, but all recognize that a large proportion of Japanese are born with double-lidded eyes. There is also a high degree of variability in eye shape among people throughout East Asia, and popular writing in China also gives estimates of half or more of the population as having double eyelids (Brownell 2003). The Japanese population is the outcome of successive immigrations in the prehistoric period. One group is thought to have originated in Southeast Asia or South China. These were the Jōmon people, the earliest inhabitants of Japan (ca. 13,000 B.C. to ca. 300 B.C., though recent findings may stretch this date back considerably). A later wave, or waves, of newcomers came from

Korea and are known as the Yayoi (ca. 300 B.C. to ca. A.D. 300). Skeletal remains and reconstructions show that the Jōmon people tended to be shorter and had wider faces than the Yayoi. They had more pronounced noses, raised brow ridges, and rounder eyes. The Yayoi people were somewhat taller, with longer, narrow faces and flat brow ridges and noses. For centuries, the rounder, double-lidded eye of Jōmon-descended Japanese was not considered beautiful, since it did not resemble the Yayoi nobility. We see this preference in centuries of Japanese art, in which the North Asian facial type was considered the most beautiful. There were even colloquial terms to describe this type, the Courtly Face *(kuge zura)* and the Kyoto Beauty *(kyō bijin)*.

From 1876 to 1905, a German named Erwin von Bälz taught at the Tokyo Medical College, later to become the Medical School of the University of Tokyo. According to Hanihara (1999), von Bälz was something of a self-made medical anthropologist who claimed that there were two physical types of Japanese, whom he termed the "Satsuma type" and the "Chōshū type." The Satsuma type was described as having large eyes with the double eyelid, while the Chōshū type was taller, with narrow single-lidded eyes. Von Bälz used photographs of nude Japanese women to illustrate each type. His effort to document racial identifiers was part of a general project of the nineteenth century referred to as "scientific racism." Although the sort of racial anthropometry he produced is avoided today, Hanihara (1999) has suggested that von Bälz's dual classification may correspond somewhat to what we have learned from archaeology, with the addition of a third type. Thus, the Satsuma type may be traced to the earliest Jōmon population and the Chōshū type linked to the immigrant Korean Yayoi population. He also suggests that we recognize a third line, the Chūkan type, represented by the mixed Kofun-era ( A.D. 300 to A.D. 710) population.

Today there is some popular interest in pseudo-archaeology that claims to trace Jōmon and Yayoi features in modern populations.[11] Writing in the *New York Times,* Kristof (1999) described a visit to a museum in Aomori where visitors may consult a computer screen that tells them the proportion of their blood that comes from the Jōmon, based on their eye shape, body hair, and other characteristics. Various popular Japanese media claim that there is regional differentiation, with the north and the Ryūkyū islands having a larger proportion of people with pronounced features of the Jōmon-type face, and the western regions having the thinner and flatter faces of the Yayoi type. Kristof (1999) quotes archaeologist Okada Yasuhiro of the Aomori museum as saying, "People in northern Japan can be 60 to 80 percent of Jōmon origin, while those from western or southern Japan are 40 percent Jōmon or less." It's highly improbable that such exact tracing of ancestral affinities is possible, yet Okada's words are an indication that there is a recognizable diversity in contemporary Japanese facial features, including variation in eyelid shape.

Popular recognition of variation in eye shape is seen in the native physiognomic system known as *ninsō*. The physical traits of the face and body are used to determine a person's characteristics and personality (Miller 1998b). *Ninsō* recognizes six possible eye categories, based on criteria such as eye size, shape, pupil placement, and pupil proportion to whiteness. The types are Big Eyes, Narrow Eyes, Hang-Down Eyes, Enticing Eyes, Pupils-at-the-Top Eyes, and Different-Sized Eyes. Each type has associated personality traits. For example, people with Hang-Down Eyes *(sagari-me)* give an impression of easy intimacy, but their main weakness is that, although they are lovable, they are easily dominated by others. Those of the Big Eyes type *(ōkii-me)* are intuitive, with sharp powers of observation, and are artistic and fickle. Enticing Eyes *(tsuri-me)* wrestle with the ephemeral nature of the world. When their own agenda is advancing, they are fine, but they get upset when things do not go their way. Companies that sell eyelid glues and tapes often propose other eye classification systems. For example, one company proposes three types that are in need of its products: the Crescent type *(mikkazuki)* has small eyes, the Folding Fan type *(suehiro)* has eyes that are set low beneath the eyebrow, and the Parallel type *(heikō)* has eyes that are set close to the brow ridge.[12]

A problem with the idea that it is massive postwar Hollywood-inspired beauty ideology that has solely created the eyelid product and surgery business is that, unlike the new craze for larger breasts and circumcised penises, which we can date from the mid-1980s or later, the desire for larger eyes has a much longer history in Japan. A surgeon named Mikamo (1896) pioneered Japan's cosmetic surgery industry in 1896, when he performed the first double-eyelid procedure on a woman who had only one natural double eyelid (Sergile and Obata 1997; Shirakabe 1990). Mikamo was trained in Western medicine and was undoubtedly influenced by Western culture, but he made it clear that he was not attempting to reproduce the white person's eye shape in his patients. He strove to maintain a Japanese-style double eyelid, one that resembled the portion of the population that naturally had this feature. The main difference between the double eyelids of Japanese and Euroamericans is that Japanese eyelids have more fat. Japanese who have surgeries that remove too much fat from the eyelid are considered weird-looking.

The method for creating the double eyelid pioneered by Mikamo has undergone sophisticated development, and now takes around twenty minutes in an outpatient clinic. A short incision of around 2.3 millimeters is made in the lid, and is then sewn up. Now aesthetic surgery clinics offer a noncutting suture alternative. An extremely thin, nonabsorbable thread is sewn in to create a crease. These sometimes disappear over time, so a newer technique adds double stitches with some twisting to make it more permanent. This procedure takes only ten minutes. The double-eyelid procedure is part of a growing industry in minor cosmetic surgery that is sometimes called *puchi seikei,* "petite surgery" (*Mainichi Shimbun* 2003). Also included in the category are chemical peeling treatments, underarm gland removal, and something termed "VFR," or Virgin Face Reduction, a surgery involving removal of part of the jawbone to make the face look smaller. The petite surgery folk classification suggests that these transformations are considered trivial and not extreme, and are therefore more acceptable than "real" surgery. This idea that some surgical alterations are negligible is seen in the way the Sapho Clinic describes its cosmetic surgery services as "surgical makeup." Japanese spent $25 million on cosmetic surgery in 2002, 50 percent more than in 1999 (Schaefer 2003). Cosmetic surgery among Japanese high school students has reached levels comparable to those in the United States (1.2 percent, as compared to 1.3 percent in the United States; Shōgakukan 2001: 484). A popular television program named *Beauty Colosseum* features contestants who receive makeovers and cosmetic surgery.

Critics of double-eyelid beauty work are eager to dismiss the claims of Japanese women themselves, who say they are not creating the extra fold in order to appear Western. Scholars insist that these women have already internalized the white-woman beauty ideal and that, although they say they like the bigger eye shape because it looks "more awake" or "younger," what they *really* mean is that it looks more "white." There is some truth to this, given the historical context of Japanese relations with the world, and a certain degree of internalization of Euroamerican beauty ideals has occurred. But it may also be instructive to look at the way eyelid beauty work is described and discussed in Japan.

Articles and advertisements on eyelid surgery, eyelid tapes, and eyelid glues rarely claim or suggest that the person getting the change will look more Western, foreign, or white, although this may be implied in the few advertisements that feature white models. Japanese I interviewed who disapprove of this fashion insist that it is straightforward emulation of the Caucasian face. This suggests that Euroamerican beauty ideals have indeed played a role in promoting this feature. On the other hand, the most common word for the double-eyelid look is *patchiri,* "bright, clear eyes." Indeed, surgery that makes the eyes appear too Western is disliked, since it looks too obviously artificial. People with eyelids that have had too much fat removed are sometimes denigrated as "looking like a Kewpie doll." Instead, the desire is for an eye shape that looks bigger but is still Japanese. An eighteen-year-old male university student told me he got the double-eyelid operation so he would look cute, like the celebrities Nakai Masahiro or Hyde. He said he wanted to look *patchiri* and be attractive to girls. His parents approved of the procedure because they thought it would help him in his career later in life. He also plucked his eyebrows and shaved his chest, male beauty work I will address in the next chapter, suggesting that he has a hybrid *Japanese* model of appearance in mind.

Many women I interviewed who had had the surgery said it was just too much trouble to put on eye makeup with the single-eyelid shape. We see this concern with eye shape in a poll of young readers of a magazine who were asked to name the aspects of their eyes they were dissatisfied with (*Ranking Dai Suki!* 2000a: 102). Their list was:

1. Single-layer eyelids
2. Eyelids are puffy
3. Eyelashes face downward
4. Eyes are too far apart
5. Left and right eyes of different sizes

Unlike centuries ago, when the double-lidded eyelid was associated with the lower classes of society, it has now become the preferred form. In 1998, *Asahi Shimbun* ran a series on aesthetic surgery, in which stories of everyday people who had elected to have some type of surgery were published without commentary (*Asahi Shimbun* 1998d). A few of these stories are useful to note, as they tie anxieties about eye shape to a range of local situations. For example, a twenty-eight-year-old woman tells how she decided to get the surgery when she was twenty-one because she had been born with only one eye with the double-eyelid fold, like Mikamo's first patient. For years she had used glue on the other eyelid but always worried about rainy days and going into pools. After she had had the surgery, her husband was unhappily shocked at the change in her appearance, and she now worries about what will happen as she ages. A sixteen-year-old said that she got the surgery when she was in the third year of middle school (around age fourteen). She said she wanted it in order to look "cuter." At the clinic she was told that all the high school students were doing it. A thirty-one-year-old told about a complex she had had since grammar school. Because of her small, single-lidded eyes, a teacher had called her an "eyeless goblin" *(me nashi yōkai)*, a nickname that stuck. She recalls always looking down when walking or talking to others. She wanted the surgery desperately, but her father forbade it. Another woman said that when she was twenty-three, she had considered getting the surgery, not because she thought she was unattractive, but to look just slightly more *patchiri*, but decided at the last minute to just live with the face her mother had given her. In another article (Cullen 2002), a woman told how, before her ten-minute surgery at age twenty-one, she had been using eyelid glues for about three years and "lived in fear of discovery, rushing off to the bathroom several times a day to reapply the glue and never daring to visit the beach." Kawazoe's (1997) thesis on cosmetic surgery also contains many personal stories of women who have had double-eyelid surgery after years of secretly applying eyelid tapes and glues.

These stories indicate something different from a simple desire to look "foreign." The process of normalization has created a sense that the double eyelid is the "average" for *Japanese* people, in the same way that American media has made it seem that huge pointy breasts are normal for American women. The normalization of the double eyelid has occurred within the context of Japanese culture and is not simply a comparison of an individual's self to Euroamerican media. When she gets her double-eyelid surgery, the Japanese girl or woman is probably not thinking of Britney Spears, but of the large eyes of J-Pop sensation Hamasaki Ayumi or the enormous saccharine pools of emotion found on her favorite *manga* characters. She is not looking to Hollywood or Madison Avenue, but to Shibuya and the pages of *GirlPop* magazine. An interesting term that also points to the contemporary locus for beauty ideals is "Cyber Beauty" *(saibā bijin)*, used to describe women who have the small face and huge orbs of Japanese anime and computer game characters, rather than the features of American movie stars.

Unlike Davis (1995), I am not an advocate or supporter of cosmetic surgery. I do not think that extending beauty work into the realm of the surgical is a good thing in any culture. My interest in drawing attention to the problem of the double eyelid is to understand it in the context of Japanese cultural history and contemporary beauty notions, not to excuse or condone it. I believe that critical appraisals of the practice are important and valuable. At the same time, doing things to the eyelid is cultural behavior, and so it and other aesthetic practices need to be interpreted in the settings in which they are found. When I first began to think about the global beauty industry, I was amazed that anyone would submit themselves to a treatment in which botulinum toxins would be injected into the face. Yet within a few years Botox had become the most popular nonsurgical cosmetic procedure in the United States, with an estimated 2.3 million injections performed in 2003. A beauty procedure that is so obviously strange has become completely normalized and common. It is important to recognize a similar process in Japan, where eyelid surgery is no longer considered to be particularly odd or unusual.

## Warped Imitation or a Locally Driven Syncretic Aesthetics?

Although all forms of beauty work, from ancient to modern, entail a degree of artificiality (consider the scaffolding of the buttressed and shellacked Edo-era *shimada* hairstyle), today's artificial styles are often interpreted as nothing more than imported Western culture. Because the classic signifiers of Japanese "race" are hair color and eye shape, any beauty work that alters these features is tied up with a politics of racial identity. Yet in the same way that Mercer (1990) illustrates for black hairstyles in the United States, these changes may not just reflect the imposition of a dominant (or foreign) culture's values, but are also expressions of syncretic forms of aesthetic culture. Mercer celebrates this possibility of creative appropriation: "Black practices of stylization today seem to exude confidence in their enthusiasm for combining elements from any source—black or white, past or present—into new configurations of cultural expression" (1990: 262).

I do not deny that the politics of appearance in Japan is inextricably bound up with Euroamerican dominance. New beauty conventions in Japan also involve aspects of mimicry, appropriation, and reworking. Japanese exist in a Western-dominated world order, but we are missing something if the only interpretation we imagine is the "wretched imitation" (Mercer 1990: 247) of an outside culture. If white or black American looks are being studiously copied, it is often from an American world of the imagination or the comic book, where men with big eyes also have hairless legs, chests, and arms, and sometimes blue hair, and women have little stars and highlights glistening next to their pupils.

When Meiji-era gentlemen began mixing Western accoutrements and clothing into their wardrobes—things like hats, umbrellas, and pocket watches—they were viewed as manifesting efforts at being "modern," not as racial sellouts. The Meiji gentleman's wearing of mixed styles is comparable to the hybrid Native and European fashions seen among Chinook males during the 1820s and 1830s, which similarly was intended not as an imitation of white fashion but rather as a reflection of cultural capital, of knowledge of forms of European ornamentation (Moore 2001). Although contemporary Japanese fashion has extended further to encompass the body itself, any evidence of body transformation that disrupts racial significations and blurs some observers' cozy categories is interpreted as slavish emulation of the West. In addition, it is psychologized as a desire to *be white*. To press it further, consumers are reduced to the status of psychologically infirm fashion dupes who lack any facility for creating alternative meanings. But at this late hour, Japanese body and beauty work has moved beyond a brute stage of emulation. I also find it slightly ethnocentric that whenever Japanese appropriate some aspect of Euroamerican body aesthetics, foreigners assume that it reflects their burning desire to become something other than Japanese, but when Americans, for instance, borrow things like nose piercing or dreadlocks from other cultures, it is seen as evidence of their creativeness and tolerance. As noted by Kawashima (2002), people outside Japan are unwilling to see traits like hair and eye color as performative, but instead view them as expected, essentialized racial markers. So Japanese figures in *manga* that are supposed to be self-representational are read as "white" by non-Japanese, and J-Pop stars like Gackt are accused of trying to "look white." Kawashima says that "race" is "generated through a visual reading process in which certain features are highlighted and others are suppressed or ignored" (2002: 164).

In his recent book, Tanja Yujiro relates a story about cruising Shibuya with a friend named Tom, who asked him why so many Japanese dye their hair. Tanja expresses anger at this question, wondering why Tom and others expect Japanese to still be walking around in kimono with black hair, as if these have anything to do with "being Japanese" (Tanja 2003: 106). It seems that non-Japanese have an inflexible and outdated model of what Japanese ought to look like. The biological anthropologist Hanihara (1999) claims that the Japanese face has in fact undergone morphological change during the last century. Facial changes are mostly the result of chewing, diet, and increased height stemming from improved diets. He compared averaged measurements of facial shape for high school boys in the

1950s with those of today and found that several physical changes have oc-curred. People nowadays are less likely to have overbites, and they have thinner and straighter noses and more angular chins. Despite this general change, most foreigners expect all Japanese to carry the pre-1950s face.

Young Japanese are experimenting with different surface identities, not primarily in an attempt at deracialization but to underscore severance from the older generation. A smooth youth with plucked eyebrows, long red hair, and big luminous eyes is a powerful form of *oyaji* ("old man") re-jection. When a teenager in Harajuku puts on her white lipstick and loose socks, she knows she does not look like any teenager in Westwood (she knows because she has seen the television series *Beverly Hills 90210*). When huge platform shoes became popular in 1994, the fad was inspired by the fashions of J-Pop stars, not by any foreign fashion industry. (Indeed, the style later spread to the United States from Japan.) As far as I know, Japa-nese girls are not thumbing through vintage issues of *Glamour* magazine for fashion ideas. Japan's own thriving popular culture industries are pro-viding them with their own models for beauty. America and Europe have not been given proprietary rights to technologies of beauty. Japanese use of hair-dying technology, for instance, has given us styles like the gray-or pink-streaked tresses popular in the late 1990s, and the blue hair once found on a member of the band Glay.

While beauty practices such as eyelid adjustment and bleached hair got their early impetus from Western media images, it is necessary to ask why they became popular only recently, since technologies for these changes have been available for half a century or more. What has changed to make their use more common? Perhaps a critical component is a shift in atti-tudes about the possibility of changing the body. People now believe that, with the assistance of commercial beauty services and products, the vul-nerable body can be liberated from its smells, oozings, growths, and imper-fections and that scientific beauty will triumph over the body's natural propensity to be ugly, hairy, and smelly.

# CHAPTER 5

# Male Beauty Work

---

In 1992, the young women's magazine *With* featured an interview with actor Akai Hidekazu, who had just starred as Miyazawa Rie's love interest in the hit television series *Tokyo Elevator Girls* (*With* 1992). Akai, a former professional boxer from Osaka dubbed the "Rocky of Naniwa," epitomized in physical form a version of standard male attractiveness. His large, bloke-ish, somewhat doughy appearance suggested desirable male traits such as strength, dependability, resolve, and commitment. In a poll from 1987 asking single women what male characteristics they liked best, respondents overwhelmingly stressed inner personal traits over external physical attributes (*PHP Intersect* 1987: 4). Akai's popularity was visible evidence of this preference.

More recently, Miyazawa's sultry costar in another hit television series, *Concerto,* was of an entirely different sort. Kimura Takuya exudes a frank sexuality that does not so easily endorse an uncomplicated portrayal of traditional masculinity. Yet Kimura—or Kimutaku, as he is affectionately called—is invariably ranked as one of the most popular male stars by both men and women. For instance, the young men's magazine *Fine Boys* ranked him number one in a survey of "favorite male celebrities" (*Fine Boys* 1998). Similarly, female readers of *An An* magazine have consistently voted Kimutaku the celebrity they like most, describing him as both "sexy" and "manly" (*Mainichi Shimbun* 1995).[1] In 2004, he captured this honor for the eleventh year in a row. Each year, Kimutaku heads the list of "guys we want to have sex with." Kimutaku fandom was fostered not only through his work as an actor but also through his singing in the

J-Pop group SMAP (an acronym for Sports Music Assemble People) and his presence in other media, such as advertising, the television program *SMAP X SMAP,* and even his selection as "Best Jeanist," a special award given to the guy who most perfectly fills out a pair of jeans. Kimutaku captured this honor two years in a row, in 1994 and 1995.

More then twenty years ago, another top male star, Sawada Kenji (who often went by the appellation "Julie"), was also notable for his striking physical beauty. Tall, slim, and with a distinctive face rendered rather androgynous with the aid of eye makeup, Sawada exhibited an external male beauty not commonly seen in mainstream media. Itō (1993) discusses Sawada's impact in more detail, but for us a significant point is that thousands of Japanese men did not try to transform themselves into Sawada look-alikes in the same manner in which they now eagerly emulate Kimutaku and a whole spectrum of other beautiful male media stars. The importance of noting the emergence of Sawada, however, is that he was an early expression of a male interest in being the object of female and/or male observation and desire.

The ascendancy of male stars such as Kimutaku reflects a shift in Japanese canons of taste for young heterosexual men. While previous generations were evaluated primarily on the basis of character, social standing, earning capacity, lineage, and other social criteria (Applbaum 1995; Plath 1980), young men these days are increasingly concerned with their status as objects of aesthetic and sexual appraisal. The recent emphasis on externalization of personal or social identity has given birth to new businesses that sell beauty products and services to those wanting to change or upgrade their appearance.

In this chapter, I outline some of the new services and products now sold to men in their pursuit of beauty. These efforts at body and beauty transformation suggest that the ideological sphere of reference of masculinity has widened to include a greater diversity of physical styles. In other words, I do not see current male beauty practices as a type of "feminization" of men, as others have, but rather as a shift to beautification as a component of masculinity. For example, critics often interpret new fashions and beauty work among young men as evidence of the loss of male power and martial virility (Kobayashi 1998). Questions I pursue are: What new practices became part of men's beauty work? What parts of the body have become the objects of beautification? What is driving these efforts at surface change?

One obvious change is that, for many young men, consumer culture and the construction of masculinity are tied to body presentation and female desire. Men's consumption of beauty products and services expresses a form of masculinity that resides in the beautified body, created in response to media-based discourses (such as the new genre of men's style magazines). Men reflexively monitor their own and others' bodies, tailoring themselves in relation to imagined female desire. This self-objectification is part of the shift in how identity is constructed in late capitalism, and is not unique to Japan. Of course, although outward appearance is only one aspect of contemporary masculinity in Japan (see Roberson and Suziki 2004), consumption is increasingly a primary method for establishing and maintaining identity (Clammer 1997: 46).

Historically, attention to male beauty is not unusual in Japan, so I am interested in understanding how current efforts at body improvement relate to aspects of contemporary social life. Outward style manifestations found among young men may have little to do with their internal shifts in gender politics, in terms of how they think about women's roles and statuses. Even so, because of the importance of heterosexual marriage for establishing adult male identity (Edwards 1989), young men must be able to successfully attract wives in an era of intense marriage resistance among women. Although I describe multiple influences that have created the new emphasis on male beauty work, I suggest that men's beauty consumption is linked to intertwined forces: it is informed by female desire, while it concurrently symbolizes consumption-driven identity and rejection of their fathers' model of masculinity. Consumption-based identity and rejection of older male appearance are not unique to Japan, but anxiety over one's ability to attract a wife is tied to a specifically Japanese demographic problem.

The model of maleness being opposed is age-graded, associated with an older generation of *oyaji* (old men) with different values and aspirations. During the postwar period, men were de-eroticized by a corporate culture that emphasized a "productivity ideology of standardization, order, control, rationality and impersonality" (McVeigh 2000: 16). During the 1970s, the creation of the desired male type shifted from scholar types or athletes to the salaryman as the preferred marriage candidate. Contemporary *oyaji* rejection surfaces in women's popular media, where we find expressions of derision and dismissal for old-style salaryman types (Miller 1998b). An emphasis on male appearance counters the salaryman reification of men as workers, while women appreciate these new styles because they are aesthetically pleasing and erotically charged.

New forms of male beauty work go hand in hand with fashion trends and are integrated into a visually structured look. Morgan, noting a similar process in the United States, states that the new focus on men's fashion and lifestyle magazines "certainly points to the elaboration of consumption-led masculinities. The healthy body, the stylish body, and the athletic body become part of a range of bodies that are available in commodified form" (1993: 87). Among Japan's fashion styles for young men dating from the late 1990s are Mode, School, Punk, and American Casual. Other popular vogues are French Casual, Military, B-Boy, Surfer/Skateboarder, Outdoor, and Dread. The Mode look, a nostalgic dandyism situated somewhere between Lord Sebastian Flyte and Antonio Banderas, requires dieting to obtain a long, thin silhouette, hairstyling to delicately frame the face, and facial-care and depilation treatments to eliminate uncivil body hair. The School style, which also entails bodily adjustments, borrows the familiar symbols of that bureaucratic world, particularly the schoolboy's short pants, which are worn in a cheeky mix with other unlicensed garb. Other looks, such as B-Boy, Surfer/Skateboarder, and Dread, may also require skin darkening processes, tattooing, or body piercing in addition to hair modification. In each case, some type of external alchemy is a necessary component of the selected style.

Edwards (1997) has shown how the male body, and the idea of masculinity itself, became objectified and commodified in British media imaging, particularly in men's style magazines. Similarly, the media in Japan has had a major role in turning the male body into an object for public assessment. Since the 1990s, there has been an explosion in a new genre of magazine that is specifically about being male, with a focus on male appearance (table 4). Of course, there are precedents in older magazines that carried an occasional article or feature on men's fashion. The July 1946 issue of the magazine *Style,* for example, included a few pages of fashion advice for the postwar man. Many of the new magazines, however, are entirely devoted to male appearance and lifestyle.

Magazines specializing in the new retro sensibilities and surface identities include *Bidan, Men's Non No,* and *Fine Boys,* all of which offer a mix of fashion advice, facial-care and hairstyling tips, interviews, sports, music, travel, horoscopes, and surveys of trends and fashions. Also available are special publications, such as *Men's Body Manual,* which promises to provide "face and body grade-up" for men (Gakken 2000). These publications provide an endless visual pedagogy (Miller 1998c) of the new male beauty work. Frequently, readers are taught about new beauty ideals through a format that provides meticulous visual representation of the beauty process, together with before and after photographs of the aesthetically upgraded man.

TABLE 4. Men's Fashion and Lifestyle Magazines

| Magazine | Monthly Circulation |
|---|---|
| *Smart* | 600,000 |
| *samurai magazine* | 300,000 |
| *Bidan* | 250,000 |
| *Men's Non No* | 235,000 |
| *Men's Brand* | 230,000 |
| *Get On!* | 180,000 |
| *Boy's Rush* | 150,000 |
| *Fine Boys* | 150,000 |
| *Boon* | 111,417 |
| *Men's Ex* | 69,000 |

NOTE: This is not a complete list of men's fashion and lifestyle magazines.

SOURCE: Japan Tsushinsha (Japan News Agency), www.japan-tsushin .co.jp/.

## Beauty Services for Men: The Men's Esute Salon

During the 1980s, esute salons began offering beauty treatments for men. Salon workers in Kanazawa, where there were no men's salons in 1997, told me they frequently got calls from men asking if they could receive beauty treatments. One of the first salons to provide men's esute was Men's Joli Canaille Salon in Tokyo, which began doing so in April 1984. By 1989, esute salons solely for male customers were an established part of the urban landscape (*Nihon Keizai Shimbun* 1989b). Male-only salons, which cater to the beauty needs of both straight and gay men, are now quite common and include establishments such as Ichirō, Prince, Cosmo, Dandy House, and Tokyo Hands. Many of these became so successful they were able to open franchises. For instance, Dandy House has more than eight salons in the Tokyo area and fifteen elsewhere in the country, and Men's Esute Raparare has eleven shops in the Tokyo area and thirty-three salons elsewhere. Kommy Corporation also had a chain of salons for men (Ono 1999).

Men's esute salons typically offer services that address skin problems, body hair, and body weight or shape. Some salons compete for customers in a manner virtually identical to the women's salons, selling not only an elaborated menu of body treatments but specialized packages such as "men's bridal esute," a bundle of prenuptial treatments to prepare the groom for his big day. Men's TBC in Shibuya (an offshoot of the women's salon chain Tokyo Beauty Center), for instance, sells a mixed groom's esute package consisting of a face tanning session, a face slimming treatment, and a hair removal treatment, and in 1999, it sold "millennium party esute," a special package of facial and massage to prepare men for the special New Year's event (*Asahi Shimbun* 1999b). Advertising for the men's esute salons frequently refers to the effect the beauty work, or a lack of it, might have on women. For example, in an advertisement for Tokyo Aesthetic Salon, under a caption warning, "So that this doesn't happen to you," we see a drawing of a man crying as a woman walks off with a *bidan* (beautiful man), saying, "Bye bye."

In 1999, I visited several men's esute salons in the Tokyo area, where I spoke to receptionists and managers, obtained informational brochures, and looked around to see what types of men were going there to get beauty work. It is clear that, as in women's esute salons, there are a few different micromarkets targeted by the salon proprietors. Some go after a cohort of men of high school or college age, while others target older professional males. Some salons appeal to a largely gay clientele, while others hold out a promise of complete transformation to decidedly frumpy men.

In 1999, Kimutaku was the spokesmodel for Men's TBC, so I wanted to be sure to visit one of their salons (figure 21). TBC originally entered the men's esute market around 1989, with shops named TBC Homme, but these were later revamped as the "new" Men's TBC salons, reopening in January 1999. I went to the branch in Shibuya, which was located on the seventh floor of a narrow building in a very busy area. The salon reception area was furnished in ultramodern chrome and glass, painted in dark colors with touches of black and gray. There were small cafe tables and folding chairs, a television monitor broadcasting information on treatments, and a poster of Kimutaku on the wall. Speakers piped in music from Glay and other crucial J-Pop. This stripped-down practicality contrasts with the prissy ornateness one customarily finds in women's salons, thus reassuring the client that he is in a truly masculine space. The lack of baroque ornamentation is also a key element of the "modern." There were two very small counseling rooms for meetings with prospective and returning clients. I was told that the typical customer is between twenty and thirty, although some younger men also go there. Some of the slogans Men's TBC was using at the time of my visit were "Men's new power" and "Support for all the world's male beauty." Customers at this salon are usually not working-class, as the prices are rather steep. TBC's "entry fee" is roughly $160, an outlay handed over before one receives or pays for any treatments.

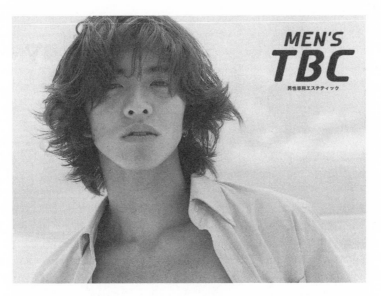

FIGURE 21. Kimutaku in Men's TBC aesthetic salon advertisement, 1999.

Because I was entering space reserved for the protection of "male pride," it was often difficult for me to gather firsthand information on the men's esute salons. Employment of exclusively male receptionists and staff at some shops worked to reassure entering clients that women would not see them before the benefit of their beauty treatments. In a few instances it was assumed that, as a foreign woman, I was just confused about where I was. In most cases, salon staff would quickly answer my questions in the hopes that I would soon leave, concerned that my presence would deter those entering.

I wondered if the men's esute salons operated like women's salons, so I convinced a male friend, Masa, to accompany me to Dandy House. Both men's and women's salons insist that potential customers first telephone for an appointment rather than simply appearing on their doorsteps. The grilling and screening of new clients begins at that time, when the caller is asked a series of questions. When he called to schedule an appointment, Masa was asked, "Where did you learn about our shop? What is your body concern? What services are you interested in? Do you have friends who go to esute?" and "How old are you?" I tagged along with Masa on his initial visit, in the role of his older female sponsor or sugar mommy, to eavesdrop on the "counseling session," during which a salon employee asked him to fill out a series of forms and tried to sell him a collection of treatments. Given its location in Shibuya, a center for cutting-edge youth style, I had expected to see many hip, trendy fellows waiting for their beauty appointments. Instead, a mixed trickle of furtive, average-looking, and not-so-attractive men arrived for their facials, weight reduction treatments, and electrolysis. I was told that Dandy House had been in business for around thirteen years and that there were five aestheticians at that branch. Although there are a few male aestheticians in the Dandy House chain, the majority at this salon are female.

The same sales tactics and questionable practices seen in women's aesthetic salons are also prevalent in the men's salon industry. Aestheticians are urged to use the salon visit as an opportunity to sell multiple products and services. One beauty worker at a men's salon told a reporter, "First and foremost, we estheticians are told that it's our job to sell. Sell tickets for treatment. Sell cosmetics. Sell home esthetic kits. Whenever we're treating a customer, we're continuously thinking of what we can sell to him next" (Connell 2004).

For those timid about exploring the men's esute salons, men's magazines regularly feature articles or advertisements that illustrate what one might expect when visiting one. In a piece in the magazine *Bidan,* three models are depicted as they try out the Men's Joli Canaille Salon (*Bidan* 1997e). One man goes for the facial, after which his skin goes "one rank up"; a second, worried about maintaining his "charm point" baby face, gets a hair removal treatment; and the third opts for a slimming course that also is said to help blood circulation. All three report on how good the esute felt and how wonderfully effective it was. Several of the salon's young attractive female cosmeticians are also pictured, urging readers to come in to meet them. In a different editorial advertisement, a certain "Takahashi-kun" leads us through each of the steps involved in getting a facial (Bidan 1997d).[2] Claiming that "this is the era of the small face," the piece shows the transformation of Takahashi as he receives counseling, individual skin analysis, facial technology that uses a suction cup device to extract oils and blackheads, a peeling treatment, massage, application of a green seaweed pack followed by a white face pack, and a final massage. Whole sections of special beauty magazines for men are devoted to precise information about the esute salon experience.

As the salon business grew in popularity, so did related or spin-off services, such as esute tours or esute included as part of the travel experience. For example, men may now go on a one-day tour by sightseeing bus to various esute salons and beauty parlors. On one tour, sponsored by a Tokyo-based travel company, men got a haircut, facial esute, makeup application, manicure, and at the end of the day, a formal portrait by a professional photographer (*Asahi Shimbun* 1999a). Overseas salons that have been providing beauty services to traveling Japanese women, such as the Hanako Esute Salon in Bangkok, now offer facials and other treatments to men. Esute treatments have also been incorporated into travel entertainment packages to places such as Korea or Bangkok, popular sex-tour destinations.

When I asked salon employees at several locations about the leading treatments sought by men, I was told that hair removal is certainly one of the most popular services. For example, during the late 1990s the number one service at Men's TBC was body hair removal, followed by facials and tanning sessions (other salons report that facial-care treatments are more common). At Men's Joli Canaille Salon, body hair removal together with weight loss tops the list. For those who are too shy or too poor to go to an esute salon for a treatment, home-use products may be purchased that will help the consumer achieve bodies that are hairless and smooth.

## Controlling the Horrible Hirsuteness of Men

Critics note that Japanese attitudes toward male body hair have undergone dramatic changes since the postwar period (*Across* 1989).[3] From the 1950s until the 1970s, a new masculine ideal was promoted through be-whiskered or bushy Euroamerican movie stars such as Sean Connery and Charles Bronson. For example, Bronson became one of the most popular advertising models through years of commercials for Mandom, the Japanese men's cosmetics firm. But a male desire to depilate took hold in the late 1980s, and chest hair ceased being a symbol of a masculinity (*Nihon Keizai Shimbun* 1989a). Although recently beards have become fashionable among some young men, hairy chests are decidedly démodé. Some men want to rid their bodies not only of chest hair, but of leg hair, armpit hair, and arm hair as well.

Separate product lines of depilatory creams and lotions, wax treatments, hair removal tapes, gels, and various shaving or extraction devices are actively targeted at men who desire smooth bodies. Advertising socializes men to think they need predepilation gels, oils, and lotions for topical anesthetic, antiseptic, and conditioning, as well as postdepilation gels, oils, and lotions to diminish redness and moisturize the skin. A variety of devices for use at home are widely sold as high science that is almost as good as electrolysis. These usually have names that sound densely technological and masculine, to distinguish them from identical female products. For instance, the Elimina 6X and the ProCare II are both dressed up shaver-tweezer gadgets that are connected to electric or battery-powered units. (They also resemble computer mice.) As early as 1988, Matsushita Electric came out with a men's combination esute set, a unit with three attachments for hair cutting and styling, face shaving, eyebrow trimming, and body shaving. The expansion in the number of drugstores and *kombini* (convenience stores) operating during the 1990s has contributed to increased availability and sales of these products.

Various explanations have been offered for young men's interest in body hair removal, but women's preference for nonhairy men must be considered a primary reason for its growing popularity. A positive descriptor commonly used by women to catalog desirable men is *subesube* (smooth), and not surprisingly, this is a term that routinely appears in advertising for male beauty products. One advertisement shows a woman gazing at her boyfriend, a speech bubble floating from her mouth with the words "*Tsurusuru* [sleek] feels good!" Occasionally banners with the text "Women really do like *subesube* [smooth]" run across the page. Male fear of negative female evaluation of their hairiness is frequently exploited by the esute salons. Men's Joli Canaille Salon urges men to "get a sleek body that girls love," and the text for a recent Men's TBC advertisement claims, "If you have arm or chest hair, it's hateful to be so embarrassed!" The embarrassment presumably issues from the derision from women this uncivilized hair might provoke. In an advertisement for a hair removal product named 10 Sex Functional Remover, there is a photograph of three young women expressing various forms of disgust at hairiness: crossing their arms in the "no good" pose or with speech bubbles saying things like "It doesn't matter how cool he is; if he has a full-on hairy body, I'll pass." In smaller accompanying comic drawings, women looking at two hairy men say, "What's with that hair?"; when they see two smooth guys, they unanimously say, "Cool."

Young women queried in a 1999 magazine poll about what they find unpleasant about the male body ranked chest hair and other forms of body hair the most offensive (*Ranking Dai Suki!* 1999c). The detestable attributes, in descending order, were:

1. Chest hair
2. Body hair

3. Leg hair

4. Beards

5. Fat body

6. Long hair (on the head)

7. Skinny body

8. Body odors

9. No muscles

10. Small penises

A drawing accompanying the poll shows a woman repulsed by the sight of a hairy man, saying, "Chest hair is gross!" (figure 22). It is noteworthy that the masculine traits so often focused on in the American (male) imagination, mainly muscles and penis size, do not receive the same attention on this list as does body hair.

In a poll of one hundred young women (Gakken 2000: 56) asking, "What do you wish a guy would take care of in his personal appearance that you become aware of when you have intimate relations with him?" the resulting list included (1) body hair, (2) beards, and (3) pimples. As a twenty-year-old female aesthetician said, "I hate men with thick leg hair. If I even see chest hair, I feel revolted" (*Akita Sakigawa Shimbun* 1996).

Most of the men's hair removal products are careful to indicate that the target audience includes heterosexual males by attaching admiring female commentary or endorsements. For example, a hair removal product named Valoir includes the words "to get the skin girls love" in its advertisements. Valoir presents a survey of women's tastes in this area, in which one hundred women between the ages of sixteen and twenty-two were asked, "Which do you like, smooth or hairy men?" According to this poll, most women (seventy-two) prefer smooth men, while only two favor hairy men. The remainder said they are "indifferent." Zero Factor, another product line of depilatory creams and lotions aimed at the young male market, also uses anxiety about female evaluation in its advertising. In a two-page advertisement, the benefits of hair removal are presented as a narrative in comic form. The story begins with a young couple on a shopping date, during which the woman asks her boyfriend to try on some shorts. When the fellow comes out of the dressing room showing his hairy legs, she reacts with disgust and suggests hair remover, but he balks at this notion. She notes, "It's a waste with your nice legs." He still protests that it takes too much money and is bothersome, but she insists that "with

FIGURE 22. "Chest hair is gross!"
Illustration for a poll ("Women think
that, as for the male body, this is not
allowed!") in *Ranking Dai Suki!*
magazine, March 1999. Reproduced
with permission of Bunkasha Publishing.

Zero Factor it's no worry." He gives in and later they frolic together hap-
pily on the beach with his smooth legs.

An article investigating the new trend interviewed men in Tokyo
about why they rid their bodies of hair (*Across* 1989). An eighteen-year-
old man said he noticed that friends were using depilatories because "girls
hate things like thick beards and body hair, and chest hair especially is
loathsome. I myself haven't had chest hair for some time." A twenty-two-
year-old says he developed thick body hair during his high school days
and was so embarrassed he would not wear shorts. He claims that since
he hates thick beards himself, it is only natural that he likes women who
also dislike body hair.

The new focus on the slim and smooth male body means that entertainers take every opportunity to flash their bare, oiled torsos in concerts,
television dramas, and advertising. Men in everyday contexts likewise display their smooth chest to onlookers. Many foreigners and older Japanese have difficulty comprehending this new male body aesthetic, a point
that hit me while on a school trip with a group of Japanese and American
college students. In the evening I stood with others who were waiting
for friends outside the entrance to the hotel's public bath. One Japanese
lad came out wearing shorts without a shirt. He was tanned, smooth, and
hairless, and looked as if he had applied some oil to his chest. One of the
American men, who fancied himself quite a ladies' man and was working
hard to draw attention to himself, looked at this bare chest and sneered,
"Gross" as he walked by, completely oblivious to the fact that all the young
Japanese women were staring at this smooth fellow with obvious interest and approval.

The popularity of male beauty work has attracted its share of criticism,

FIGURE 23. Making fun of male beauty work. Reproduced with permission of *Asahi Shimbun* and artist Fukuda Toshiyuki.

however, primarily from middle-aged men. Newspaper scandal sheets often carry nasty tidbits about hot young athletes who are sporting trimmed eyebrows, bleached hair, or unnaturally smooth and hairless skin. One article that frets over the fact that some young baseball players are engaging in depilation, body piercing, nail manicures, and hair removal is accompanied by a cartoon showing two men engaged in beauty work (figure 23). One is shaving his eyebrows while the other is trimming under his arm. A distressed observer watching them says, "Enough, the underarm is fine!" (*Asahi Shimbun* 1998a).

There is also some resistance among some young men over the issue of manscaping. Interestingly, university students I interviewed who claimed to not like it used sexist rather than homophobic logic to justify their positions. They felt that it was wrong not because it renders the male body more feminine and thereby suspect, but because it signals that the hairless man has no pride and has given in to women's demands and desires. Their denigrating term for men who remove body hair is *Tsurutsuru-kun*, "Mr. Smooth."[4] *Tsurutsuru-kun*, they told me, are only interested in getting girls by whatever means necessary.

An episode that highlighted the contrast between American and Japanese attitudes toward male body hair happened at the building where I was housed with other foreigners associated with a Japanese university.[5] Japanese students frequently came by to hang out on an upstairs balcony. One day I went up there to talk to a small group of them about male beauty work. This school had been an all-male university until only a few years prior, when it began admitting women. There are still very few female students, and the ones who are there have entered by virtue of superior math and science skills, which enabled them to beat out male competitors. All the women I met were highly intelligent, straightforward, serious, and unpretentious. As I talked with them on the balcony, an American male student came up and, not understanding, asked for a translation. When I explained that many Japanese women find body hair on men unattractive, which has led to the development of new products and services for male body hair removal, he was incredulous. He refused to believe me, claiming that chest hair in particular indicates that one is a "real man" and that women universally "dig it." I suggested that different aesthetic sensibilities were in operation, but he continued to protest such an idea. Just then "Naoko," a female student as bright as any I met, came up to join our group. The American chap, deciding to simply test my theory empirically, lifted his shirt to display his hairy chest, asking her what she thought. Naoko screamed, "How hateful!" *(Iyā da!)* in a shrill voice and ran to hide behind a door, periodically peeking out to whimper at the unspeakable sight.

Although an old Japanese proverb says something like "a hairy person is a sexy person" *(Kebukai mono wa irobukai),* the majority of young Japanese women these days just do not like hairy men. Although esute marketing must have played some small role in establishing this preference, it is also the case that distaste for hairiness is another form of *oyaji* rejection. Other scholars have noted that an aesthetic preference for hairlessness accompanies a penchant for youth and downy innocence. According to Dutton (1995: 306), speaking on male beauty in general, "Nakedness, a hairless body and smooth skin texture are all forms of social neotny, signaling a childlike nonthreatening quality and thus denying messages of aggression." For many young women, patriarchal values, or at the very least a dowdy conservatism, go hand in hand with the cloned salaryman body style. A rejection of this aesthetic, therefore, and an appreciation of the ephebe style can be viewed as a veto of male dominance and an assertion of an independent sexuality.

## Cosmetic Beauty Work

Cosmetic products targeting men have long had great success in Japan. This may be related to the fact that from the beginning, the product category roughly equivalent to "cosmetics" *(keshōhin),* was never strictly

FIGURE 24. Meiji-era unisex cosmetics: Bigan Sui (Beautiful Face Water).

gendered in Japan, as it is in the United States (Fields 1985: 91). It is a category that has always included body products for both men and women, as can be seen in advertisements from the Meiji era (1868–1912) for products such as Bigan Sui (figure 24), a "face water" for clearing up and beautifying the skin (Machida 1997).

The bulk of a young man's beauty work is devoted to his head hair. For this important task, according to one recent poll, the majority of young men (76 percent) prefer to use the services of a specialized hair salon rather than an old-fashioned barber (*Fine Boys* 1998: 186). Hair dyes and various hair-growth products, along the lines of Grecian Formula in the United States, have long been available for older men worried about gray hair and hair loss. For years the cosmetics firm Kanebo has offered such products for men under the name Valion. Men also bought a variety of pomades, waxy hairdressings, and liquids, such as Vitalis hair liquid.

Beginning in the mid-1990s, a fad for brown hair, or *chapatsu,* took hold for both men and women. The *chapatsu* look ranges from nutty brown to mahogany or chocolate tones and is popular all over Japan, not just in the urban centers. Men who sport orangey or caramel hair colors are sometimes teased with the name *purin-kun,* or "Mr. Pudding Head," but whenever I heard this, mainly coming from young women, it was used both affectionately and approvingly.

Hair may also be streaked with various colors or dyed blond or orange. At the Salon de Kosson in Tokyo, men may have their hair dyed one or more of thirty-six different colors. At Hair Bar Ogiso, men are able to first select and preview the style on a computer simulation screen. This

FIGURE 25. How to get Kimutaku-style hair. Reproduced with permission of *Bidan* magazine.

fad has resulted in the creation of new product lines of hair dyes and bleaches for young men. For that fluffy, thatchy look, one can buy any number of male-targeted hair coloring products, such as Gatsby, Bolty, or Nudy, and magazines routinely carry visual guidance on how to bleach and style one's own hair at home. In many cases, instruction is given for how to style the hair to resemble top celebrities such as Kimutaku (figure 25). Some older, originally female-oriented products, such as Bleacha and Beauty Labo, are now being sold in more neutral packaging to take in this growing male market. Concerns about hair are even incorporated into *Bidan*'s regular monthly horoscope, in which readers are offered "Lucky Hair" tips (*Bidan* 1997c: 118). For instance, in one issue the astrological sign Virgo was advised to go with long hair, Cancer with bleach, Gemini with shaggy, and Libra with Dread.

Separate non-unisex lines of men's cosmetics have been sold in Japan for almost two decades. In 1984, Isetan department store opened up a makeup corner for men, and in 1986, Gear introduced a male line of face packs, eye liner, and foundation products. New high-end department store lines of men's cosmetics include Jinnous Men's Skin Care line from Fancl House. Currently the Mandom company produces twelve cosmetic products under the Mandom name, but most of these are the more prosaic hair tonics and aftershave lotions targeted at older men. Advertising for the *oyaji* crowd emphasizes masking gray hair and concealing bald spots so as to look young and plucky as part of their work identity. For the younger market, Mandom created a newer line of products sold under the name Gatsby. There are more than twenty Gatsby products, including facial scrubs, facial paper, nose pack, facial cream, facial astringent, deodorant, two types of hair bleach, and various hairstyling foams, gels, and sprays. Mandom also created an Internet advice web site for male skincare and hairstyling tips. The Gerald line of male cosmetics, from Shiseido, sold more than $1 million worth of products in one year (Ono 1999). The hottest items in young men's cosmetics are the oil blotting papers and nose packs, and Shiseido, TAG, Biore, NUDY, and Gerald all offer versions of these products specifically for men (*Asahi Shimbun* 1997b). Manicures for men may include the use of brightly colored nail polish, and men's magazines often offer advice on how to buy and use nail polishes and nail-care products. A *Fine Boys* article on manicures tells the reader that "if men do their nails, it's cool!"(*Fine Boys* 1997: 107). There are gender-neutral nail-care products as well as male-coded lines available.

For men concerned about how to apply these new cosmetic products, classes and training programs are available to assist them. For example, in September 1999 the Asahi Culture Center in Tokyo, an adult continuing education service, offered a two-hour "Men's Makeup" workshop. Flyers for the workshop included before and after photographs of a newly beautified man and announced that men should "take advantage of the era when even men can be glamorous." In a clear move to address the reason for the beauty work, the flyer specified that wives and girlfriends should accompany the men in order to observe their beauty transformation.

## The Elegant Crescent

Perhaps more than any other cosmetic procedure, the contemporary manipulation of the eyebrow is presenting a challenge to the "naturalness" of gender stereotypes. Male cosmetic treatment of the eyebrows has a long history in Japan, dating to at least the Heian era (794–1185 A.D.). Tsuda (1985: 2) points to the refined eyebrows seen on many of the first Buddhist statues, such as the Chūgū-ji Buddha in Nara, as possible inspiration for this beauty practice. Eyebrow plucking and shaping is just one of numerous beauty activities many contemporary women do in order to create female gendered looks. When men engage in such craftsmanship, the degree to which women's faces are the product of beauty work and cosmetics is exposed, or at least it is brought to another level of conscious awareness.

The current preference among young men is for thin rather than thick eyebrows. Men emulate celebrities who sport plucked eyebrows, including Funaki Kazuyoshi, the Japanese gold-medal winner in the ski jump, who impressed fans with his carefully plucked and shaped eyebrows and engendered a widespread desire for the *Funaki-mayu,* "Funaki eyebrow," look. The press has taken note of this fad, often linking it to the beauty of someone like Kimutaku. For example, a *Yomiuri Shimbun* article reports on the fad among teens and men in their twenties, citing Kimutaku and pop music star Ishida Issei as good eyebrow men (*Yomiuri Shimbun* 1997b). All this media attention to the male eyebrow is likewise reflected in polls of male tastes, such as a 1998 *Fine Boys* poll, in which 70.9 percent of the respondents said they think men look better with thin eyebrows (*Fine Boys* 1998: 187). Of course, really bushy eyebrows were always frowned upon, as indicated by the insult *gejigeji mayuge,* or "centipede eyebrows," a rude term used for both men and women. In explaining why he went to get an eyebrow cut at a department store men's makeup corner, a thirty-four-year-old said it was because his girlfriend called him centipede eyebrows (*Asahi Shimbun* 1999c: 5).

Advice on how to create a nice eyebrow shape is found in many men's magazines (figure 26). One such article claims that it "seems like 100 percent of the cool guys on the street are shaping their eyebrows," and gives explicit and detailed instructions for eyebrow creation and management (*Bidan* 1997b). Before and after photographs instruct readers in the improvements to one's looks possible through this beauty work, and advice is tailored to various eyebrow types. For instance, a guy with an eyebrow in the shape of the Chinese character for "one" (a single solid horizontal line) is advised to pluck between the eyebrows, cut the lower edges and upper outer edges of the eyebrows, and form curves that narrow at the ends by drawing out the tail with an eyebrow pencil. To insure that eyebrow work is seen as an acceptable heterosexual activity, articles and advice pieces insert quotes from admiring girlfriends or testimonies from the guy on the street who reports that his girlfriend approves or that, in fact, it was a girlfriend who first taught him how to do it. One fellow even positions this beauty work as a form of courtship: "Doing eyebrows together with a girlfriend is my dream."

Special tools for eyebrow construction are available so that, together with proper hairstyling, one may get the Kimutaku look. The Gerald for Men Eyebrow Design Kit, launched in November 1996, comes with eyebrow brush, tweezers, scissors, and eyebrow pencil. There are also eyebrow templates one may buy with ready-made shapes, such as the Make Line, clear plastic guides with exact measurements imprinted on them. One may

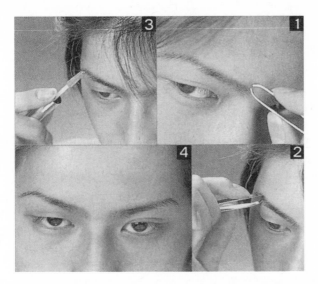

FIGURE 26. Men's
eyebrow beauty
work. Reproduced
with permission of
*Bidan* magazine.

do eyebrows at home or go to a beauty parlor for eyebrow shaping, a service many hair salons are now extending to men. In Tokyo men can get eyebrow cuts at the Ritz salon for $20, at Herb's for $25, or at CAP for $15.

Just as male body hair removal has its detractors, so too eyebrow plucking is viewed by some critics as unmanly, debauched behavior. In the controversial yet bestselling comic castigating postwar moral decadence, Kobayashi (1998: 8) depicts young men plucking their eyebrows as an example of the vile self-indulgence that accompanies democracy. The macho, war-glorifying principles espoused by older men like Kobayashi, however, are despised by younger generations.

## Dabbling in Beauty

Young men actively experiment with many types of cosmetic and beauty products but often feel a bit inept or inexperienced in their explorations. One way to reassure consumers that it is normal, everyday practice to use cosmetics is through feature pieces that highlight what some men carry around with them to maintain their appearance. In an article on the beauty goods men have in their pouches, readers get to examine the contents of the small cosmetic bags carried around by a group of young men (*Bidan* 1997a: 30–31).[6] Inside a Lolita pouch that was a gift from his mother, one man carries a portable shaver, wash packets, face powder (which he claims to use before meeting girls), a Gerald Eyebrow Design Kit, lip gloss, a hair brush, pimple medicine, and a Hello Kitty lighter. An eighteen-year-old student's pouch contains a mirror, a hairbrush, a vial of perfume he got from his current girlfriend, an eyebrow comb and pencil left over from an ex-girlfriend, nose hair scissors, lip cream, and a hair band for when his teacher makes him pull his long hair back.

Ear piercing, body piercing, and tattoos have become more common among straight men after decades of being seen as having strictly underworld or gay connotations. But style advice for the heterosexual man warns that if one does get piercing, cute or sweet earrings should be worn to soften the potentially "hard" look. Ear and body piercing is available at some beauty salons and at cosmetic surgery clinics. Both procedures are relatively inexpensive. The Shibuya Sarah Beauty and Health Salon offers piercing services to men for as low as $4 for the ears and starting around $40 for any other part of the body.

Of course, the existence of men's cosmetics and beauty goods does not really tell us much about how many men really use these products. It is difficult to determine the percentage of men who buy or use cosmetic products, since not everyone is confident about their excursions into this domain or the degree to which their beauty secrets should become public knowledge. Surveys suggest that men are relatively open about hair coloring and bleach, which is hard to disguise, but less so about other procedures. For example, when I was a visiting professor at an engineering university in 1997, I mentioned the new eyebrow plucking fad to some of the professors in my office. They looked at me with disbelief, but a few days later excitedly told me that, now that I had made them aware of it, they were seeing that indeed at least a fourth of the men sitting in their classes had plucked their eyebrows. A poll of men between the ages of twenty and twenty-four by the magazine *Nikkei Trendy* (table 5) found that 65 percent of the respondents had used hair coloring products, 38.2 percent admitted to shaping their eyebrows, and 17.2 percent had received some type of hair removal treatment (*Nikkei Trendy* 1997). A different survey of a younger cohort in *Fine Boys* (table 6) gave similar results but included other body treatments, such as tattoos, makeup use, and body piercing (*Fine Boys* 1998: 187).

Both surveys make it clear that there is a great deal of experimenting with the body, especially with hair color, body hair removal, and eyebrow shaping. A smaller survey of young men in *Seventeen* magazine were asked, "Have you done eyebrow work?" The majority (89 percent) said yes (*Seventeen* 2001a: 126). When one hundred young men ages ten to

TABLE 5. "Which of These Have You Done?"
Nikkei Trendy *survey of men aged twenty to twenty-four, February 1997*

| Practice | Percentage Answering Yes |
|---|---|
| Dyed hair | 65.0 |
| Grew a beard | 48.4 |
| Grew long hair | 42.2 |
| Eyebrow shaping | 38.2 |
| Facial pack | 31.8 |
| Piercing | 24.2 |
| Hair removal treatment | 17.2 |
| Tanning salon | 11.5 |

TABLE 6. "Esute I Did, Esute I Want to Try"
Fine Boys *survey, February 1998*

| | Percentage Answering Yes | |
|---|---|---|
| *Practice* | *Did It* | *Want to Try* |
| *Chapatsu* | 40.0 | 14.3 |
| Hair color | 39.0 | 47.6 |
| Depilatory | 19.7 | 25.9 |
| Growing a beard | 19.0 | 35.1 |
| Body piercing | 10.2 | 17.8 |
| Foundation makeup | 5.1 | 21.1 |
| Manicure | 4.4 | 23.4 |
| Tattoo | 2.2 | 28.7 |

twenty were asked, "Do you want to try esute?" half (53 percent) said yes (Gakken 2000: 56). Young men are trying out a spectrum of new types of beauty work, from facials to makeup, and are curious and interested in delving further into this new terrain. In an interview, a twenty-year-old university student says he uses a women's electric eyebrow shaver and does a facial pack once a week. He says, "Even when I turn fifty, I'll continue to do it." A fifteen-year-old uses oil-blotting paper and foundation and, when he gets enough money, wants to try a salon (*Asahi Shimbun* 1999c: 5).

While older men may be reluctant to try out makeup and eyebrow plucking, many are still interested in improving their appearance with the assistance of salon facial treatments or tanning sessions. Among the *oyaji* set, a good tan is considered a masculine attribute, perhaps denoting an active outdoor sports life or youth and robustness. It suggests that the man is dedicated to work-related activities, such as corporate-sponsored golf. To combat the unhealthy pallor of the office, middle-aged men go to tanning salons such as Sparkys Solar or Cyberspace Sun Muscle in Tokyo (*Asahi Shimbun* 1998c; *Nihon Keizai Shimbun* 1999). A father and son getting tanning treatments together may therefore be doing so for very different reasons—the young man to look good for women, the *oyaji* to look good for his clients and company.

Male engagement with many of these forms of beauty work not only challenges conventional gender constructions, it also contends with traditional notions about the malleability of the self. Earnest efforts to accommodate to the new aesthetic are also seen in the development of other services, both surgical and less permanent, for modifying the body.

## Other Body Modifications

It is often said that Japanese women hate three things: the short, the bald, and the chubby. Advertisements for weight-loss and hair-growth products exploit this anxiety by referring to women's opinions or including surveys of female tastes. For example, an advertisement for a product named Men's Super Speed Diet HCA 780 includes a survey of two hundred women that asked them, "What type of man do you hate?" The majority, 89 percent, gave "chubby" as their pet peeve. Most of the weight-loss products sold to men are similar if not identical to those targeted to women, and include so-called miracle seaweed soaps from China, herbal remedies that are supposedly based on traditional Chinese-style medicine, and diet suppressants, teas, and elixirs.

The average height in 2000 for a man between twenty and twenty-four was 171.8 centimeters, or around 5 feet 7 inches (*Asahi Shimbun* 2002: 204). But these days young men do not want to look average; they want to look like the models and stars they see on television and in magazines. According to Hashimoto (1994: 320), the typical Japanese male celebrity or model is around six feet tall—for instance, Sorimachi Takashi, who starred in the television drama *Beach Boys* and is often featured on lists of favorite celebrities. For those who see Sorimachi and other tall men as their aspirational yardsticks, a quest for methods to increase height has led to a variety of dubious products being huckstered through every media form. The Kyōrin Medical Company sells something called the Gulliver #3, which employs pulleys and a traction extension machine to straighten the legs and lengthen the body. The company guarantees that if the buyer uses it for twenty minutes every day, his stature will increase by four inches within three months. Models in the advertisements for the Gulliver #3 exclaim that "with this I'll be a regular guy and get a girlfriend," and that sports ability will also improve. Instead of using an apparatus or taking a medicine, a business named the Nihon Health Academy (the same mail order outfit also offers a home breast enhancement training program to women) sells what it terms the DNA System. This too is coated with a smooth layer of fraud when it announces that it works through the activation of the "growth hormone," so that getting taller may be accomplished "naturally." Advertisements feature scales and photographs of a young DNA System user towering over a poor sod who simply let nature take its course.[7]

Increasingly, surgery is also called on to beautify the body. According to the director of a hospital in Tokyo, "Especially for young Tokyoites, it is merely an extension of having your nails done or your ears pierced. It is a more active form of an esute salon" (Itoh 1996). Another cosmetic surgery clinic in Tokyo has noticed a gradual rise in the number of its male clients, so that now they comprise around 30 percent of the total (Stuhlman 1999). For men, the face is the most frequent site for what Balsamo (1996: 62) dismisses as "fashion surgery," particularly operations that build up a flat nose, sculpt the nasal tip, enhance the chinline, or change the eyelid. The ubiquitous eyelid tapes and glues are also sold in gender-neutral packaging and are advertised in both women's and men's magazines.

## Interpreting Change

Why has there been a change from the decades in which men who wore anything but dark blue suits were suspect to an era in which eyebrow plucking and hair coloring are de rigueur? In trying to understand the male quest for surface beauty, one market researcher suggests that use of cosmetics by men is just the outcome of "copying everyone" (Ono 1999: B1). Although there may be a degree of peer pressure involved, this still does not explain why such fads began in the first place, nor why it is the body that is the object of change. Others have suggested that a change to a new model of masculinity, in which mass media images of hairless men are prevalent, is linked to the sports craze, especially cycling and skateboarding (*Across* 1989). Hanihara (1999) claims that some of these beauty changes actually reflect an evolution in Japanese facial anatomy.

Evolutionary psychologists have a slightly different angle on why young women might like "feminine" male faces. In studies conducted at the University of Tokyo and the University of St. Andrews in Scotland, researchers claim that women in their study preferred men with "feminized" faces for long-term relationships, while men with masculine facial types were selected during the point in the ovulation cycle when a woman is most likely to conceive. The researchers suggest that these putative preferences show that supposedly the "masculine" type will deliver better sperm, while the "feminine" type is, well, nicer. Setting aside the ahistorical nature of these studies, among other problems there were defects in the methods used (for instance, women chose from a collection of digitized, composite faces instead of actual faces). The primary impact of these studies worth noting, however, is that the popularity of less harsh-looking men is becoming a marked global phenomenon, one that calls out for an explanation (*U.S. News and World Report* 1999: 56).

Various political, economic, and social perspectives have also been used to interpret changes in the modern representation of gender and masculinity. In much classical sociological theory, it is not shifts in the culture, changes in the conception of masculinity, or gender politics that fuel this change, but rather changes in the economic system. The advancement of consumer capitalism promotes the beauty and fashion industries (McCracken 1988; Simmel 1957; Turner 1980; Veblen 1925). So, for upward-hustling Japanese men, having the right look—the right hair, face, skin, and clothes—means that one has both the sensibilities to recognize this new aesthetic and the time and resources to achieve the socially desired body for compulsory heterosexual marriage. Their bodies are now "projects" (Featherstone 1991; Shilling 1993; Frühstück 2000) that fuel an economy of beauty goods and services.

In sorting out the reasons for the expansion of interest in men's fashion, Edwards (1997) sees it as linked to developments in marketing and advertising and to the nature of modern consumption. He says: "It has become more socially acceptable for men to be consumers per se and, more importantly, to be consumers of their own masculinity, or in short, to look at themselves and other men as objects of desire to be bought and sold or imitated and copied" (Edwards 1997: 73).

Masculine identity, once defined through work, now hinges on consumption, a sort of "commodified selfhood" (Langman 1992: 734). Some observers claim that men who work hard at improving their surface appearance are not doing it to please others, but are working from a narcissistic urge to look good for their own consumption. The androgynous writer Tsutamori (1990) suggests that rather than accommodating the female or male "gaze," such work enables one to "redeem the body for oneself." He sees the body as the last refuge from social discipline to which members of society might cling. During an interview, the social critic and writer Seki claimed that the new beauty work is an outcome of "aesthetic communication" in which men have acquired female sensibilities and bodily sensuality as an aspect of self-expression (*Mainichi Shimbun* 1996; see also Seki 1996).

Japan is a major coparticipant in a common consumer-oriented ethos diffused through transnational corporations, advertising agencies, and media. Many critics and scholars interpret the rise of new body aesthetics as emanating from an imported racist beauty ideology that denigrates Asian physical appearance. For example, Kaw (1993) vehemently disparages cosmetic surgery among Asian American women as the result of a colonialist and racist discourse. The late film director Itami Jūzō also insisted that young Japanese who change their bodies are earnestly trying to "become American."[8] For example, the desire to have eyelid surgery is usually interpreted as wanting to look more foreign (see chapter 4). I find it odd that, even though a large percentage of the Japanese population already has natural eyelid creases, no one suggests that individuals are modeling themselves after that segment. New male body styles that include a preference for a large eye shape and new and diverse hair colors should not automatically lead us to claim that they are simply emulating non-Japanese. Would that not be confounding the rejection of older Japanese models of male identity, particularly the salaryman, with a rejection of ethnicity? When American ravers or cyberpunks appropriate non-Western forms of body modification, such as nose piercing or tattooing, we do not hear anyone accuse them of trying to turn themselves into Dani warriors or Maori islanders. Of course, Dani and Maori never occupied the United States in the way Americans occupied Japan in the postwar era through the military and imported media. Even so, if looking Euroamerican includes having a hairy body, I doubt that very many young Japanese men would be interested. It seems to me that this is an aesthetic that combines many features and is not merely "failed Western" or "faux-American." It pulls in ideas from outside Japan for inspiration in certain of its traits, but it also draws on local concepts and proclivities.

This new male concern with beauty work may also be linked to sociopolitical issues. In his discussion of British youth styles of the 1970s,

Hebdige (1979: 28) sees their significance as a political phenomenon that disrupts the dominant culture. Youth styles are characterized as an aesthetic that merges individualism, polymorphous sexuality, and a fragmented sense of self. This way of thinking also accounts, somewhat, for the new body aesthetics for men in Japan. In a similar manner, the transformation of the body surface "asks to be read" (Hebdige 1979: 101). It is a style that "offends the majority, challenges the principle of unity and cohesion, and contradicts the myth of consensus" (Hebdige 1979: 18). The rejection of imposed and proscribed norms, especially images of short, stocky, dark-suited *oyaji* with pomade-plastered hair, is notable in the fashion trend in which affluent urban young men, nicknamed *taorā* ("towelers"), wrap white towels around their heads in an appropriation of a style commonly found among day laborers, fishermen, and construction workers. (Kimutaku wore such a towel style in the television series *Concerto.*) Ironically, their fashion insurgency ultimately supports the status quo by accommodating female desire, thus leading to participation in a state-endorsed ideology of heterosexual bonding and reproduction.

This is perhaps most clearly seen in the appeal of hiphop subcultures (Condry 2000) and the fashion rebellions of early groups such as *bōsō-zoku* ("hot rodders") who created tough-guy images from blended accoutrements and hairstyles (Sato 1991), adumbrating today's mixed styles. The wearing of uniforms in schools and suits in the business world diverts attention away from individual, particular bodies. Similar to how the aloha shirt has become the antithesis of business "success" dressing in the United States, representing a minor act of defiance, beautification of the body denotes a refusal to accept the bland imprint of corporate sameness. Many high schools have a "Lifestyle Guidance Leader" who polices and tries to enforce rigid dress codes and rules for hair color and style. Big corporations in Japan, including IBM, often insist on strict conformity to canons of appearance. For example, only a few firms, such as Nissan Motors, Kirin Beer, Sega, and Japan Steel, allow workers to wear the dyed-brown *chapatsu* style (Gray 1997). Young men who give detailed attention to their surface ornamentation are rejecting this suppression of individuality. Their visible grooming activity creatively opposes the rigid male salaryman icon, or at the least provides a "refuge" from the suffocation of the salaryman ideal.

According to some observers, the new focus on androgynously erotic men reflects what Seki (1996: 36) and Lunsing (1997) term Japan's "gay boom," in which gay sensibilities and tastes have informed wider social trends and aesthetics. Although a gay boom may well be under way, and a female receptiveness to gay men as characterized in popular culture reflects changes in attitudes and feelings toward traditional masculinity, gay culture is probably not the inspiration for female preferences in male appearance. As pointed out by McLelland (1999), the over-the-top masculinity of the male body as presented in gay media is not at all the same as the beautiful young men espoused in girls' comics but rather is a hypermasculine embodiment of the very traits women are rejecting (particularly aggressiveness). The taut men pictured in gay magazines such as *Barazoku* are quite different from Kimutaku and other stars who make it onto *An An*'s annual lists of "men I want to have sex with." The idea of "gay" best friends for women and the new beauty norms for straight men both stem from a similar rejection of a narrow and traditional capitalist-dictated masculinity.

New male beauty work indicates a deconstruction or breakdown in rigid 1970s gender categories and images, and hence it disturbs many critics, who see it as unwholesome or creepy (Imamura 2000). Yet rather than see the new emphasis on male beauty as contributing to a reconstruction of masculinity, critics often view it as straightforward "feminization" of men. This is based on the assumption that "beauty" is de facto "feminine," and supports an extremely polarized view of gender. In Robertson's (1998) investigation of historically situated constructions of androgyny in Japan, she finds that, despite the workings of a normalizing principle, neither femininity nor masculinity has been deemed the exclusive province of either male or female. When based on a blunt contrast with mousey-gray salaryman drabness, men like Hyde, lead vocalist for the group L'Arc~en~Ciel, and Kimutaku might indeed seem "feminine." But viewed from the perspective of women's desires, these men retain their masculinity, which is concurrently presented with a surface beauty. So-called feminine-looking men are not read as fastidious prickmedainties—overly fastidious about their bodies and hairstyles. When a woman says of an androgynous J-Pop icon, "He's not vulgar, and seems like he'd be calm and steady in bed," she is hardly describing someone lacking masculinity (*An An* 1997: 20). Fans perceive no contradiction when, for instance, in a description of Hyde, they express sentiments such as "Those eyes. That voice. He's really beautiful, masculine, and sexy" (Imamura 2000: 48).

Hirota (1997) describes the transformation of male beauty as seen in artistic representation of the male heroes of *The Tale of Genji,* the Heian-period classic by novelist Lady Murasaki. She notes the contrast between male beauty as visually depicted in medieval scroll paintings, which feature men with plump faces, narrow eyes, thick eyebrows, and tiny mouths, and that found in modern-day comics, in which Genji characters are often slim and tall with long legs, oval faces, small jaws, huge round eyes, and small noses. Here we see a clear influence from the realm of girls' comics on contemporary constructions of an ideal masculinity. The beautiful young men *(bishōnen)* depicted therein influence more than contemporary representation of characters from classical literature, however. The degree to which female *Comickinder* have succeeded in insinuating their own preferences into modern life is apparent even in ostensibly male domains, such as popular music.

This is most evident in the prominence of "visual-*kei*," bands and singers who focus energy on their appearance as much as, if not more than, on their music. Some observers claim that the male styles found in visual-*kei* have inspired the interest in eyebrow shaping, skin care, and other beauty work among ordinary men (Shōgakukan 1999: 290). Nonetheless, I see both the music fad and the beauty trend as having identical roots in cultural productions from girls' culture, especially the popular *bishōnen* comics. J-Pop artists such as Gackt, Hyde, Izam of Shanza, and others seem to have all stepped out of the pages of girls' comics onto the music stage, providing living manifestations of readers' fantasy men. The blue hair of J-Pop boys is modeled not after ancient Anglo-Saxons but after Japanese *manga* characters. Male images in *manga* have their own complex histories and meanings, and while some critics perceive a type of deracialization at work in them, it is also true that their hybrid ideal for male appearance does not reflect hypermasculine Western norms. If the representations of men in comics do not look like Japanese to outsiders, neither can one say that they look like foreigners or "white" people either.

One of the hottest entertainers in Japan is a megastar with the stage name Gakuto or "Gackt." A former member of the Japanese Goth band Malice Mizer, he started his solo career in 1999. Over the years, Gackt has appeared with hair dyed many shades, from silvery white to reddish brown. He often wears contact lenses that change his brown eyes to blue or green. Indeed, fans of Gackt love to hunt for his look-alikes in domestically produced media. In 1999, Gackt was into the romanticized pseudo-European antique look, with red hair and obvious makeup. We see this most easily in his inaugural solo release, the *Mizérable* mini-album, music video, and photobook. It is obvious that Gackt's baroque, androgynous indeterminacy draws heavily from the classic *manga* by Ikeda Riyoko (1972), *The Rose of Versailles,* a series set in France in the years before the French Revolution. Later in 1999, Gackt dyed his hair very white and wore blue contact lenses. I thought he looked suspiciously similar to the character Griffith in Miura Kentarō's (1990) *Berserk* comic series. In early 2000, Gackt had straight reddish hair with dark roots. He permed his hair after a few months, and by August had changed his hair to fluffy dark auburn and wore green contact lenses. By November his hair was browner and straightened. In 2001, he was back to the core *chapatsu* or brownish-red look, and in December of that year, he had short, spiky red hair. In June 2002, his hair was blond again, and he was wearing blue contact lenses. It was during this period that he posed nude for the cover of the July issue of the women's magazine *Frau*. In October, his hair was back to red but with extensions. In March 2003, it was red with streaks. During the same month he was voted the "guy I'd most want to paint nude" in a magazine for teenagers ( *Junion* 2003). Gackt explicitly modeled himself after a character when he dressed up as a Meiji-era (1868–1911) samurai straight out of the popular series *Ruroni Kenshin*. At other times, Gackt himself has claimed that media characters were created after his likeness. His nickname for Squall Leonhart of the Final Fantasy VIII role-playing game is "Gackt Number Two." In August 2003, the game company Taito announced that it was working on a new Sony Playstation game named Bujingai, in which the main character is patterned directly after Gackt. Gackt also worked on voice acting and motion-capture for the project.

The recent appearance of living specimens of *bishōnen* such as Gackt calls into question past scholarly analysis of androgynous or gay male characters in comics. Some scholars have suggested that they serve as vehicles for girls to fantasize themselves as these characters and to thereby escape gender role restrictions, a type of displacement necessitated by a sexist culture. Others have interpreted *bishōnen* love as avoidance of womanhood, or as a covert opportunity for girls to aspire to masculine ideals. Beautiful young men in comics are supposedly projections of the female reader's own desires and imagined agency, or some other type of displacement (Matsui 1993; Fujimoto 2004). Yet, as McLelland (2001) reminds us, such explanations can be reductionist and deny the complexities of both desire and identification. He noted, "Underlying these arguments is the assumption that in a non-sexist world women would 'naturally' choose heterosexual fantasy" (McLelland 2001). Treating the interest in androgynous or gay *bishōnen,* real and imaginary, as problematic and in need of explanation negates the possibility of uncomplicated erotic interest.

Numerous feminist scholars have claimed that when women do beauty work, they are making themselves the "object and prey" (de Beauvoir 1968: 642) of men or of an imagined male connoisseur. Does this in turn mean that when the male body is the candidate for assessment, it legitimizes women as the observers of male bodies? A few intellectuals would say no. Gay and lesbian scholars have pointed out the many ways in which "straight" culture is saturated with homoerotic imagery (Fuss 1995). Their explanation for how this can exist in a homophobic culture is that representations of male bonding and the attendant reification of the male body in areas such as sports or television are necessary components of patriarchy (Sedgwick 1991). Consequently, an increase in the so-called feminizing of male behavior or appearance could be viewed as a means of reinforcing patriarchal masculinities (Horrocks 1995: 11). According to Chapman (1988), male narcissism and fashion interest amount to a confiscating of femininity, in which men adopt only the behaviors without suffering the consequences. Social critic Ueno created the term "transvestite patriarchy" to describe just this process in the "feminization" of Japanese men: "Even when it cloaks itself in femininity," she says, "patriarchy is patriarchy" (1997: 21).

From this perspective, it appears that women have become doubly marginalized and that the rise of male beauty aesthetics has done little to change existing power relations between men and women. One wonders, then, if the creation of beautiful men is truly for appreciation by a female audience or if it is simply providing a space where men, both gay and straight, may safely view and admire each other. Fuss (1995) noted that for female fashion photography to "work," the female consumer, be she heterosexual or lesbian, must look at and appreciate eroticized images of the female body. Is it possible that the new body aesthetics for men is merely a similar principle in operation and that it is completely unrelated to women's desires or social roles?

Even acknowledging this last point, it is still the case that Japan's heterosexual marketplace is suffering some serious problems. During the first decades of the postwar era, the man of "pure action and sincerity" (Plath 1980: 51) was attractive to women because of his dedication to family, community, and emperor. Whereas previously men were not expected to be beautiful as long as they offered economic stability and social capital, women now employ a differently critical eye, which includes aesthetic criteria, when they evaluate potential lovers and spouses. A man who is unwilling to remove a little body hair might have an autocratic, dictatorial husband *(teishu kanpaku)* streak hidden in his soul. If he doesn't make any effort to make himself sensuously appealing, just as she must, does that not mean he'll be unbending, inflexible, and selfish in other ways as well?

Among the many theories that have been proposed to explain the new beauty fads for Japanese men, few of them acknowledge the role female desire might be playing in male anxiety about appearance. In his review of the literature on cultural notions of human beauty, Gillmore (1994) points out, in perhaps too delicate a fashion, that most scholars use their own models of male beauty when they set about this task. The result is that they consistently link cultural notions of proper character and be-havior to understandings of male beauty, and in turn view purely phys-ical beauty as being the sole province of women. Such assumptions, produced from a mostly Euroamerican male imagination, ignore the con-siderable cross-cultural data to the contrary. One of the most overlooked aspects of the esute fad among Japanese men is its erotic meaning. The beauty work of heterosexual men, after all, is intended at least partly to stimulate women's interest. Perhaps this point is overlooked due to wide-spread acceptance of the idea that all visual codes serve to position women as the objects of a viewing "male gaze" (Mulvey 1975; Pollock 1988). Yet, according to M. Miller (1998: 432), the position of the viewing subject in Japanese visual media is not exclusively male; she notes that "the female gaze is recognized and incorporated." In pre-Meiji prints, for example, men are often depicted as objects for the female viewer, par-ticularly in erotic prints or *shunga*. Increasingly, other scholars are questioning the complete dominance of the so-called male gaze (Chow 1995).

There is also a cultural bias against women openly expressing erotic desire, and a consequent erasure of this when they do so. Yet female ex-pression of desire for the beautiful male body is commonly found in a variety of popular media. For example, a woman's magazine asked read-ers to talk about the latest crop of beautiful male idols and what they find most appealing about them (*An An* 1997). A few women used the term "boyishness" as one of the qualities they find attractive. They say these men bring out their maternal instincts, or that they make them want to "indulge" *(amayakasu)* them. But these lads also inspire more carnal impulses. When beautiful men turn up in unexpected places, such as knit-ting how-to manuals for housewives, where cute male stars model the latest designs, we know something is going on. The following assess-ments from the *An An* poll, which I have also heard echoed in conver-sations, suggest something other than a maternal urge. A thirty-year-old housewife, commenting on one of the young idols, says, "He's manly, yet there's still some boyishness remaining. If you have sex with him, he'd have good energy," while a twenty-six-year-old says, "At one glance, I want to have sex, to go to a resort hotel, and spend some leisurely time there." Speaking about Sorimachi Takashi, a twenty-four-year-old worker at a publishing company notes, "With his beautiful eyes, suntanned skin, and wide eyebrows, I think I'd want to have lusty sex with him." Entertainer Takenouchi Yutaka has a unique sort of slightly dangerous image. A twenty-three-year-old woman who works for a food corporation says, "He's got that cool, wild image, and those long fingers . . . he'd definitely be good at sex," while a nineteen-year-old bank worker says, "Although he's slim, he's got muscles, so has a body you want to have sex with." About Kimutaku, with his air of impudent carnality, women say, "I want to spend a passionate week with him at some villa in the mountains" (a thirty-one-year-old computer specialist), "He seems like a guy who would use various techniques to give you pleasure" (a twenty-two-year-old student), and "I want to press my face into his chest!" (an unemployed twenty-four-year-old). About J-Pop idol Gackt, a teenager says, "He has a body so beautiful it's like an art object; if I hugged him, I'd get dizzy. I'm filled with fantasies of the excitement that would happen if we were in bed" (*Junion* 2003: 28).

That women are willing to take on the role of epicures of male flesh is further illustrated by a new business that offers "party support"—male companions for year-end parties and other gatherings held by groups of women. A Kobe escort service will provide a sleek, cute twenty-year-old boy who will pour beers, smile sweetly, say charming things, and flirt with clients for two hours at a cost of around $80 (*Asahi Shimbun* 1998b). In 2004, Skynet Asia Airways began offering all-male cabin attendants to attract female passengers on round-trip flights between Tokyo and Miyazaki (CNN 2004). The male staff was supposedly selected on the basis of their handsomeness and unmarried status. There is also a significant increase in the number of "host clubs" catering to female patrons who are seeking flirtatious banter along with their cocktails. The new host clubs cater to a younger clientele and are often less expensive and more casual than those in past decades. It is estimated that twenty thousand men are working as hosts (Onishi 2005).

Sexual selection resulting from demographic transformations might very well be the most important reason for the new male beauty work industry.[9] Jolivet (1997) discusses the contemporary problems related to women's refusal to enter marriage and motherhood, and the resulting increase in the numbers of "old bachelors" who cannot find wives. The number of unmarried women and men doubled in two decades, leading to what some critics have labeled a "marriage drought" and an associated birthrate decline, dropping to approximately 1.39 in 1997 (Shōgakukan 1999: 277) and, despite optimistic predictions to the contrary, to 1.34 in 1999 (Ministry of Health, Labor and Welfare 2001). This demographic shift, which presents a serious threat to Japan's pension system and portends future health-care woes, is predominantly due to women, who are reluctant participants in marriage and childbirth. The overall marriage rate per 1,000 people was 6.1 in 1999 (compared to 10 in 1970), and the average age of first marriage for women rose to 27 in 2000 (Ministry of Health, Labor and Welfare 2001). The Prime Minister's Office conducted a survey in 1999 that found that 40 percent of the women polled said that marriage is a "burden" (Japan Now 2000: 4). Because marriage is a rite of passage for heterosexual men, who are dependent on women's domestic labor, unwed men are seen as immature losers and are negatively sanctioned in their professional and private lives for their failure to get wives.

Of course, men worried about physical appearance before the 1990s, when the boom in male beauty work began. But their earlier concerns about receding hairlines, height, and penis size reinforced traditional ideas about masculinity. By denouncing frumpy middle-aged salarymen and approving groomed *subesube* men, young women are manifesting refusal of postwar patriarchal culture and exposing the sexist nature of beauty ideology. When they express contempt by calling salarymen *kuso jijii* (shitty old geezer) and *chibidebu no kimochi warui oyaji* (short, fat, creepy old fart) while applauding cute and hairless young male bodies, they are asking of men that which has long been required from women—youth and physical beauty.[10] While a change to new forms of beauty work may accomplish two things—signifying rejection of corporate conformity and attracting women—it has done little to alter the structure of basic gender relations. A young man may get a heterosexual date and show how unique he is with his dyed hair and plucked eyebrows, but he will still expect the women in his life to fulfill traditional and subservient gender roles.

During the bubble era, the media claimed that Japanese women had three requirements before they were willing to tie the knot. Dubbed the "three highs," these were high salary, high educational credentials, and high physical stature. The three Hs were actually the product of an in-house customer survey conducted by the Altman Marriage Service, and therefore reflected only the "requirements" demanded by women who were interested in getting married. One wonders what women interested only in dating or sleeping with men were after. There is said to be a new list, this time with three Cs: men must be comfortable, communicative, and cooperative (Shōgakukan 1999: 283). Perhaps we may look forward to a time when a media spin doctor creates a new set, such as the three Es: egalitarian, easy-going, and elegant.

# CHAPTER 6

# The Well-Behaved Appetite

Since 1979, the Nestlé company has sold the most popular liquid coffee creamer in Japan. A few years ago Nestlé launched a new product aimed at weight-conscious women. Called Krematop Super Slim, it is said to "make it easy to diet as a habit while enjoying full flavor." This version has not only 40 percent fewer calories but some unusual ingredients as well. Added are garcinia, derived from a Southeast Asian fruit said to curb the appetite and to prevent the synthesis of body fat, and gymnema, from an Indian vine that purportedly inhibits the absorption of sugars. Nestlé thus joined numerous other companies that have also produced a deluge of novel products containing such peculiar additives.

In this chapter I look at the recent explosion in new products like Krematop Super Slim. At a time in Japan's history when food supplies are at their most varied and plentiful, young women are fearful of this bounty. Changes in beauty ideology have created an incredibly lucrative industry in weight-loss services, diet goods, and fads. Some of the more curious of these, as well as the desire for ultrathin bodies that drives their selling power, have caught the attention of the domestic and foreign media, and are even reported in the Chinese press (*Shanghai Star* 2001).[1] For example, Mintier (1996) mentions diet advice like brushing your teeth left-handed, which stimulates the right side of the brain (the side that controls fat digestion), and Kojima (1999) writes about the growing popularity of spicy foods as a dietary fad.

The media ideal of attractiveness and one's divergence from it create the conditions for the dieting industry. In this chapter, I describe a few products and weight-loss regimens in order to document how some of the major themes of the beauty system emerge in this domain. As in other beauty realms, dieting is linked to scientific rationalization, health, and postindustrial worry over cultural authenticity. One way marketing exploits these worries is by selling diet goods and products as "natural" or traditionally "Asian." My interest is not in whether or not these are effective; rather, I wonder what Japanese women are really after when they buy Mannan Foods Bust Keep Diet or try the Karaoke Diet. This discussion of the dieting business is not intended to expose the tsunami of poppycock that seems to engulf it, but to show how dieting, albeit tied to beauty ideology, is also an activity with potential symbolic meanings. Dieting is a cultural behavior in which discipline and effort are rewarded, and it may therefore be linked to specifically Japanese cultural ideas about struggle and perseverance. At the same time, the Japanese example may in some respects be typical of the way dieting is sold and consumed elsewhere, illustrating common elements found in late capitalist consumer societies.

Although there are many possible explanations of this dieting craze, most agree that women who diet are at least partly influenced by media images. A famous photograph of a wine-drinking woman from a 1922 advertising poster shows a beauty of the era with a plump face and sloping shoulders (Fraser, Heller, and Chwast 1996: 20). It would be difficult to find such fleshy voluptuousness in a contemporary model. No matter which beauty trend young women emulate, from intentionally tacky Kogal to demure debutante, all of them emphasize extreme thinness. Media-disseminated normalizing images (Bordo 1993) tell women about new forms of "fatness" they were unaware of in past decades. Even the otherwise priggish Japanese government has come to acknowledge the power of the media.

In 1997, when the Ministry of Health, Labor and Welfare released data on the average physical stature of women at age twenty, they felt obligated to explain why height had continued to increase each year while body weight had not (*Japan Times* 1997). This trend had been documented a decade earlier, when it was noticed that weight increases seemed to have stopped in 1970 (Takahashi 1986), but no one has ever accused the Japanese government of acting quickly. In 1949, the average weight of a twenty-year-old was around 112 pounds, the same as in 1997, although women were taller by around 2 inches in 1997. The ministry attributed the trend to an obsession with slimness and widespread dieting, and in turn linked this to a desire to emulate ultrathin pop idols. They pointed to J-Pop celebrity Amuro Namie as one such model for slimness. The average weight for women between twenty and twenty-four dropped to 110.66 pounds in 2000 (*Asahi Shimbun* 2002: 204).

Not surprisingly, the extreme thinness that is considered attractive and is promoted by the media has resulted in an increase in eating diseases. Anorexia and bulimia, once considered American disorders, are now thought to be at a comparable level in Japan, afflicting one in a hundred women (Efron 1997). A desire for thinness really began to escalate around 1980 (Kiriike et al. 1988; Suematsu et al. 1985; Nogami et al. 1987). An interesting finding is that even though Japanese female college students in one study did not have a high rate of eating disorders, they were nevertheless more likely to perceive themselves as overweight and reported greater body dissatisfaction than American female college students did, despite the fact that they were thinner than the American cohort (Mukai, Kambara, and Sasaki 1998). Other researchers, such as Mizuki (1991: 119), confirm that there is a growing gap between young women's ideal size and their real size. Their concern about ideal body weight surfaces in the expansive discourse about food and control of eating, and in a cultural frenzy over weight loss fads.

## Tantalizing Food and Diet Food

Kaoru, the main character in a novel by Ogawa Yōko (1991), keeps a food diary that chronicles everything she consumes. She retastes the food she has eaten each time she reads it. Anxiety over eating often surfaces in contemporary Japanese literature—in comics, poems, and fiction that reveal food obsessions and trepidations.[2] Ogawa (1991) and Matsumoto (1991) have both written novels in which the female characters suffer from eating disorders and view food as alluring and addictive. Their work and that of other writers reveal attitudes ranging from gustatory glee over pork and noodles to repulsion and fear of dioxin-laced vegetables and other polluted foods.

In the midst of a cultural milieu that surrounds her with media images of thinness, a young woman is also presented with an unprecedented variety of wickedly fattening foods to eat. Unlike the Victorian cult of thin, ethereal fragility described by Brumberg (1997), in which many items, such as meat or spices, were rejected outright for their sexual or coarse connotations, young Japanese women enjoy eating available foods and suffer when they cannot indulge in the pleasures of the appetite. Magazines often feature surveys and polls of favorite teenage foods. On lists of most-loved yummy things we find McDonald's Teriyaki Burger and the Mos Burger. Favorite chocolate snacks are ranked by brand name: Melty Kiss, Sasha, White Crunky, and Men's Pocky are a few of the favorites (*Rank-*

*ing Dai Suki!* 1999e). On other lists of favorite foods, we find items like pork-stuffed steamed buns, the Kentucky Fried Chicken Sandwich, and Seven-Eleven's Yakisoba Beef Croquette Sandwich. Another poll lists Fast Chicken Jaga Butter Potato, McDonald's Teriyaki Burger, and Mos Burger's Yakiniku Rice Burger as the top three pig-out foods (*Fine Surf & Street Magazine* 1999c).

An unusual and sexist interpretation of the lust for these new food items was reported in *Shūkan Gendai* (June 26, 2002). A doctor at the Stress Hibiya Clinic in Tokyo blames fast food for schoolgirl nymphomania. He links fast food to bulimia, which in turn, he says, leads to the development of sex addictions. According to the doctor, the sinfulness of these new foods may relate to their status as putative Western food items or food practices. Eating food (other than noodles) on the run, while standing and without rice, is a custom that evolved in the postwar era with the arrival of American-style fast food restaurants such as McDonald's (Ohnuki-Tierney 1997). Implied in this theorizing doctor's conservative critique is the idea that if women ate decent Japanese foods, such as fish and rice, there would be no need for a diet industry. Conservatives claim that the decline of the female diet is due to contact with tantalizing non-Japanese foods and degenerate eating behaviors. Tokiko, the heroine in Matsumoto's (1991: 45) novel about eating, appreciatively describes the food seen in a supermarket as "an edible art gallery." The tension between a quest for slimness and tantalizing food choices buttresses the market for new diet products and services intended to counteract the desiring appetite. It is to some of these that I now turn.

In the 1980s, food and pharmaceutical companies in Japan began producing new enriched products intended to offer benefits beyond their nutritional value. This idea spread globally, and now there is a huge industry for what has been dubbed designer food, pharmafood, or nutraceuticals. Initially designated as "functional food" and later renamed "food with a specific health claim" *(tokutei hokenyō)*, it is a $2 billion market, with over two thousand new products launched since 1988. Although the Japanese market for health foods surpasses that elsewhere, there is also a market for such products outside Japan, especially in the United States (Kubomura 1999). The functional food category encompasses items like health teas, cocoa drinks, yogurt, and no-cal biscuits that supposedly neutralize harmful substances or prevent disease or weight gain; examples include Diet Mousse Yoghurt and Super Diet Water. One of the more interesting functional foods is Dr. Nakamatsu's Yummy Nutri-Brain Drink, whose cerebral nutrients include shrimp, chicken liver, and eel. The Ministry of Health, Labor and Welfare began a system of official scrutiny and classification of functional food, but it examines only fat, sodium, and sugar content, and government-approved foods constitute only a small fraction of the market. The approval system is voluntary, so fraud claims continue (Center for Science in the Public Interest 1998).[3] Even so, functional compounds, such as vitamins, collagen, calcium, amino acids, garcinia, and gymnema, are often touted as diet aids. For instance, one may buy Garcinia Coffee to complement Krematop Super Slim coffee creamer. Another garcinia product is Kanebo's Cut and Cut Diet tablets, also containing yucca and vitamin B1. The label claims that the consumer "can eat but still lose weight" and control her craving for oily and sweet foods. Claims about the health effects or weight-loss results of all these new products are unconfirmed or of doubtful validity, and some of the same diet fads and questionable diet products also appear in the United States (Willis 1982).

Many diet fads are inspired by trendy functional food ingredients, such as the 1995 gymnema craze, when all sorts of teas and other products appeared. Their success depends on the consumer's assumption that because these ingredients are "natural," they are pure and not harmful. The cosmetic company Shiseido entered the competition with Gymrind Neo tablets, which contain gymnema, tamarind, cayenne, and guava. Diet supplements form a one-trillion-yen market, and many food companies are creating new diet products as fast as they can. For example, House Foods has been selling fifteen types of diet supplements since July 2000, while Fancl sells about one hundred diet products (*Mainichi Daily News* 2002a). New diet food fads also get a boost from media attention. The television program *Omoikkiri Terebi* focuses on health news, and when it announced in 1996 that cocoa lowers cholesterol and prevents hardening of the arteries, sales of cocoa increased by 24 to 25 percent. Soon afterward, many cocoa-based diet products appeared, such as Cocoa Diet (with garcinia and vitamins) and Lisura Cocoa Diet laxative. A friend of mine somewhat sheepishly revealed that she had tried Lisura, which she said operated with efficiency equal to any other laxative but at least had the advantage of tasting sweet and comforting.

## Any "Diet" You Want

The linguistic anthropologist Stanlaw (2004) spent many years investigating the use of English loanwords and made-in-Japan English in a range of new products, discovering few with the word *diet* (2004: 239). But *diet* (*daietto*) eventually did find its way into the Japanese lexicon and product naming. Once borrowed into Japanese, its semantic range was broadened to include behaviors and items beyond what an English speaker means by the term. Almost anything that is related to weight loss may be put into the "diet" category. Thus we find something called the Hot Pepper Diet.

Advocates of the Hot Pepper Diet claim that you can eat whatever you like, as long as you put hot pepper on it. This is because eating peppers induces perspiration, so they help "burn" off fat. In addition, one eighteen-year-old told me, "You don't want to eat any sweet things this way." If consumers would rather not douse their McDonald's Teriyaki Burger with Tabasco, they can always ingest the ingredient in pepper that makes it hot, called capsicum, in tablet or tea form. Products such as Maximum Hot Diet, Hot Fire Diet, and Spicy Diet Super contain capsicum along with ingredients such as ginger, garcinia, collagen, guava, and gymnema. The label of one jar promises, "Get slim with the hot sauna feeling." Another big seller is Kimchi Slim, which earned over $4.5 million its first year on the market. Kimchi is a traditional Korean pickle made with hot chili pepper, and these tablets supposedly contain kimchi extract. The producer claims that it regulates energy uptake, promotes the excretion of lipids and waste matter, and burns off body fat.[4] (Also expressed in some advertisements for kimchi tablets is a racist and offensive suggestion that one will not have the garlic smell said to be characteristic of kimchi-eating Koreans.) Within the industrial beauty system, these ideas about "hot" foods are occasionally linked to the native *kanpō* medical system, in which some foods are classified as having "heating" qualities. The advertisers of the products deliberately draw this link to tradition, but very few young women are aware of these ethnomedical beliefs before buying these products.

Women who do not want to give up all those Yakisoba Beef Croquette sandwiches are enticed by one of the many diet products that claim to help the dieter lose weight while sleeping. Products such as Sleep Slim, Night Diet Super, Magical Diet, and Night Esute purportedly contain amino acids that dismantle fat while one snoozes. An illustration from Sleep Slim explains how it works: reading a "diet diary," we learn about mean white fat cells inside the body that swell up. Taking four to six Sleep Slim tablets before going to sleep induces the amino acids to create brown fat cells that diminish nasty white ones. When the dieter wakes up, she will be surprised at her weight loss "achievement."

"Asian" diet teas are also quite popular. Kanebo entered the market with a canned Chinese diet tea drink with ginseng added. Another, Banaba Diet Tea from the Philippines, guarantees that if you drink it twice a day without sugar or honey, you'll lose weight. However, one dieter told me, "It's a bit grassy tasting." The distinction between marketing angles for new products trying to cash in on the diet boom and established Chinese-style *kanpō* is not always clear, however. Some bona fide *kanpō* apothecary shops are also active in the production of diet goods and market herbal and other natural weight-reducing medicines. For example, the entire reverse side of a flyer from a *kanpō* shop in Kanazawa named Kusuri Nihondō is devoted to diet products. The names and descriptions of these products are indistinguishable from those found elsewhere. A "diet medicine scare" developed in 2002, after the deaths of four women and one man and more than 833 serious illnesses linked to use of imported Chinese diet products (*Mainichi Daily News* 2002b).

There are numerous "eat only x" diets, in which the dieter almost exclusively eats the same food item for every meal (Uemori 1997). Some of the popular ones have featured pineapple, apple, yogurt, honey, egg, and jelly *(kanten)*. A variation is to regularly eat certain items to control the appetite. An example of this type is the Honey Diet, in which a teaspoon of honey is added to hot water or tea three times a day or more to control a craving for sweetness.

Many "diets" involve not ingestion of a product but rather modification of behavior. Diet fads given media attention include the Video Diet, the Dumbbell Diet, the Walking Diet, the Bracelet or Earring Diet, the Sex Diet, the Acupuncture Diet, the Bath Diet, the Reflexology Diet, the Massage Diet, the Mentholatum Diet, the Blood Type Diet, the Karaoke Diet, and the Manicure Diet (figure 27).[5] Some of these also play off an appropriation of ancient "Asianness." For instance, a big hit was an imported Chinese seaweed slimming soap that earned more than $28 million in sales. The soap, which promises to "wash away fat in seconds," carries the endorsement of the Chinese gymnastic team and the Traditional Chinese Medicine Science Cosmetic Institute of China. Many bath diets incorporate soaps like this, or else Korean bamboo-based soaps and lotions. Also popular are products that activate images of an exotic ancient South Asia and its philosophical-medical system, ayurveda. In the mid-1990s, a line of soaps, creams, and oils called India Esthe appeared that claim to improve skin and weight loss and are featured in various massage diets. One brand contains sesame and coconut oils and "oriental herbs" *(orientaru hābu)* and is sometimes featured in sex diets.

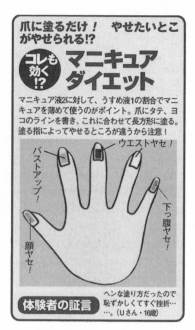

FIGURE 27. The Manicure Diet. From *Ranking Dai Suki!* magazine, 2000.

For the Karaoke Diet, the dieter sings and dances to her favorite hit song at least once a day ( *Japan Echo* 1999). The dieter is encouraged to select an upbeat tune in order to burn more calories. The Daiichi Koshu company sells a calorie counter software program that calculates, at the end of each karaoke number, how many kilocalories were expended. For example, singing along to Amuro Namie's "A Walk in the Park" burns 17 kilocalories. The company claims to have "scientifically" tested the program at a fitness center.

Some diets operate on the principle that the sense of taste suffers when pleasant but not appetizing smells are presented to the nose before eating. In the Mentholatum Diet, menthol Chapstick is rubbed on the lips and under the nose two to three minutes before each meal, dampening the appetite. Similarly, in the Perfume Diet, the dieter sprays on perfume (of whatever scent they like) whenever they feel hungry. This is said to put them in a good mood while curbing the appetite. The aesthetic salon Slim Beauty House often combines two or more diet fads, such as the *Kanpō*-Aromatherapy Diet, which also uses smell as an appetite blocker.

Another diet fad is the Keep It Closed Diet, in which the woman wears a tight bra and belt so that she will not feel like eating much when mealtime comes around. The Ear Pinching Diet works by stimulating the ears to suppress the appetite. Dieters are told to pinch both ears every day for three minutes. This is the same principle as the Mimi Hari Diet, a traditional acupuncture treatment in which very small needles are left in the ear for a week. Many aesthetic salons sell treatments based on stimulation of the ear, such as the *mimi tsubo* treatment (described in chapter 2).

Proponents of the Sex Diet assure that "you'll be more than happy losing weight this way!" This diet exploits the fact that doing "average" sex once a day burns the same number of calories as running 1.5 miles. The Salt Rub Diet is promoted as a method handed down from ancient times and even used by Cleopatra. Salt is massaged into the skin every day during bath time. Perhaps salt has connotations of purification deriving from its use for that purpose in Shinto, so that here the body is purified of fat. For the Towel Diet, a towel is placed on the head every time one has a meal or eats a snack. The towel must stay in place and not fall off while eating, thus forcing the dieter to eat slower. Finally, in the Small Face Diet one inserts a mouthpiece or other apparatus, such as the Mouth Fitness, over the molars.[6] Once a day the dieter faces a mirror and chomps down fifty times.

According to the Manicure Diet (figure 27), all one does is lacquer the nails. Depending on which finger is painted, there will be different results. The thumb is for face slimming, the middle finger for waist slimming, and the little finger for stomach slimming. However, painting the index finger has the opposite effect—it will result in "breast enhancement." Related in principle to the Manicure Diet is the Reflexology Diet, in which certain points on the foot are pressed to activate weight loss. The waist in particular is said to be receptive to this method.

An unusual dieting belief is that there is an interconnection between one's blood type and the best diet plan (*Ray* 1997b). Classifying people by blood type is a popular Japanese indigenous system called *ketsueki-gata* (blood typology, Miller 1998b). In this scheme, there are four basic types—A, B, O, and AB—and each type has associated personality characteristics. The Blood Type Diet suggests that one should select a diet strategy based on the qualities of one's particular blood type. For example, the B-type is assigned the keywords "enjoyable," "results-oriented," and "can do it quickly," so diets suited to this type include the "eat only x" or "drink only x" regimen. B-types are also said to get results from the slimming programs offered through aesthetic salons and at spa resorts, especially one of the thalassotherapy diets (from the Greek word *thalassa*, "sea," its name refers to a treatment using sea substances, such as seaweed, sea mud, or sea water). B-types, however, do not do so well with calorie counting or graphing diets. A-types should try garcinia diets, boxing diets, and bath diets; O-types should try bath massages and body wrapping diets; and AB-types should try wearing "slimming sandals."

## Dieting as a Knowledgeable Activity

After learning about karaoke diets, manicure diets, sex diets, and massage diets, it is evident that dieting is not only about self-denial. Indeed, Japanese eating disorder therapist Moriyama Nachiko (Mizuki 1991: 115) suggests that dieting activity is a type of "female entertainment," something like a hobby. I agree with her that many of the diets are not taken completely seriously and are tried with little expectation that they will succeed. Diet fads are often discussed in female media with humor and arch drollness—it is hard to imagine that the Manicure Diet could be talked about with gravity. However, in this section I present a critical assessment of Moriyama's theory about dieting in order to draw out some of the neglected aspects of dieting as a behavior. Moriyama maintains that dieting is popular because it offers the following attractions: the rules for dieting are easy to learn; dieting does not require a particular place or much money; dieting does not necessitate any special abilities; and dieting is something one can do alone. While intuitively her assessments seem reasonable, I would like to examine them in more detail.

Moriyama asserts that the rules or methods for dieting are easy to master. Yet, in looking through books, magazines, and the Internet, I have been astonished at the pragmatic yet methodical manner in which the whole issue of dieting is approached. From the very beginning, the principles of scientific rationalization have been applied to weight loss. Some will understand that there is a parallel here with Ritzer's (1993) theory of the McDonaldization of society. According to Ritzer, the model of the fast-food restaurant, with its apparent stress on efficiency and predictability, has become the form of rationalization extended to all areas of everyday life. McDieting begins and proceeds with rational management, with an emphasis on exact measurement and calculation. Before selecting a diet, a woman could easily wade through several questionnaires and tests to help gauge the sort of diet that suits her best. For example, she can examine her dietary life with the Diet Psychology Test. Questions she will be asked include "Why are you fat?" "What diet is right for you?" "What

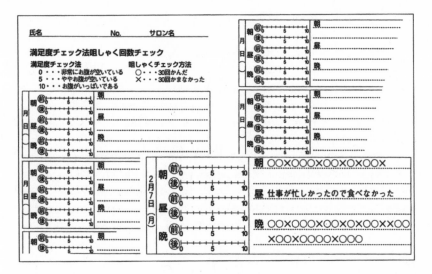

FIGURE 28. The dieting journey weight-loss diary.

stresses are in your life?" and "Why can't you stick to a diet?" Or else she can go to an interactive computer program that leads her through a series of twenty-four categories, in which she considers her food habits with the help of questions such as "Do you weigh yourself each day?" "Do you ruin your diet by eating forbidden foods?" and "Can you say exactly what you ate yesterday?"

Once she has embarked on a dieting journey, she must keep vigilant track of her progress by recording weight loss in diet journals or diaries and by graphing weekly and monthly results. A graph supplied by the Takano Yuri Beauty Clinic tracks weight over a seven-month period. Takano Yuri also offers "Five Points for Dieting to Make a Cinderella Body": write down what you eat every day, do esute calisthenics at home, check your level of satiety and monitor your chewing method when you are eating, and eat a balanced diet. Another type of record tracks the daily nutritional career (figure 28). Diaries for the purpose of reflection or reconsideration *(hansei)* are common in institutional settings, such as schools and corporations, so the self-disciplining dieter is accustomed to this form of surveillance.[7] In one diary, the dieter ranks her feelings of hunger or fullness on a scale of zero to ten before and after each meal, also noting the number of times she has chewed her food. Books and pamphlets are available that teach one how to create diet diaries and graphs, and cute decorated forms can be downloaded from the Internet or purchased in fancy goods stores.

Another important method is to monitor calorie intake. Computer programs are available that will determine an individual's caloric limits based on his or her height, weight, and age. Thereafter it is possible to keep track of calories by using a pocket-sized personal calorie counter. These come in all styles and colors and are priced higher than an average hand-held calculator; an example is the Poketto Esute (Pocket Aesthetics) calorie counter, which sells for $28. Omoron makes a delicate pastel-pink device called the Slim Step, which promises to help the buyer diet "correctly" and "reliably." Slim Step also tells the owner facts such as how much exercise one needs to do to compensate for overstuffing oneself at a meal. Contrary to Moriyama's assumptions, the rules and methods for dieting may be quite complex, requiring advance planning, diligent surveillance, and subsidiary technology.

Moriyama says that dieting does not require a special place or much money. That would be true were it not for the willingness of capitalist industries to provide both diet settings and goods. I have already mentioned a few of the thousands of functional foods and diet potions available. Most of these are rather expensive: Sleep Slim costs $94 for 150 tablets, and a Chinese diet tea named Birehō costs $84 for 70 tea bags. Suzuki Sonoko, proponent of the *bihaku* (beautiful white) hyperpigmentation boom, was once known as the "Diet Queen" after publication of her bestseller *If You Want to Lose Weight, Eat!* (Suzuki 1980). In 1999, I waited in a long line of extremely thin women for Sonoko's Ginza retail shop to open one morning. Many of Sonoko's disciples had copied her odd bony white body. Once the doors opened, they rushed in to buy up her expensive low-fat, low-salt food products and some of the many diet books she has written. A single small sugar cake made without oil sold for around $20.

Another way to spend money on the dieting effort is to enroll in classes about dieting offered through adult learning centers. For example, the Asahi Culture Center in Tokyo teaches courses entitled "The History of Dieting," "Get Slim and Beautiful with Chinese Tea," and "Boxing and Diet for Women," at $68 per course.

The same reliance on technology—or, more commonly, a pretense of scientific management—extends to expensive products sold for use at home. Many of these devices are electric or battery-powered, creating an aura of order and management. Fat or cellulite can also be attacked with products that disperse an "anti-fat" lotion from an internal tank as it rolls over the skin. Of course, thousands of creams, lotions, and gels are also peddled as slimming agents, including products named Leg-o-Slim, Hippi Dip, Eliminator, Ashi Bijin Foot Cool Slimming Lotion, and Profael Massageless More Glamourous, which, according to the English on its package, "helps losing extra flesh." Also sold for home use are masks, harnesses, and packs. There is Svelt Patch, a sort of bandage applied to the skin that supposedly assists in the decomposition of body fat. Although it is not necessary to go to a special place or to spend money in order to diet, in fact most dieters are also busy consumers of slimming services and products. Even smart, sensible women I know have purchased diet goods at least once, on the slight chance that they might work.

Moriyama declares that it does not take any special abilities to diet. Yet aside from graphing and math know-how, a socially hip dieter would need to study the latest diet fads and the special ingredients specified for weight loss. Dieting formulations therefore become intellectual property that confers prestige value on the dieter. Dieting products take on the role of social media, which gain value through interaction. If the dieter is supposed to take her Virgin Body Diet tablets, Gymrind Neo, or Estro Slim pills before each meal, she may do it in front of others, who will ask about them. She may then pedantically explain about the garcinia, the gymnema, the amino acids, and so on. An ability to keep up with the latest global trends and to pronounce the foreign names of exotic diet substances becomes a form of cultural capital. As Bourdieu (1984) makes clear, knowledge acquisition equips a social agent with appreciation for particular cultural codes. Class and individual identity construction may then be tied to elevated taste and refined appreciation for particular consumer goods. A Japanese woman who is able to expound on the esoteric ingredients in her diet products is demonstrating superior social status.

Moriyama says that dieting is something you can do alone. While this is definitionally the case, dieting often becomes a very public endeavor. What may start off as a competitive individual struggle with food gets bound up with many opportunities for public display of the dieting effort. The dieter is enmeshed in an extensive industry in which there is corporate interest in making the activity open and subject to positive sanctions. The year 1996 was the debut of the *Dieters TV Game Show*, in which contestants wearing bathing suits were weighed publicly and booted off the program if they gained even one pound. Recently many restaurants have begun participating in the diet industry by providing calorie information on menus, so that eating out also has become a public forum for dieting.

For example, the Century Heights Hotel restaurant in Shinjuku offers menus with the calories for each item listed.

Additionally, the work of dieting is socially rewarded regardless of the results. This is because it demonstrates that the dieter is at least making an effort at self-improvement, thus addressing the general cultural value of *gambaru,* doing something with tenacity (Amanuma 1987). Common translations include "persevere," "do your best," "give it your best shot," "hang in there," and "don't give up." The word is often used when encouraging someone in a demanding task. Great emphasis is placed on *gambaru* in the educational system (Singleton 1993), and women have learned the value of symbolically demonstrating effort. For years company workers have been rewarded for taking English language courses, even if they never improve their proficiency by even one word or phrase. Now, in a similar manner, women are being socially rewarded for a display of dieting work. I have a friend who loves her Men's Pocky and Mos Burgers and has been the same somewhat chubby shape for over a decade. However, she has prominently displayed and drunk a Chinese diet tea at work for years, demonstrating to others that she is at least making a stab at weight loss. Her co-workers are rather impressed with her long-standing dedication to self-improvement.

In fairness to Moriyama, it should be mentioned that her idea of dieting as "female entertainment" is reflected in an amusing product called the Hello Kitty Mecha Esute (Hello Kitty Extreme Body Aesthetics). The success of the Tamagotchi "virtual pet" who lives on a tiny LCD screen on a keychain was followed by an explosion in keychain pet products, including Hello Kitty Mecha Esute. The package says (in Japanese), "From tomorrow I don't have to be a fatty anymore" and (in English) "I want to be dynamite body!" The game is based on the idea that Kitty-chan has to get back in shape in six days before her big date. A player begins the game with a chubby or skinny Kitty-chan, and he or she has to choose the right diet (foods are given with different caloric values) and exercise.

## Craving the Thin Body

If one were inclined to look for individual or psychological motivations for the diet craze, one would find numerous theories proposed as explanations. Not to be taken seriously is the suggestion of a journalist in Tokyo who interviewed a college lecturer who had queried her class about the thin trend. According to the professor's vague survey, some respondents said that while they realize there is something unhealthy or weird about the phenomenon, they follow the trend anyway because being thin is "cool" and is also a "prerequisite to wear clothes" (Galer 1999: 13). Galer cites Japanese commentators who naively interpret the thinness craze as an event emanating not from beauty politics and gender ideals, but rather from an individual's personal desire to conform to or integrate into general group behavior.

I will mention one additional analysis of the dieting craze, proposed by Inoue Shūji, a professor of nutrition at a women's university. Inoue claims that women work at losing weight because they are washouts in other areas of life (Kojima 1999). He says: "Women diet as an excuse for failing in our competitive society. If she fails an entrance exam, she satisfies herself by making a dieting effort." He goes on to express concern that young women are damaging or weakening their reproductive potential this way. But Inoue's sexist condemnation overlooks critical aspects of the dieting endeavor. Dieting gives women an opportunity to satisfy various social imperatives: the imperative to approximate gendered media ideals, the imperative to work at self-improvement, the imperative to consume status-conferring commodities and services, the imperative to participate in social conversations about ratified topics. Indeed, it is usually successful women, those who *do* pass exams and are wonderfully competitive, who make the best dieters. Research on anorexics also finds that they are typically "good girls" who do what they are expected to do (Bruch 1978).

Although theories about why women diet that begin with individual motivation may have some basis, scholars caution that we also need to link the obsession with slimness to broader social, political, and economic factors (Chernin 1981; Bruch 1978; Bordo 1985). Dieting is an arena where social and individual needs converge. It is multidetermined, emanating from a combination of beauty politics, cultural proscriptions, and individual desire. The Japanese food and diet industries include many of the same companies, which seduce consumers with savory foods like Coffee Cream Pan and Fast Chicken's Italian Tomato Fried Potatoes yet concurrently chasten them with products like Fat Spark, Hyper Slim, Sugar Away, and Glamour Slim. According to Counihan, "The economy depends on manipulating consumers to buy as much as possible and one way is to project simultaneously the urge to eat and the need to diet" (1999: 87).

In many cultures, food is symbolic of home, motherhood, and fertility, qualities that are in turn manifested by valuing bodies that are curvy and cushy. "In the majority of cultures for which data exist, plumpness is preferred, especially for women, because it is associated with fertility, hardiness, power, good nurturance, and love" (Counihan 1999: 11). Sobo (1997) describes a juicy body in Jamaica as one that exudes fertility and sexiness through plumpness. The idea that a pursuit of slimness may be correlated with a rejection of motherhood and reproductivity is proposed by Fallon (1990: 88).

Spielvogel (2003) takes up this theme and links the quest for "selfishly skinny" thinness not simply to beauty ideology but to resistance to gender roles through dieting and food refusal that counters the other-directed Japanese model of femininity. Dieting by Japanese women is an expression, therefore, of rejection of the social roles of domestic food preparer, family nurturer, and fertile progenitor of future salarymen. Her study admirably describes the tensions and interconnections between discourses on beauty, diet, and fitness, and the acceptance or rejection of these by individual women. We see this same ambivalence in the way that even sensible women consume questionable products such as Ayuruba Drink Glamour Slim, which claims that weight loss will occur only on parts of the body other than the breasts.

Not only are women rejecting the body shape that symbolizes fertility and nurturance, but they are rejecting marriage and motherhood itself. Indeed, there has been a shift in the marriage market (and in reproductive effort) such that men must become more active consumers of beauty goods and services in order to attract women. Yet the voluptuous bodies adored in the cultures Counihan (1999) and Sobo (1997) describe are still seen as horribly grotesque in Japan. Even women who desire motherhood and a self-sacrificing caretaker role do not desire the voluptuous earth-mother body. They too want the slim body they see in mass media. Most studies in Japan therefore insist that dieting and a desire to become thin are linked to mass-mediated concepts of beauty. In some studies, eating disorders are additionally connected to an internalization of Euroamerican beauty ideals (Mukai, Crago, and Shisslak 1994).

Dieting advertisements, as well as ads for other beauty work, rarely show the admiring male gaze, which reinforces the idea that the desire for slimness extends beyond a simple longing to attract men. If not to get a boyfriend or a husband, who is the woman starving herself for? Perhaps fasting and dieting are ways to exert control without challenging male power. Bordo (1993) accounts for the way that normalizing practices train the body in obedience to cultural norms, yet are nevertheless *experienced* by the individual in terms of self-actualization and individual power, which is exactly what the industries that sell dieting want consumers to believe.

It is important to keep in mind that, like all the beauty work found in the body aesthetics industry, slimness and the attainment of "beauty" symbolize individual success, moral improvement, and self-transformation. For Japan's younger generation, self-control over the appetite is, in addition to an aesthetic issue, a moral problem that reflects the internalization of *gambaru* values in Japanese society.

# CHAPTER 7

# The Language of Esute

An advertisement in a women's magazine for something called Slim Sauna Metal Alpha shows a woman wearing what looks like a space suit in order to achieve weight loss. Like many other advertisements for body transformation products, this one uses English lexemes in both the roman script and the Japanese *katakana* syllabary. The product name is represented as *metaru alpha* (メタル α), using *katakana* graphs and the Greek alpha letter, and also as METAL α, using capital roman letters with the Greek alpha. The use of both *metal* and *alpha* imparts a scientific veneer to the product (as does the astronautical styling of the ensemble), indicating cutting-edge technology. This chapter focuses on the intentional use of language in beauty advertising to impart such nuances.[1]

In his description of the difficulty of writing about the game of chess, Menand (2004: 87) says, "You can ignore the technical stuff and write about powerful queenside attacks, hammering rook assaults, intense positional struggle, and so on; but the truth is that the game *is* the technical stuff." Similarly, the beauty industry uses the resources of language — its phonology, morphology, textures, and nuances — to perform some of the beauty system's core semiotic content for producers and consumers. To understand the role of language in structuring the cultural model of beauty, it is necessary to look at how, as a linguistic system, this cultural model is bent, teased out, and packaged to do this work. This chapter looks closely at the technical stuff: the words and sets of words that appear frequently in industrial beautyspeak.

Selling beauty is "a business of storytelling, an industry where market forecasts and number crunching inevitably yield to adjectives and atmosphere" (Gavenas 2002:11–12). I will analyze the adjectives, product names, and other words that are used in beauty advertising for the stories they tell. How is the language of esute intertwined with cultural symbolism and gender iconography? We can retrieve some of these meanings through close examination of collections of words used to name and describe a range of products. One friend accused me of indulging in linguistic microscopy, and another of being redundant by including the Japanese along with English translations. In offering copious examples of Japanese words, my goal is to reveal the great innovation, playfulness, humor, and artistry used in esute language. For this reason, translation alone fails to unveil the unique properties of beauty language.

My analysis is confined to print advertising for body and beauty items and services found in magazines, newspaper inserts, flyers, brochures, and other promotional materials. These are not just fancy propaganda attached to goods or used to describe salon treatments, but are themselves linguistic commodities that consumers appraise for their aesthetic, expressive, humorous, visual, and euphemistic value. In addition to the artful use of language, esute advertising may also deploy images or symbols that suggest science, technology, health, and an Asian identity, themes also explored in the examples that follow. Particularly prominent is the plethora of English-derived words which characterize this domain. Viewed in isolation, product names such as Slim Sauna Metal Alpha may look like warped English. What I hope to show is that English in Japanese advertising is not an inept language attempt or a form of linguistic larceny. Rather, within the world of beauty, English and other foreign-derived linguistic materials are part of a domestically created semiotic system with its own webs of nuance.

Bourdieu (1991) uses the metaphor of the "linguistic marketplace" when discussing the necessity of using sanctioned forms of discourse within specific realms if one wishes to be successful. It is a useful metaphor that asks us to view language as something exchanged or displayed as a product that is given a certain symbolic value. Depending on the setting in which these linguistic commodities occur, they are evaluated according to local sensibilities and values. The language of the beauty market, for example, usually does not command great value in the "official" language markets of Japan as taught in schools or used in newspapers. The beauty world's extensive use of English, odd clippings, and new slang is not considered worthy language among the self-appointed custodians of the Japanese language. When beauty products and advertising draw on youth culture and knowledge of esoteric trends for their currency, they are creating a different level of value, one that appeals to a consumer with her or his own models of distinction.

## English in Japanese Advertising

Advertising in Japan is a six-trillion-yen industry. It is no wonder that examination of Japanese advertising has proven to be quite fruitful for social science researchers, who have unpacked numerous intentions and symbolic values manifested in advertising text and images (Larrabee 1994; Moeran 1985; 1993, 1996b; Tanaka 1994). Despite this social science attention, however, Japanese advertising has usually been treated in business literature as a uniform enterprise that is said to exhibit remarkably unique tendencies. Analysts generally depict these ads as different from those found elsewhere because they are more impressionistic or atmospheric, have less content, or avoid use of a "hard sell" approach. This chapter examines the variation and creativity found in advertising language, which such brute characterizations ignore or dismiss. My interest is not in discussing Japanese advertising as a production process. The product names and copy I look at are cultural products that may be legitimate objects of analysis for readers, who will come away with their own interpretations. Whether or not these were intended by the ad's creators is moot. Regardless of the people, political considerations, or compromises that go into the creation of products and their presentation in ads (Moeran 1996a), creators ultimately rely on the same linguistic devices that are used by readers.

For more than a century, English has been appearing in Japanese product names and in print advertising. During the Meiji period (1868–1912), most goods were sold as nameless bulk without fancy packaging. Exceptions were early brand-name commodities, such as Kaō soap, Ajinomoto seasoning, and Shiseido cosmetics, which were advertised in newspapers, on telegraph poles, and with chalk on city streets (Rubinfien 1995). Yet even then English was incorporated into ads and product names: one Meiji-era brand was a tooth powder named Lion Dentrifice. Shiseido used the alphabet in 1898, in one of its earliest product names, Eudermine lotion, and later created one of the first roman script name logos in 1929, one that is still in use today (Yamada 2000). A popular Meiji-era product named Naisu (The Nice) was a unisex hair dye used to cover gray (figure 29). The use of English in advertising and product names became firmly established over the next several decades, and should no longer be

FIGURE 29. *Naisu* (The Nice) hair coloring: an example of English in product naming during the Meiji era.

considered unusual. Unlike the referential or prestige functions seen in earlier times, the recent use of English is a deliberately and carefully orchestrated innovation valued as a linguistic achievement.

Contemporary ads invariably contain English written in either roman script or the Japanese *katakana* syllabary, as in the Slim Sauna Metal Alpha ad. No matter how it is orthographically represented, the use of English in many beauty ads is not necessarily intended to designate the product as somehow of foreign or Euroamerican derivation, but rather to do other socio-semantic work. As Larrabee (1994) showed regarding roman text in Japanese advertising, both English and the alphabet have become so "naturalized" that they are often associated with products positioned as new or innovative rather than foreign or Euroamerican. An essential aspect of all advertising is the clever use of language, and in the Japanese beauty industry wonderfully creative innovations are readily apparent. Given that esute is a relatively new domain, it is not surprising that hundreds of new terms incorporating English have been created during the last few decades.

## Japan-Made English

Analysis of Japanese treatment of foreign language material as both a linguistic and cultural phenomenon is an old enterprise. Until recently, most critics have viewed it as a straightforward form of linguistic borrowing. A few scholars (Horvat 1970; Quakenbush 1974; Higgins 1984; Miller 1997; Stanlaw 2004), however, have acknowledged that some loanwords are not, in fact, true loans at all, but rather foreign morphemes or lexemes manipulated or consciously invented in Japan, sometimes labeled as "Japan-made English" *(wasei eigo)*. One customary form these homemade words take is a composite of two English morphemes that together create a new word or concept. The original English usually undergoes significant semantic and phonological renovation in the process, a sort of "off-English." We see, for instance, the current use of *hair manicure (hea manikyuā)* in some ads. Pressed, companies who sell this would have to concede that it is just another way to say "hair coloring." Another example of newly contrived compounding is the use of *UV cut ( UV katto)* in sunscreen products to refer to the "ultraviolet cutting" of harmful rays.

Sometimes there is a realignment of already entrenched loans, which are remodeled as part of new combinations. The use of *home care (hōmu kea)* to refer to take-home esute products after a visit to a salon derives from the earlier coinage *after care (afutā kea),* meaning "after-sales service." This is wedded to the firmly established *home (hōmu)*. One aesthetic salon offers a service described as *order made sensation (ōdā mēdo kankaku)*. The term *ōdā mēdo* (with a slight variation in the representation of the word *made*) has already been in use for a few decades to mean "custom-made" goods, mainly clothing. Through semantic extension, the ad conveys something like "customized, individual treatment." The same intended meaning is also found in a salon ad that asserts that it will supply "personalized handmade technique" *(dokuji no hando meiku tekunikku)*.

In his book investigating loanwords in Japanese, Loveday (1996) views the use of English as primarily related to the referents' alliance with the West or with Westernized versions of particular items, which bestows symbolic power that enhances a product's value. Although this may explain some uses of English, it will not do much to help us understand English in ads that are unquestionably trying to index a non-Western identity. For instance, one salon offers *Ejipushan surimingu* ("Egyptian slimming") for a weight reduction program. When we look at the Egyptian slimming ads, we find English represented in both *katakana* syllabic characters and roman letters, together with random Arabic script, a model dressed up as Cleopatra, pharaonic tomb paintings, and Japanese text displayed in an archaic style that suggests the ancient or traditional. A complex ad like this, in which reference is made to multiple genres and meanings, using multiple writing systems, is common in the world of esute and extends beyond simple notions of Western indexicalization.

Scholars are not in agreement over the degree to which Japanese use of foreign-derived lexemes should be attributed to the emulation of a prestige language and culture. Haarman (1989) and Higa (1979) are two of

the strongest proponents of this view. Others, however, see the proliferation of English not as more evidence of Euroamerican cultural imperialism but rather as an imaginative exploitation of an already fully domesticated linguistic resource. Stanlaw (1992, 2000, 2004) has perhaps
made the case most often for recognition of alternative functions served
by Japanese use of English, arguing that English is a creative and critical
part of the Japanese language. Uses he has discussed include communi-
cating modernity, enabling expression of changed attitudes, a personal
way to creatively utilize available linguistic materials, and as ambiguous
descriptors and nebulous names for new food products, flavors, colors,
art, and fashion.

While earlier generations of Japanese encountered English mainly as
a foreign written language in books, this is no longer the case. Because
of the widespread implementation of mandatory and long-term English
language education, coupled with the use of English and roman script in
all aspects of daily life, Japanese now learn about English and the roman
alphabet from birth. English is in everything, from train station signs to
Hello Kitty artifacts and pop music lyrics (see Stanlaw 2000).

The sheer volume and history of English in Japanese contribute to its
loss of power to exemplify the foreign or Euroamerican. Even so, some
conservatives have attempted to curtail the use of English or English-
derived words. Most recently, the National Institute for Japanese Language began working with a group of dictionary editors, translators, and
journalists to come up with replacements for foreign loan words in government documents. It is unlikely, however, that their efforts will in any
way hinder the creative use of English in beauty advertising, where it is
utterly entrenched.

## Beauty Up

Once a nativized English word has been firmly established in the Japanese
lexicon, it lends itself to endless new combinations and experimentation.
A few of the more serviceable workaday words in the beauty industry include *slim (surimu), my (mai), gold (gorudo), rich (ritchi),* and *body (bodii).*
Surely the most frequent, however, would have to be *up (appu)* and *make
(meiku).*

Popular English-based coinages such as *image up (imēji appu),* to improve the image of something or someone, and *base up (bēsu appu)* for a
salary increase, were introduced into the Japanese vocabulary decades ago.

FIGURE 30.
The productive
use of *up* in
product names:
bust-up products
T. Este Bust Up
Tool Home
Esthetic Tool and
Best Bust Up Gel.
Photo by author.

In succeeding years, newer forms ensued, such as *charm up (chāmu appu)* for enhancing one's looks or allure, and *sense up (sensu appu)* for heightening or refining one's taste. Countless new *up*-based constructions have been created specifically within the context of the beauty system. *Up* is a good word for beauty advertising; it is optimistic and full of promise. We have already seen it in *bust-up (basuto appu)* for breast enhancement. *Up* is also used for other beauty endeavors, such as *slim up (surimu appu)* to mean weight loss or reduction, and *hip up (hippu appu)* for buttressing the bottom. More recently the coinage *beauty up (byūtii appu)* has appeared, as in a Slim Beauty House claim that customers will get "beauty up" through its services.

*Up* written in roman letters and/or in the *katakana* syllabary is frequently used as part of a product's name, as in two breast products named T. Este Bust Up Tool Home Esthetic Tool and Best Bust Up Gel (figure 30). Shiseido sells a facial astringent named Face-Up Water.[2] Helene Curtis once ran a Color Up campaign for its hair coloring products, and Daimaru department store featured a Kirei Up (beautiful up) campaign. Other examples are Kanebo Fresh Up Bodywash and Exercise Body Up Lotion, Skin Lift Up Profael Lotion, Moisture Up Essences, Lunalena Fresh Up, Upper Cut Rolling Up Essence lotion, Bright Up Cleanser, Aquaspa Up and Gloss Hip, and Hip Care Series Up and Smooth Scrub. A hair treatment product named Up pledges, "Still more up!" *(sara ni appu)*. One reason *up* is so popular in naming beauty goods is that it implies attainable progress and improvement. Cute Up Bust Cream promises to make the breasts go "two size up" in twenty days, while Tense Up is a collagen- and vitamin-enhanced drink that moisturizes the skin from the inside out.[3]

Another trustworthy indication that esute is not far off is the use of the *make* lexeme. *Make* was originally used as a clipped form of "foundation makeup," alternatively seen as "base make" *(beisu meiku)*. By extension it is currently used for many kinds of products, including "hair make" *(hea meiku)* for hair-care products such as styling gel, and Make Cleansing, for facial cleanser. Cosmetics for removing makeup include Shiseido Lip Make Cleansing, Shiseido Naturals Make Purify, and Sofina Make Clear Speedy Gel. One may also do "bust make" *(basuto meiku)*, so *make* refers not only to foundation makeup and lotions but also to the activity of making something beautiful happen. Esthense sells, for $8.50, the Body Make Roller, a small pink and white device that is used to smooth out cellulite and other imperfections in the skin. Many salons advertise that they deliver "body making" *(bodii meikingu)*, meaning various esute services for body transformation. The internationally known appliance corporation National offers a complete line of specialized battery-powered hand-held razors, shavers, and trimmers designed specifically for women's esute. For example, the $56 Pink Free Eyebrow Make comes with five different attachments for brushing, cutting, and shaping the eyebrow.

Other routinely used terms are *rich*, as in Face Lotion Rich, Creamy Washing Powder Rich, and Lux Super Rich, and *gold*, found in Pureraria Bust Gold, Jaws Epinet Gold depilatory cream, and Gold DX Alpha, an eyelid adhesive that adds a temporary fold to the eyelid. The American FDA has a nomenclature committee that approves names submitted for new drug patents, and names are rejected if they imply claims or sound or look too much like existing names. Perhaps a similar rule is needed in Japan's beauty industry, where we have diet products named Garcy Slim, Slim and Keep, Pure Slim, Pieras Slim Gel, DHC New Slim, Slim Queen, Slim Plan, Slim Harb Tea, Slim Get, Aesthe Slim, Activa Slim, and Slim Amin. Constellations of words such as *my, gold, body, slim, make, rich,* and *up* illustrate how deeply embedded English-derived terms are in the beauty system.

Writing about the quest for beauty among the Trobriand Islanders, Malinowski found that magic naturally enters the picture as a way to improve one's appearance. Within the repertoire of magical language are invocations meant to change male and female appearance. One formula involves repeated utterance of the words "I smooth out, I implore, I whiten" (1979: 238). Malinowski saw parallels between Trobriand magic and cosmetics advertising in the London of his day: "The advertisements of modern beauty specialists, especially of the magnitude of my countrywoman Helena Rubinstein, or of her rival, Elizabeth Arden, would make interesting reading if collated with the formulas of Trobriand beauty magic." (1979: 237). In the past, Japanese women might pray to Konsei, the Shinto god of childbirth and marriage, for white skin. Contemporary women use a different sort of magic in their pursuit of beauty, and the new alchemy is purchasable in commodities and services. It would truly be magic if Japan's Magical Cosmetic Company's bust-up gadget really worked. Miracle Spice Moisture Skin White lotion, Super Miracle Beauty Cream, and Miracle China diet pills are purchased by women who understand the point about miraculous transformations. The other side of magic is science, and that too is called on for creating beauty.

## Scientific Beauty

Through investigation of the way treatments are described and delivered within the aesthetic salon, we saw how beauty is reformulated as a commodity that may be created or manipulated with the aid of "science." The positioning of esute as a scientifically based beauty methodology is seen not only in the use of machines like the GX-99 Endermologie or the Beauty Scope but also in product naming, where consumers may now select from hundreds of well-named instruments to help remodel their surfaces.[4]

To remove unwanted hair, one may buy the Full Automatic Hyper Frequency Microcomputer Depilating System, also written with the truncated compound Micon Full Auto (maikon furu ōto). When an eyelid adhesive is advertised as a Double-Eyelid Technological Innovation, in the best possible English, we are witnessing the no-nonsense marketing of the fake cutting edge. Many of these devices are electric or battery-powered—such as the Pul Slimmer, which is used for slimming down (surimu appu). The Pul Slimmer costs $100 and purportedly employs a "science wave" to make fat cells disappear. Fat or cellulite can also be attacked with a product that disperses an "anti-fat lotion" from an internal tank as it rolls over the skin. A variant is the Octopus Roller, part of an anticellulite "system" (it comes with lotion and an exercise/stretching belt), which is said to work through a combination of suction and pressure. One new concept is to hotwire a pair of gloves and sell them as beauty technology. Two companies market the Diamond Silhouette Wave Glove and the Total Active Hand; in each case the product consists of gloves attached by cable to a stimulation machine. One slides the juiced-up gloves over the body to achieve desired ends, either weight loss or bust-up (Total Active Hand has other possibilities the maker may not have anticipated). These names tell interesting stories of products that glide over the skin and reach for the body with everything from tentacles to electrified digits.

Some products are sold as multipurpose esute technology. One of these is Estheen, a hand-held contrivance that comes with different attachments for massaging the face, extracting blackheads, slimming and firming the body, and breast enhancement. Although these products are sold as high technology, they are nevertheless a science targeted at women. Consider the Labeaul device (deliberately reminiscent of *labia*), a battery-powered multipurpose esute kit made of all-pink components. It comes with an assembly of clear pink plastic cups that can be used for waist slimming, facials, and breast augmentation.

Esute itself is often embedded in product names, such as Estheen, although romanization results in a variety of alternative spellings. Thus we have Aesthe Slim, Q's Day Face Esthe, Aesthetic Line Body Care Cool Lotion, Mellowness Cool Massage Esthetics Lotion, DHC Esute Mix Vitamins for the skin, Immediate E Esthetic Body Pack, Esthetique TBC Body Styling Sheet, and the Esteny Line of body goods and lotions. Two facial products offered exclusively through the Takano Yuri Beauty Clinic are Pure Esthe Pla Essence P Placental Extract and Pure Esthe Hya Essence Umbilical Cord Extract (each sells for a hefty $165). Some variations are unwittingly not very tasteful or appealing to a native English speaker, such as T-ESTE Cold Pack, which at a glance triggers an association with *testes*. The same company's T. Este Bust Up Tool Home Esthetic Tool (figure 30) has a queerly uncomfortable name. The large number of product names that use some variant of the term *esute* manifests its function as a key concept in the world of beauty.

English is often clipped or made into diminutive forms when used in product names, so that *maximum* becomes *max,* as in B-Max Gakurua bust-up pills, D-Max Asorbital diet pills, and Cut Max diet tablets. *Garcinia* reduces to the dainty Garcy Slim. *Epilate (depilate)* becomes Épi D'or Hair Removal Gel, while cellulite sounds much more sporty as Cellu Jet Slim. At other times, the clipping loses its essence or power, as in Moon CXc28 Wrink Gel.

Names are often created to suggest the type of ingredients found in the product, such as DHC Gymnema, Chitosan After Diet, and Chlorophyll Spots Gel. DNA Diet Cream and DNA Soap and Enzyme Special

Lotion are touted as containing some special DNA compound. One may presume that DHC Olive Virgin Oil for the skin contains olive oil and not some other ingredient. Product names also indicate the desired result, such as Bigan ("Beautiful Face") Cake for the treatment of pimples, Beauty Line C-Bust, Profael Body Tight, Fitfix No-Sleeve Zone Essence upper body lotion, and Fat Burning, which lists Kitosan, Guava, and DNA as its main ingredients. Virgin Body Diet tablets, which "support a girl's dream," are said to allow one to lose six kilograms in six days. The Wacoal Dear Body line of products uses a letter of the alphabet to indicate the targeted body area: B-Gel is for the breasts, and H-Gel is for the hips.

Occasionally transliteration conventions vary, so that we find names such as Speed Jodel diet pills as the romanized version of *supiido yōderu,* and Buste Farming Essence lotion for a "firming" bust-up product. Names might be meaningful yet carry slightly negative overtones for a native English speaker. Presumably, these names describe conditions the consumer wants to eliminate: Body Unbalance Waist and Hip Smoother cream, Kose Selfconscious Lift on Lift Slimming Lotion, Anesty Wrinkle Essence, and Funky Lotion for depilation. But any negative or erratum possibilities arise from an outsider perspective and are not really of import within the Japanese beauty industry. As Stanlaw (2004) so extensively demonstrates, the type of English we find in Japanese advertisements has little or no connection to "native" English and should therefore be evaluated not as English but as Japanese English.


## Bygone Beauty and Health

Although many esute products and salons have foreign-sounding names and may use photographs of Euroamerican models, there is also a concurrent appeal based on an exotic non-Western pedigree. One of the most common trends is to position new products as ancient, traditional, and Asian—and therefore more "natural" than modern or Western elixirs. Bust Queen, a bust-up remedy, claims to be based on a product transmitted through the "Indonesian Royal Family for women's cosmetic health." Powder Up Bust is a commodity sold as though it were a type of Chinese herbal remedy or *kanpō,* with text that explicitly distinguishes it from "Western medicines," which "only treat specific problems."

Appropriation of the Chinese-derived medical system is common for weight reduction pills, teas, and formulas, such as Miracle China, a diet drink powder. Many of these products employ dense Chinese characters and Sino-Japanese names, such as Reiron-cha and Bireihō. A product with the Sino-Japanese name Bisōgen incorporates English into its ad copy, going so far as to maintain that it is a "a Chinese diet that's easy on your system" *(karada ni yasashii chainiizu daietto)*. Packaging also supports this effort. Fat-reducing diet pills called Pure Slim are sold in bottles that resemble those used to sell ginseng, with an old-fashioned aqua label and an archaic script style. The label says it uses the "power of natural Chinese herbs." In print ads for Pure Slim, the connection with authentic tradition is reinforced by showing the bottle resting daintily on some antique lace.

Beginning in the mid 1990s, an esute fad activated images of exotic South Asian ayurvedic medicine as the basis for products and services. India Esthe, a line of products sold in most drugstores, includes soaps, creams, and oils made with ingredients such as sesame oil or "oriental herbs." *Kanpō* and other Asian-indexed esute claim to draw on "traditional wisdom," and testify to a concern about ethnic identity also seen in other forms of popular culture. Beauty products are additionally sold under the guise of being health aids with therapeutic value. Two products that explicitly call up this connotation are Medical Lotion and Herb Medic. This intent is also reflected in the naming practices of numerous enterprises that call themselves "clinic" *(kurinikku)*, such as Takano Yuri Beauty Clinic.[5] One goes to a clinic for health reasons rather than for cosmetic improvement or hedonistic relaxation, so large sums of money may be spent there guilt-free.

In other cases, the beauty product uses the English appellation *Dr.* to advance the medical. We see this in various skin-care products, such as Dr. Make Body Lotion, Dr. Ark Moisturizer, Dr. William's Water Cream, Dr. Lim Sakurai's Cosmetics (formerly labeled as Supplement Recover Lipid Supply Dr 'S Cosmetics), Dr. Schats Lotion, Dr. Mano's Bioserum Lotion, and Dr. Baeltz Medicated CPX Solution, for "science skin care," according to the label. A new twist is the Crystal Skin Care MDPhD line of facial-care products, said to be "medical cosmetics born in a clinic." The health-medical assemblage of names addresses a woman's yearning for accessible solutions to her beauty problems. Just as she may go to a drugstore and buy Excedrin when she has a headache, wrinkles or dry skin demand a medicine like Cello Chanter Cream EX.

## Pseudo-Morpheme "Ex" Goes to Japan

The letter *x* means many things. It represents the Roman number ten. It is used in scientific and mathematical notation as a variable or stand-in

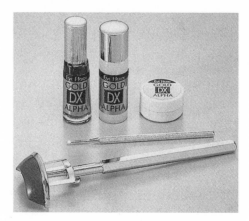

FIGURE 31. The pharma-
ceutical *ex* product marker in
Gold DX Alpha eyelid glue.

for an unspecified amount: "Let *x* be . . ." It also means "here," this spot,
where the treasure is buried, or this is a mistake, "cross out" or ignore
this. It is used to alert readers that something is poisonous. Not to be
forgotten is the racy XXX Nude Girls!! In this case, the Xs presumably
stand for the idea of extremely "X-rated." The use of *x* or *ex* in American
product names is only documented after 1920 (Sebba 1986; Pyles 1957).
Some of the earliest were Kleenex, Pyrex, Kotex, and Windex. *Ex* is not
simply a "product name marker" (Sebba 1986: 321), but a meta-morpheme
that indexes the medicinal and cosmeticological. Pyles (1957) was the first
to note its function as a pseudo-scientific suffix, and Erlich (1995) documents how professional name-creators hired by pharmaceutical companies, who gave us product names such as Xanax and Lasix, rely on *ex* or
*x* to suggest Greek. Its popularity in drug names might also be related
to the use of the pharmaceutical *Rx,* originally a shorthand form of
"recipe." The status of *x* and *ex* as markers of the cosmetic or pharmaceutical is now fully established. For decades American companies have
been exporting over-the-counter remedies like Excedrin, Ex-Lax, Maalox,
Sinex, Sominex, Drixoral, Comtrex, and Blistex to Japan. The pharmaceutical *ex* has now firmly taken hold of the Japanese consciousness
(figure 31). Perhaps the marker recalls the term *extract (ekkisu)* commonly
found on Japanese drug labels.

Although Sebba (1986) describes how *-ex* is not a typical morpheme
because it doesn't carry any specific referential meaning, its productivity
is nonetheless impressive. While *ex* is a bound form in English, which is
to say it never stands alone as a word, this is not the case in Japanese. There
we find it floating freely, appearing as a suffix, infix, and free agent, which

may be plopped into product names with abandon. Consider these instances: Shiseido UV White Refining Emulsion EX II, Optune Perfect
Sebum Off EX, Tooth Enamel Hanic EX Pantype, Hollywood Cosmetics Natural EX Lotion, Garcina EX Diet tablets, Shiseido EX hair treatment pack, Styling Body Gel Bonpresso EX lotion, Whitening C Mois-
tex skin lightening cream, and BSTA-UPEX breast enhancement elixir.

In other contexts, it is hard to determine what *ex* is doing, other than
simply being used in the "product marker" capacity. Bourbon Pickle EX
Mild is, surprisingly, a chocolate-flavored snack cookie, although it is long
and cylindrical (like a skinny brown pickle?). The package states, in this
exact English, "Enjoy the superb taste of chocolate formulated with selected ingredient, beautiful things are beyond time. Women's history
never cease to yearn for beauty," so perhaps the link with "beauty" justifies
the presence of *EX*. The important point we see here is that consumers
recognize forms such as *x* or *EX* as markers of a category of pseudo-
pharmaceutical products.


## Fomenting and Alleviating Insecurity

The beauty industry often creates new body worries for consumers, introducing them to areas of the body or beauty problems that can be cor-
rected through novel products and services. Because status and economic
success may depend on a culturally defined presentation of self, including
a sanctioned gender construction, many of the advertisements for beauty
play on the consumer's anxiety that she might not measure up to the ideal
female body. The word *worry (nayami)* is routinely used, as in an Erufurāju
headline that reminds us, "A small bust is a big worry!" Copy for an advertisement for Delsia Girl declares, "A voluptuous bustline is the greatest 'charm point' for a woman. But if you have small or droopy breasts,
your appeal gets reduced by half." From this we learn that without proper
bust augmentation, for instance, no woman can hope to be considered acceptably attractive. Most people do not conform to the ideal, which is continually reconfigured so there will always be a market for self-improvement
products. Books and other media are available as technical guides to esute.
One such "educational" product, a documentary video that reviews beauty
procedures such as eye surgery, dental work, and breast enlargement, was
created by the Takasu Clinic of Cosmetic Surgery. To lure customers into
his clinic, Dr. Takasu proposes that "instead of worrying about your complex, try to confront your true intentions honestly. All women have the

potential to be beautiful." Paperback books on home esute are also widely sold in bookstores (Asami 1997; Kenkō Shinbunsha 1994).

To alleviate worry and reassure potential buyers, many advertisements feature testimonials from people who have used the new products. The witnessing is often made more personal and authentic when it is coupled with a small photograph and personal details such as name, age, and social position (e.g., university student, housewife, office worker). After 2004, some advertisements appeared with "print club" *(purikura)* photo-stickers marked up with text that raves about the product or service.[6] An ad for the Labeaul bust-up device includes two testimonials from happy customers underneath shots of their smiling faces. One says, "I can't believe something so compact is so great." The other, from a twenty-one-year-old, will reassure those concerned about what the appliance actually feels like: "I was really surprised by Labeaul's power, but it was a really good feeling." She adds, "Thanks to this, in one month I went from A-cup to B-cup size. I'll feel good about wearing a bathing suit this year." Advertisements for Super Bust Rich include a face shot and testimonial from a twenty-two-year-old who says, "My breasts were small, so during high school I had a complex. But this spring I had confidence and was able to get a cool boyfriend." A less common strategy in esute products is the testimonial from a famous person. A hair removal cream named Rōana uses celebrities and models for testimonials, but most others rely on everyday Office Ladies and students. However, idols and celebrities are frequently recruited as models for sales campaigns for aesthetic salons.

Japanese frequently use English-derived lexemes to dodge the sensitive or indelicate. This is particularly prevalent in the pornography and sex-for-sale industries, where the prefixes *pinku* ("pink") and *ero* ("erotic") are used to indicate the sexual. In esute advertising, English morphemes are similarly recruited to discretely describe commodities or services. This is most noticeable in ads for products dealing with body hair, such as depilatory creams, lotions, and tapes, electrolysis devices, and skin or body-hair bleaching agents. An example is the Feather Flamingo, which sounds as if it might be an eye shadow brush but is really a women's face shaver.

One company sells *esute datsumō tēpu* (body aesthetics depilation tape). Here, the addition of both esute and *tēpu* serves to mark the activity of ripping off body hair seem like a normal part of beauty maintenance. In some cases, we find multilinguistic creations such as the English, French, and Japanese *hōmu esute datsumō* (at-home body aesthetics depilation). At times, however, it seems that beauty can be peddled with an in-your-face brazenness. There's a men's line of cosmetics sold under the brand name NUDY that feature confidently groomed male models.


## Esute Innovations

Japanese advertising is said to focus on mood and to rarely boast about the merits of the product (Creighton 1995: 139). One business professor claims that "in Japan, you don't directly sell the product. It's not acceptable to force people to buy something. . . . A very personalized soft sell is traditionally very Japanese, and the cosmetics industry, in particular, seems very conscious of that" (Gumpert 2000: 44). While these characterizations may be true for many types of advertising, such as cars or whiskey, the ads for beauty products and services usually prick readers' anxiety and then urge them to take concrete action. As we have seen, readers know they are meant to resculpt their forms whenever they encounter any variant of *up,* meaning enhance or increase. Some advertisements use an imperative or exhortative mode of address, thereby imparting an air of immediacy and urgency to the advice or information given. Readers are apprised of the necessity to change their bodies when they read copy such as this:

> This is the secret to weight loss!
>
> *Yaseru himitsu wa kore da!*

> Pick a reducing plan and start right away!
>
> *Genryō puran o erande ima sugu sutāto!*

> Just covering up is no good!
>
> *Maburu dake ja dame!*

Despite a widespread mythology of Japanese indirectness (Miller 1994), beauty advertisements are usually exceedingly direct and explicit. The copy for a bust-up product screams, "Say goodbye to a flat chest and drooping breasts!" *(Pechapai, tarechi ni sayonara!),* and a face cream announces, "Say goodbye to pimply faces!" *(Nikibigao ni sayonara!).* A liberal use of exclamation marks and bright magenta or red characters underscores this intensity or directness. Beauty advertisements are often garishly busy with text and multiple graphics and visuals.

Moeran (1985) investigated the semantic parallelism and opposition found in advertising slogans and copy that employ English. He notes the

TABLE 7. Orthographic Code-Switching

---

1. 夏のUV対策ケア
   *Natsu no UV taisaku kea*
   Care for summer ultraviolet countermeasures
2. スリムボディをGET!
   *Surimu bodii o GET!*
   Get a slim body!
3. 2サイズUPのメカニズム
   *Ni saizu UP no mekanizumu*
   Mechanism for going up two sizes
4. ツルツル ＆ スベスベの美肌をGET!!
   *Tsurutsuru & subesube no bihada o GET!!*
   Get slick and smooth beautiful skin!

---

poetic intent in the symmetrical slogan "Nice day, nice smoking" used by the Japan Tobacco Company, and "My life, my gas" by the Tokyo Gas Company. Likewise, juxtaposition of writing systems in beauty ads presents an aesthetically pleasing balance and contrast, as in the salon name Esute de Mirōdo (エステ de ミ ロ ー ド), where *esute* and *mirōdo* ("Milord") are written in the Japanese *katakana* syllabary, separated by a smaller romanized *de*. Indeed, the linguist Ishino (1985) suggests that the contemporary expressive power of Japanese is perhaps given its fullest play in the area of orthography, where writers routinely draw on four different writing systems.

Consider the polygraphic forms in table 7. In example 1, four different scripts are used—Roman letters, Chinese characters, and both Japanese syllabaries. In example 2, there is an interesting use of the Japanese object marker *o* with the verb *get* in roman letters, yet the words *slim body* are written in *katakana* script.[7] Example 3 highlights the thrust of *up* by writing it in capital roman letters. These examples contribute to a visual mode of consumption in which readers are presented with abundant orthographic code-switching. All three examples of multigraphic writing provide visual interest and, in examples 1 and 3, aesthetically pleasing symmetry.[8] In example 4, which is directed to the male consumer, we also find the use of *get* written in the Roman alphabet.

English is commandeered as an additional resource for imaginative punning, palindromes, and other word play. One of the more playful uses of language in the beauty business is *ateji,* writing that is used phonetically with little or no relation to meaning. Tokyo Beauty Center promotes commercial activity with an "Aesthetic Card" that allows two visits to the salon. Copy for the ad used the English *go to* in several places, and the "Aesthetic Card" had *go two* written on it in Roman letters. The double meaning of *go to/go two* is calculated. Likewise, a slimming product with the name Leg-o-Slim Original is surely intended to be playful.

Many product names express a high level of creative playfulness and a sophisticated manipulation of English, such as Shiseido Proudia Face Escort Super Fix UV and Kosé Intelligé T-Zone Tonic, "made for your skin's personality." On the other hand, it is not always possible to discern the product-naming strategy behind all names. One wonders what the motivation is for Reset Wash, Ethpital Rect Bust, or Haba UV White Lotion. Pure Doil Epi is a hair removal gel, where *Epi* is clearly a clipped form of *epilate* but *Doil* is something of a mystery.

The American cosmetics and beauty industry often uses a food angle in its product naming and ad copy, to address the hunger for nourishment that goes on the body instead of in the mouth (Tringal 2004). Although "body butters" and "strawberry bath gels" are not yet as popular in Japan, there are examples such as English Very Very Fresh Milk skin lotion and the hybrid English-French Lait Buste Bust Beauty Lotion and Gel.

Japanese readers appreciate lexical novelty, and essays in magazines, newspapers, and journals often deconstruct creative ad copy. At one time there was a regular feature in the linguistic journal *Gengo* in which guest copywriters analyzed advertising copy and slogans, many of them containing foreign loans or Japan-made English. The name of the feature was "CM Word Watching," in which the acronym CM is a Japan-made coinage for "commercial message" or advertisement. Periodicals devoted entirely to media commentary include *CM Entertainment Magazine, CM Now, Favorite CM Characters, Consumer Mind Index,* and *Up to Creation Brain*. In Japanese society there is a strong awareness of ads as artistic products, and many people know something about the advertising industry Clio awards.[9]

Other writers have explained how advertising words and language convert existing meanings into hybrid or new meanings (Williamson 1978; Goldman 1992). Viewers draw on knowledge from previously read examples and a shared cultural system to decipher these new meanings, a form of labor that turns the ability to decode advertisements into a value-producing activity. Nicely illustrating this point is an advertisement for a breast enhancement massage system that presumes exposure to previous Sony Walkman advertisements for its interpretation. For those desiring the trendiest technology, the company that makes the Delsia Girl bust-up apparatus also offers a much smaller, portable gadget that looks just like a Walkman. This is a pastel turquoise unit called the Walkfree, a new technology that, according to the copy, allows the customer to watch television, do the cooking, and perform other household chores while also working on bust-up.

The contemporary use of English in the Japanese beauty domain is a deliberately and carefully orchestrated innovation valued as a linguistic commodity. The advertisements examined in this chapter show that this use of English is not a simple process of imitation and borrowing. Esute advertising is parasitic on other genres but is also a site where a unique lexicon of words is created and circulated. Within the realm of beauty, many values are attached to beautyspeak forms. The oblique allusions and unusual coinages not only index a variety of meanings (health, a non-Western, usually Asian identity, anxiety, and so on), but also socialize consumers in ways of reading and interpreting advertisements. These ads draw on a recycled general advertising vocabulary, and concurrently provide their own specialized esute lexicon from which words are mined and to which they are added.

Specialists in beauty language are a critical part of the industrialization of beauty and body aesthetics, and the words and concepts they create and use are integral to its construction. They are selling not only cosmetics or body improving products but also hope and fantasy. Language voices the cultural meanings found in conceptions of beauty. The rationalized production of beauty goods and services for mass consumption is mediated through language that anoints them with additional layers of meaning. Beauty language is founded on shared understandings, both linguistic and cultural, that circulate in the beauty marketplace. While a deeper investigation of commodity texts, or a "commodity semiotics" (Goldman 1992), is possible, the brief survey given in this chapter allows us some insight into how beauty is imagined. Beautyspeak might be opaque to some Japanese speakers, but for those who seek beauty, it is integral to their consumption experience.

CHAPTER 8

# Esute Power

Beauty is not to be ignored. The Meiji Shrine gift shop sells aromatherapy goods and herbal beauty products, and in 2001, a Shinto shrine in Sendai selected its New Year maidens via a beauty contest competition. In this final chapter, I discuss the enduring power of the concept of esute and how beauty work gives renewed meaning to the cultural notion of self-improvement. The esute concept has leaked into other areas of culture and is often appropriated and stretched to encompass a broad range of phenomena, including baths and brothels. Industrial beauty culture sells the message that consumption of its products and services will not only perfect one's image but radically transform one's life. By embracing the possibility of bodily change and difference, consumers are manifesting a slight shift in philosophical orientation, in which everything is open to modification. Yet the intense self-involvement needed for "beauty up" does not mesh well with cultural ideals of self-sacrifice, especially for women. In order to be successful, the beauty industry has had to define beauty as obtainable through scientific management and hard work, thus establishing it as a legitimate form of self-betterment.

## Esute Expansions

In 1999, I saw a small sign for a business in Roppongi advertising "Chinese body aesthetics" *(chūgoku esute)*. Curious, I took the elevator up to the third floor of a narrow building and entered the establishment,

中国エステ

龍 宮 佳 苑
DRAGON GARDEN

MASSAGE

| | |
|---|---|
| 30分中国式マッサージお試しコース<br>30 Minutes Relaxation Mssage - Basic | 3,000 Yen |
| 60分中国式全身マッサージコース<br>60 Minutes Relaxation Mssage - Basic | 6,000 Yen |
| 60分全身オイル＋足踏み<br>60 Minutes Oil Mssage | 8,000 Yen |
| 60分アロマオイルマッサージ<br>60 Minutes Special / Aromatherepy Oil | 7,000 Yen + Oil<br>(2000円から各種) |
| 30分足裏健康療法<br>30 Minutes Foot Mssage | 3,000 Yen |

FIGURE 32.
"Chinese esute" as
a code for sexual
services.

where I alarmed the receptionist and a departing male client paying for his noontime "massage" at what turned out to be a sex-for-sale joint. The receptionist and customer were upset that I was there, but I did get information about prices and was surprised to see that services at. Dragon Garden Massage are cheaper than what it costs for real esute (figure 32).

The term *esute* has been appropriated from the beauty industry and is now used as a code word for "hot (raw) sex" *(nama esute)* and "beautiful prostitutes" in sex advertising (seen in figure 12 in chapter 3). Using English-derived coinages as coding for sexual services (such as "health massage" and "fashion massage") is nothing new in Japan. In a manner similar to the use of *soap lady (sōpu redii)* for a sex worker, flyers (called *pinbura*) advertising sexual services now feature the "aesthetics lady" *(esute redii),* who is no more than an ordinary prostitute.[1] During the World Cup soccer games in 2002, male visitors to Japan were enthusiastic about the flourishing and seemingly police-immune sex establishments they found. Many of them mistakenly assumed that, because of this appropriation, the term *esute* is synonymous with "sex." One can only imagine the confusion they might experience when confronted with the word *esute* in non-sex-related contexts, such as Body Fit Cool Freezer Esthe salt scrub or Pure Esthe Hya Essence Umbilical Cord Extract lotion. It might be supposed that through a process of semantic taint, *esute* will eventually be dropped as a catchall term for beauty work. But for now, there is no disenthrallment: the fertile concept of esute shows no signs of withering, but instead has bloomed in unexpected places.

The core ingredients of the esute concept—beauty and body—easily allow it to be poached in novel ways. It is used to describe objects such as "aesthetic shoes" *(esute shūzu)* and Esthe Support Pantyhose. At an Italian restaurant in Shibuya, I was given a packaged wet napkin instead of the usual hot white hand towel, with a label identifying it as "wet tissue esute science." An aesthetic salon now provides "divination aesthetics" *(esute uranai)* on its web page, and a Christian organization published "Beauty Treatments for the Heart" ("Kokoro no esute," by Yoko Hirano).[2] I once saw a gas station advertising a car cleaning service as "car aesthetics" *(kā esute),* and I spent many evenings cleansing my body and spirit in a small pool called the "aesthetics bath" *(esute basu),* located in a public bath in Kanazawa. A special business with branches in Paris and Tokyo is named Pet Esthé. Their aesthetic salon is only for animals, but it is not very different from aesthetic salons for people. They offer beauty work and grooming treatments such as pet aromatherapy for stress, Dead Sea Salt treatments, and special whitening shampoos for dogs. Pet Esthé sells a full line of cat and dog shampoos, named Pet Esthé Keep, which contain the trendy salon ingredient propolis, a material "created by honeybees." Other pet esute salons also offer "courses" of shampoo, teeth brushing, coat trimming, flea spraying, and massage (Nikkei Trendy 1998). Esute has been appropriated by multiple industries hoping to confer meanings of beauty, cleanliness, and status.

The body aesthetics market survived Japan's long-term recession without much attrition.[3] Consumer spending by Office Ladies and other young women is keeping esute afloat and is also fueling the growth of other luxury goods and services. Young women often live at home or in a dorm, relieving them of some housing, utilities, and food expenses. A popular term coined by a male sociologist to describe the 70 percent or so of unmarried Japanese women in their early thirties who still live at home is "Parasite Single," a nasty term that also caught the fancy of the American media (Orenstein 2001; Butler 1998; Strom 1998).

Of course, male scholars and writers interpret this trend as evidence of the selfishness and hedonistic self-centeredness of women, ignoring that these women do in fact contribute a small portion of their paychecks toward their parents' household budget (Rosenberger 2000) and forgetting the existence of male versions of the domestic barnacle. Feminist critics note that it is really an economic fallout resulting from Japan's unequal workplace culture, and that women, not much interested in suffering, are reluctant to become housewife drudges (Yamamoto 2001). Japanese mothers are also happy to let them stay home and are in no rush to see their daughters duplicate their own life trajectories of disappointing marriages with lack of help in childcare or household chores from overworked husbands. The new focus on the body and the diversification of beauty practices are enabled or encouraged within these economic conditions.

While a few big aesthetic salon chains have experienced a downturn, other body aesthetic industries are undergoing growth. A new development is travel overseas, or within Japan, with esute treatments included as part of the experience. The tourist returns from her exotic experience with her own body as the souvenir.[4] A few years ago, the Japan Travel Bureau began offering activities, such as golf, opera, or esute, as subsidiary options to a regular package. Esute tourism to Korea has become especially popular. Packages usually include air travel, hotel room, salon treatments at the hotel, some meals, and expensive ginseng-based cosmetics (*Sankei Shimbun* 1994; *Saitama Shimbun* 1997).[5]

One tour company sells the "Become a Beauty in Seoul" tour (which men may also enroll in), also named the "Mugwort esute experience." The course involves two treatments sold as "authentic" and "ancient" Korean beauty care: the mugwort sauna and the *akasuri* massage. Wormwood or mugwort aromatic plants are a valued aspect of Korean cultural identity (figure 33). Mugwort features in Korean mythology and is dried and used for medicinal purposes. It is thought to provide protection against evil spirits; people used to hang it across thresholds to repel malevolent spirits. Mugwort smoke is often used in saunas, and is now sold to Japanese tourists as an exotic esute treatment. In Korea a rough towel is appreciated for vigorous scrubbing, and public baths often have assistants who would scrub the customer's body with one. In 1999, the Korean tourist industry began selling this custom as a "traditional beauty" service to Japanese tourists. They dubbed it *akasuri* ("dirt scrubbing"), and it became a fad in Japan as well.

Young Japanese women like Korea as a destination because Korea and Korean things are on the list of what is "cool" and exotic, and it is less expensive than Japan. For older Japanese women, a desire for the Korean experience may perhaps hint at nostalgia for a more traditional Asian lifestyle or values,[6] but other foreign destinations are also popular. One can get "bridal esute" as part of a Hawai'ian honeymoon package, or "oriental esute" at the Banyan Tree Spa on Phuket island. Advertising editorials for a special Bali esute experience feature lush tropical surroundings,

FIGURE 33. Esute tourism to Korea. Reproduced with permission of Kinki Nippon Tourist Co.

unusual foods, and the possibility of receiving body treatments from esute servants (*Can Cam Beauty* 1997c). Although Bali is part of a sophisticated international tourism industry, it is represented in spa advertising as an Asian paradise that modernity has passed by. Massages are given in thatched, open-air huts without air-conditioning.

Unlike the domestic salon business, the primary market for international esute tourism is middle-aged women. According to a 1995 survey, 60 percent of female overseas travelers were over the age of forty (*Yomiuri Shimbun* 1997c). For younger women, the Japan Travel Bureau and other travel companies have been selling forms of domestic esute tourism, with the idea that two friends can afford a weekend escape. Many hotels now feature the "Esute Stay Plan," a weekend in a luxury hotel that includes meals and some body treatments in the hotel spa. The Akasaka Tokyu Hotel, for instance, sells a twin-bed package for two friends that includes gift pajamas or makeup kits.

Global media and product distribution have not eradicated all local distinctions in East Asia, despite Barber's vision of cultural uniformity and concern that transnational commodities and ideas are "pressing nations into one homogeneous global theme park" (1995: 4). There is a branch of a Japanese salon chain in Hong Kong named Esthy World that mainly targets Japanese tourists and expatriates. The "menu" of treatments is written in Japanese, English, and Cantonese. The Chinese salon manager is an employee of the Japanese firm that owns this chain, and she was trained in Japan and speaks Japanese. When I visited this salon in 1998, Japanese magazines such as *Can Cam* and *An An* were strewn around the reception area. Even so, there are services at the Hong Kong shop that one does not normally find in an esute salon in Japan. Eyebrow Shaping and Eyelash Perming are services found in the hair parlor instead of the esute salon. Something like "cupping," popular at Slim Beauty House and other Japanese salons, would never make it in Hong Kong, where home-use cupping sets, still very common and associated with frumpy old ladies, are sold on the same street at a medical supplies store. So even this very Japanese business has adapted to the local scene.

This is similar to what Ossman (2002) found in her analysis of globalization, flows of fashion, and the interaction between media and the creation of gendered looks in beauty salons in Cairo, Paris, and Casablanca. Although we live in a universe saturated with similar images and goods that move across borders and languages, these same artifacts and images are recontextualized into local settings and do not always have the same meanings or uses. Iwabuchi recognizes that both global culture and local understandings of it are deeply intertwined when he states, "The operation of global cultural power can only be found in local practice, whereas cultural reworking and appropriation at the local level necessarily takes place within the matrix of global homogenizing forces" (2002: 44). When they arrive at a new cultural setting, they take on different values and uses. For example, in cross-cultural research on beauty contests, scholars note that while Western ideals of beauty inform pageants in some ways, local conditions and ideas resist or integrate these (Cohen, Wilk, and Stoeltje 1996). In a similar vein, the ethnographic study of McDonald's social, political and economic repercussions in East Asia illustrates that although it has had an impact on some forms of cultural behavior, it has not completely eclipsed local food cultures, and furthermore, the way people use the restaurant is not always what the company of origin had in mind (Watson 1997).

## Beauty Possibilisms

In trying to understand the way beauty is consumed by the Japanese, we must recognize that consumers are not merely the dupes of audacious claims made by the beauty industry. There is a deeper core appeal to esute that runs beneath advertisements that promise straighter legs or perfect skin. Esute relates to a new trope of self-improvement that has been tied to the body. It promises the possibility of change thorough body practices.

Writers offer many explanations for the motivations and the plurality of models for becoming beautiful. Some seek explanation at the level of individual psychology. For example, a psychologist who counsels women seeking cosmetic surgery looked for answers in female psychology (Kajihara 1998), explaining the desire to become beautiful through a "typology" of women. According to her, one type believes that if she becomes beautiful, she'll be happy and will become a celebrity. Another type feels that she will demonstrate her determination to get a successful career by any means possible. A third type believes she must be like everyone else, so she needs to become just a little more beautiful. The fourth type is a "good girl," who needs to be beautiful to resemble her princess mother.

If one seeks a psychological explanation, I suspect that it has less to do with "types" and more to do with a shift in how young people think about the body and its changeability. One difference between younger Japanese and older generations is the idea that the body is a malleable surface open to modification. Although technologies for body transformation have been available since the Meiji era, the popularity of using these modern technologies for beautification is rather new. The body was once considered unalterable, as indicated by the phrase *shikata ga nai*. *Shikata ga nai* is commonly used in everyday conversation to mean "it can't be helped" or "nothing can be done," denoting a sense of resignation to aspects of life that can't be changed.

Some writers have interpreted *shikata ga nai* as the reflection of a "dangerous fatalism" (Cortazzi 2001) or a passive apathy (Wolfren 1989). But despite Buddhist philosophical support for such a stance, scholars of the postwar era found little evidence of true fatalistic determinism in Japan (Bellah 1965; Dore 1973; Plath 1966). Instead, it seems that the Japanese have pragmatically and aggressively made efforts to manipulate their stations in life. In an essay that argues against the idea that Japanese are cursed by a "despotism of the mental canals," Plath (1966: 161) sees expressions like *shikata ga nai* as an explanatory device available to allocate responsibility for unfortunate events, not as ingrained defeatism that cuts off the possibility of change.[7]

Historians have also documented the existence of an optimistic philosophy of self-help already present among late Edo-era (1680–1868) peasantry. Kinmouth (1981) writes that young samurai were avid consumers of self-help literature, and some waited all night for bookstores to open so they could purchase the first Japanese translation of Samuel Smiles's *Self-Help*. Self-improvement literature of that era aimed at moral and philosophical reformation of the self in order to better serve society (Bellah 1957). Later there were government-sponsored "daily life" campaigns intended to teach people how to improve their hygiene, diet, and consumption patterns, among other things (Garon 1997: 129). An important point is that the self-transformation these early writers advocated was limited to one's character and health, and rarely meant anything like a cosmetic change to the inherited body. The goal was never reformation of the self for individual enjoyment or pleasure. For example, Ninomiya Sontoku (1787–1856), the farmer and self-taught social philosopher, encouraged advancements in agriculture and physical health as ways to improve society. Ninomiya become a symbol of self-study through his advocacy of success via personal effort and development. He believed that each person should save money, eat well, and keep clean for the sake of the family. But now beauty prestige has replaced Confucian regard for family reputation.

The modern proliferation of "how to" books aimed at telling Japanese how to make themselves better or more successful people therefore is a legacy of this faith in self-change. Popular writing on how to get ahead in the workplace and how to upgrade your manners or decorum are now standard fare. Even timeworn American self-help books are being translated and eagerly read. There is also a specialty boom in self-help books for women, including titles like *55 Ways to Have a Likeable Self* (Satō 2000) and *Change Yourself in One Minute* (Satō 1999). One reason the idea of a "science" of beauty is so appealing is that it engages with this pragmatic worldview.

Young Japanese now believe in the ability of science to refurbish their hair, penises, eyelids, and other aspects of the body, things that were once considered *shikata ga nai*. Confidence in the transformative power of beauty technology and beauty work is often manifested in the phrases "before aesthetics" *(esute mae)* and "after aesthetics" *(esute ato)*. In other words, a profound difference occurs as the result of the aesthetic work. However, optimism in the possibility and desirability of change also gives birth to a more damaging attitude. In the same way that some prewar Japanese thinkers believed that poverty was the result of individual laziness, young men and women judge those who refuse to participate in active forms of beauty work (or are too poor to do so) as suffering from character flaws. Beauty does not just "happen" but is an accomplishment that requires much effort.[8] This means that it is an individual's own fault if he or she fails to meet today's standards for appearance.

Beauty advertising often operates on this belief in the possibility of change. For example, Takano Yuri Beauty Clinic's "Cinderella book" brochure has bubbly proclamations such as "I became a new self!" A bust-up product named Redo Bust promises women that they will "discover the new you" once their bodily conversion has occurred. A television advertisement for Tokyo Beauty Center once featured a vignette entitled "The Day That Naomi Changed." Naomi, an average-looking, ordinary young woman, leaves her house to go off for her salon treatment and returns home as supermodel Naomi Campbell. A powerful appeal of the esute business is its claim to egalitarianism. Anyone can become beautiful if they work hard enough, have self-discipline, and follow the models presented to them.

This last point relates to an entrenched cultural focus on models of precise "ways of doing" (kata) that are followed as a learning device. In her work on the sentimental ballad genre called enka, Yano (2002) discusses the role of mastering kata in creating a proper enka singer, who constructs a performance from set patterns and formulas. The concept of kata is found in diverse and wide-ranging areas of Japanese traditional arts, including karate and flower arrangement. There are likewise fixed routines and templates for becoming beautiful, established patterns for the doing of esute. Because beauty is a concretized quality, something that is measurable and not just existing "naturally" in some people, it is attainable through beauty kata by anyone with enough self-exertion.

How does this intense self-involvement correspond to cherished Japanese cultural ideals about female self-sacrifice? The new images of beauty and the beauty work required to approximate the new ideals send a message that is contradictory to some enduring cultural proscriptions. The earnest narcissism required to obtain new body styles runs counter to a long-standing gender norm which dictates that, more than any other trait, women should never be self-centered or selfish. In survey after survey, selfishness or self-centeredness (wagamama) is always the most despised female trait (Miller 1998d). Therefore, such intense focus on the body must be masked as a health concern or as admirable self-discipline. Women and girls are admonished to be hypervigilant about body minutiae, yet the time and money spent on body change and upkeep must be concealed, lest she be thought selfish or self-centered. Spielvogel (2003) describes the fitness club as a space in which women must juggle contradictory messages. They are urged to use exercise as way to demonstrate discipline and self-control and to get a slim body that can be revealed in sexy leotards. Yet they are concurrently told that the self-discipline required for obtaining such a body is selfish and that display of the sexy body is narcissistic. In a society that relentlessly pressures them to be other-directed, the business of beauty affords a little slice of life where one may focus on the self without accusations of being selfish.

Recently scholars have questioned the apparent political apathy of contemporary Japanese youth, asking why they are focused on the self rather than social responsibility (Kotani 2004). Hashimoto (2004) suggests that widespread disempowerment, withdrawal, and apathy are linked to the narcissism fostered by late modernity. The massive attention young people now give to body aesthetics and beauty upkeep raises the question: if they weren't engaged in beauty work, what might they be doing? There is no way to answer such a question other than to acknowledge that beauty work absorbs an enormous amount of time and energy that might otherwise be used for other endeavors.

## Conclusion

This book provides a description of Japanese beauty culture as it developed during the mid-1990s to the early 2000s, detailing some of the ways in which it has driven expanded forms of beauty work for both women and men. Through examination of aesthetic salons, dieting products, weight-loss activities, breast enhancement efforts, beauty language, and beauty imaging, I have traced how beauty consumption and meanings are embedded in changing cultural, historical, and economic circumstances. The discussion of beauty has also been linked to larger issues concerning the construction of femininity and masculinity, ethnic identity, and the international flow of images that all converge in the production of body aesthetics and new forms of subjectivity.

Although the beauty industry is an outgrowth of global tendencies (especially the creation of identity through consumption) and conventional media representation, it may nevertheless allow for forms of individual resistance, as well as the symbolic expression of socially sanctioned self-improvement. The beauty work described in this book can be viewed as both empowering (by recognizing the agency in consumption activities) and as constraining (by admitting that beauty discipline ties consumers all the more firmly to gender norms). For women, new beauty ideals symbolize the collapse of the patriarchal cult of innocence and the expression of self-confidence and adult sexuality. For both men and women, new beauty work represents nonconformity and the importance of the body and beauty in modern identity construction. Young people may simultaneously reproduce normative femininity and masculinity while contesting notions of ethnic homogeneity.

There are two final lessons I hope this book has illustrated. One is that beauty language and beauty ideology reflect ongoing interaction between Japan and the foreign, in which formulations continue to evolve and emerge. We should be especially careful not to assume that young Japanese who experiment with innovations in self-presentation and identity management, in which body modification is part of the beauty system, are engaged in deracialization or emulation of the foreign. Contemporary beauty in Japan may index older indigenous ideas about body and beauty yet also look similar to something we see in Euroamerican contexts, so trying to classify all that we see as *either* authentically Japanese or imitation Euroamerican is not always very illuminating. It also denies the Japanese the creativity and agency accorded other groups and freezes our conception of what is acceptably "Japanese."

A second lesson is that beauty is culturally and historically molded and is never obvious or "natural." By looking at beauty in the Japanese context, its changes and diverse contradictions, we become aware of the contingent and culturally constructed nature of beauty ideology. At a time when English-language media is saturated with "scientific" studies of beauty in which evolutionary psychologists claim to have discovered universal, biologically based human preferences in appearance, it is important to keep in mind that these studies lack cross-cultural depth and are culturally skewed. Studying beauty in a non-Euroamerican culture is a corrective to such inherent naturalizing.

Many of the body "problems" the Japanese beauty industry sells — breast size, weight, and dry, wrinkled skin — are no different from the defects women in other societies, especially the United States, are taught they must hide or correct. Yet the way that beauty is produced in aesthetic salons, with dieting goods and treatments, diligent hair removal activities, and other controlling efforts, is linked to specific Japanese notions about beauty. As seen in the popularity of both black face and white face styles, Japanese young people do not have a single concept of beauty or share identical notions about the way to achieve it. The Japanese beauty industry is not simply a vassal to Euroamerican beauty culture. However, this does not indicate that the local meanings of consumption in Japan have released consumers from the dominating influence of the capitalist profit motive. The power of esute is its quality of attainability, but it is attainable only through consumption of products, services, and ideology. The beautification process's inherent optimism and potential for human agency are attractive to consumers, but this process rests on a mythology of transformation created by domestic and transnational corporations, which are happy to promote multiple local, embedded meanings.

# Notes

## Introduction. Approaches to Body Aesthetics and the Beauty System

1. *Consumer Reports* magazine regularly publishes test results on the efficacy of skin moisturizers, and, except for the Retin-A-type creams, all products, regardless of price, do nothing more than moisturize the surface of the skin.

2. Aspects of positionality in this research are found in Miller (2004d).

3. *Californio* is the term used for individuals descended from settlers from Mexico prior to the Treaty of Guadalupe Hidalgo in 1848. My Afro-Mestizo-Spanish ancestors were among the expedition that founded the Pueblo of Los Angeles in 1781. An outcome of decades of endogamous marriage, I am descended from the *poblador* Luis Quintero and the escort soldiers Eugenio Valdez, Roque Jacinto de Cota, José Manuel Machado, and Francisco Xavier Sepulveda.

4. Some people have wondered if the term *esute* has any relationship to the name of the world-famous cosmetic company Estée Lauder, founded by Josephine Esther Lauder. Although they sound similar, the derivations are different.

5. Two of these films are *Fit Surroundings* (1998), directed by David Plath and Jacquetta Hill, about women shellfish divers, and *Women of Japan: Memories of the Past, Dreams for the Future* (2002), produced by Joanne Hershfield and Jan Bardsley, about the work and life trajectories of six women from a variety of backgrounds.

## Chapter 1. Changing Beauty Ideology

1. Although I will argue otherwise, one scholar claims that, based on an examination of Edo-period "manuals" for makeup application, beauty ideology con-

cerning eye shape and nose shape has not changed much since that time (*Hokkoku Shimbun* 1995).

2. See Kashiwagi (1987) for a similar analysis.

3. Amuro became so popular that, beginning in 1995, young women who imitated her hairstyle, clothing, makeup, and body style were dubbed *amurā*, a term formed from her name and the suffix *-ā*.

4. There is a deeply entrenched folk etymology surrounding the term *kogyaru*. Folk etymology is the common assignment of meaning to words based on similarity with known morphemes rather than on research into the history of the word. My research into the term indicates that it was coined around 1990 by male staff at discos and live houses, who called the under-eighteen crowd *kōkōsei gyaru* (high school girls), later clipped to *kogyaru*. In popular rationalization, the morpheme *ko* in *kogyaru* is instead assumed to mean "small," yielding the intuitively logical meaning of "small girl." Many scholars insist on retaining and repeating this erroneous folk etymology.

5. Kogal and *ganguro* style is also discussed in Kinsella (2002, 2005) and Miller (2000, 2004b, 2004c).

6. The *ganguro* style, as confounded with the B-Girl style, is seen in Wood (1999) and in description of the work of artist Iona Brown.

7. In 1873, when the Meiji empress appeared in public with white teeth and unshaved eyebrows, she caused a major controversy (Shibusawa 1958). The practice of teeth-blackening, called *ohaguro, nesshi,* or *kanetsuke,* was officially stopped, yet advertisements for ready-made blackening products continued to appear in Japanese newspapers for decades (Machida 1997: 142). When Mattel's Barbie was first redesigned for the Japanese market, prior to current changes in beauty ideology, her parted lips, which disclosed white teeth, were firmly closed. Tooth-blackening is found in other places, such as Vietnam, Peru, and the Philippines, and is listed as one of the cosmetic arts in the Kama Sutra (Trumble 2004).

8. A collection of photographs of *ganguro* is found in Klippensteen and Brown (2000).

9. The lack of maidenly reserve is seen in published interviews as well, such as one with Hitoe in which she openly calls herself a narcissist (*Myōjō* 1990).

10. Because some women have always disguised an independent attitude beneath hypersubmissiveness, this is simply another avenue for its expression.

11. It should be kept in mind that not wearing any makeup at all is also symbolic. The middle-class women interviewed by Ashikari (2003) assumed that those without makeup must be troublemaking feminists, lesbians, or farm women.

12. White skin has been valued in other parts of East Asia for centuries as well, and similar face-whitening products are sold in China and Korea. For example, the Korean company Jutanhak sells Temptation White Up Creme. Even so, the selling of skin-whitening products is fiercely contested in places like India, where advertisements for skin-lightening products create heated debate.

13. "*Nihonjin no hada ishiki*" (The skin consciousness of Japanese), a Shiseido skin-whitening product information insert.

14. Metallic whiteners were still used until the Meiji period, when less harm-

ful replacements were sought. Lead was also used in American cosmetics in pre-FDA days.

15. Similarly, Maybelline sells a sunblock product in Asia called White Stay UV Base. Shiseido sells its whitening skin-care products in a few stores in the United States, such as Japanese-frequented shopping areas, but not often in high-end mainstream department stores.

16. These new eyebrow types are not the same thing as the traditional Chinese-derived body reading system, *ninsō* in Japanese, a divination method used to determine character and personality traits. In *ninsō* there are seven "eyebrow types," each indicating future prospects. For example, women who have eyebrows that resemble the Japanese syllabic character for *he* are said to like work better than marriage (Miller 1997).

# Chapter 2. Aesthetic Salons

1. Information on profit estimates and structure are from a market report compiled by the Société Centrale d'Echanges Techniques Internationaux (2004).

2. Both salons and spas are slippery businesses to pin down. Estimates of the number of day spas in the United States are unreliable as well, ranging from 840 to 3,000 (Benson and Elliott 1999).

3. In Japan, health clubs such as Tokyo Kenkōland and Healthy No Yū are more spa-like.

4. The advertisements were found in *Healing Retreats and Spas Magazine,* July/August 1998.

5. It is possible to continue Foucaudian self-monitoring and scientific management of weight at home with one of the recent fads in consumer products, the personal calorie counter.

6. Many of my ideas about the role of science in the beauty industry are mirrored in Postman's (1993) book about the role of technology in American culture.

7. Thanks to Debra Occhi for bringing this school to my attention.

8. Personal communication from Kazuko Watanabe of Kyoto Sangyo University, who has sadly passed away.

9. French words are also found in product names as well as bogus school names, such as the Ecole Internationale de Esthétique Française and the International French Aesthetic Academy (Kokusai Furansu Esuteteikku Gakukan).

10. French Antique's association with beauty is not unique to Japan. The plush office of a CEO at Estee Lauder's New York headquarters contains a voluptuous Louis XIV desk (Rybczynski 1986: 12).

11. The elevation of the aesthetic salon through naming is similar to Chicago beauty parlors' use of names that include the designations *castle, chalet, emporium, manor,* or *terrace* (Byrd 1982).

12. In their product description in brochures and sales catalogs, the manufacturers of the GX-99 Vibratory Endermatherapie System, for instance, stress that it requires no special license or certification to operate.

13. At another aesthetic salon, the salon manager even sent a letter to my university address afterward, insisting that although I would be departing Japan in less than a month, there was still time for me to have more and better esute treatments.

14. This contrasts with the high degree of sociability found in American beauty shop culture (Furman 1997; Nardini 1999) and in beauty salons in Cairo, Paris, and Casablanca (Ossman 2002).

15. Another machine with a similar function is the Paragon Skin Scanner System. This one drenches the customer's skin in black light and then reflects it in 3-D magnifying mirrors. According to the maker, the fluorescent light highlights imperfections and surface debris and thus helps sell more salon services and products.

16. The first historical record of cupping in China dates to the Jin Dynasty (265–420 AD); see Mi (2004).

17. Similar practices have been reported in other societies. The Greeks, Romans, other Mediterranean peoples, and indigenous North Americans used procedures similar to cupping. In Russia it is known as the "blood therapy."

18. This fad has spread to other areas of popular culture; for example, see New Age artist Miyashita Fumio's *Ying Yang Five Elements Music Therapy* CD (Biwa Inc.).

19. Skov (1996) also discusses the reformulation of orientalist stereotypes within the avant-garde Japanese fashion world.

20. Although green tea is much too ordinary to fully capture the fancy of most Japanese consumers as a beauty ingredient, it has entered America mainstream marketing as an element in products such as Dove Essential Nutrients Day Cream.

21. Some public baths in Japan still provide radon baths, as well as *denki buro* or the "electric bath," water with a mild electric charge.

## Chapter 3. Mammary Mania

1. Morohashi (1993) examined *Non No* and *Cosmopolitan* (the Japanese version) from the mid-1980s and did not see any advertisements for breast augmentation.

2. American hypermammary fixation reached a new high when the June 1996 issue of *Playboy* magazine featured the freakish basketball-sized breasts of a stripper who goes by the name "Twin Peaks."

3. In the poetic convention of pairing particular nouns with formulaic qualifiers (called "pillow words"), *tarachine no* came to refer to the mother, the parent, and sometimes even the father. I would like to thank Linda Chance for bringing some of this etymological background to my attention. Nonsexual associations found in other cultures are also quite common, as when they symbolize fertility and life. Dransart (1987) describes some Nasca ceramic beakers from Peru, dating to A.D. 100–800, on which images of life and death are commonly juxtaposed. Among excavated artifacts are beakers with flesh-colored rows of "mammiform protuberances" painted alongside warriors with their weapons and enemies. "Apparently, breasts, warfare and the taking of a trophy head are conceptually linked and expressed visually" (Dransart 1987: 68).

4. Baumslag and Michels (1995) trace this societal discomfort with breast-feeding partly to the aggressive advertising campaigns of formula manufacturers.

5. Not only are breasts flattened, but waists are filled in to get the desired shape. In her research on the Miss Cherry Blossom beauty contest in Honolulu, Chris Yano watched a kimono dresser using towels of varying thickness to fill in the waist, fill out the hollow of the small of the back, and slightly pad shoulders. Prior to the kimono fitting, she examined each contestant individually and told them how many towels they would need to bring for her to accomplish her magic work of "tubing" their bodies (personal communication).

6. A similar practice is found in the ancient Roman *strophia,* a chest-flattening band of cloth.

7. Orbaugh (2003) also writes about the emergence of the busty heroine.

8. According to both Haiken (1997: 247) and Byrne (1996a: 43), this is actually a decade later than when an American doctor named Kagan is said to have started injecting a form of silicone, Dow Corning 200 Fluid, into breasts. The fact that this date is earlier than their attributions of a 1950s invention of the practice in Japan is never explained.

9. For additional descriptions of the toxic effects of breast injections, see Miyoshi, Tomioka, and Kobayashi (1964) and Yoshida et al. (1996).

10. A common finding in the Japanese literature concerns cases of connective tissue disease, particularly the incidence of progressive systemic sclerosis from paraffin injections.

11. The transplant debate also hinges on the cultural definition of death (Ohnuki-Tierney 1994).

12. Woman interviewed by Kawazoe (1997: 51).

13. Reading the descriptions of some of the bust-up services and products also suggests that a certain degree of autoeroticism is covertly involved in their appeals. Advertisements frequently point out the physical response one might expect from using their goods. For example, they often include testimonies such as the claim by one user that the product is "soft and easy, with good-feeling stimulation."

14. Thanks to Jan Bardsley for sharing the Busteen ad with me. Frühstück (2003: 172) finds the same idea of education having a negative effect on girls' bodies in 1904.

15. Many of the bust-up products currently being sold have an uncanny resemblance to the "Princess Bust Developer" advertised in 1897 in the Sears, Roebuck, and Co. catalogue (Yalom 1997: 167–70). This is actually a set of items: a jar of cream, a bottle of lotion, and a bathroom plunger–like apparatus purported to be "new scientific help to nature."

16. Some of the products are indeed of French origin, although it is difficult to distinguish many of these from their Japanese clones. Examples are Decö Buste Eve Firming Gel and Creme, Lait Buste Bust Beauty Lotion and Gel, and Lierac Phytrel Bust Firmer Soluté.

17. McCombe (1995) has written a review of a few Barbie studies.

18. The first Barbies were actually manufactured in Japan, and then packaged for the market in California. Ruth Handler, Barbie's creator, sent the original de-

signs for the doll to Kokusai Boeki Kaisha, a Tokyo-based novelty maker. Another reason Japanese disliked Barbie was her "mean" foxlike face.

19. I thank A. Elizabeth Enciso for the *milagro* related to this chapter.

20. Thanks to George Tanabe for bringing this shrine to my attention.

21. There is a similar idea found among Ndembu, who believe the *mudyi* tree stands for human breast milk (Turner 1967).

## Chapter 4. Body Fashion and Beauty Etiquette

1. Some material in this chapter is based on Miller 2004b.

2. Distress over the shared shaver also relates to concepts of purity and ritual contamination from strangers.

3. Thanks to Roger Thomas for helping me locate this passage in Enchi's work.

4. This is similar to the older Chinese practice called "pulling the face," in which taut strings are twisted across the face in preparation for bridal makeup. A wonderful description of the preparation of a Taiwanese bride's face for wedding photography is found in Adrian (2003).

5. In the 1930s, when American cosmetologists started to offer certain types of facial services at beauty parlors, they upset the brotherhood of dermatologists. The dermatologists wanted to protect their domain and accused the beauty parlors of "practicing medicine illegally" (Fox and Lears 1983).

6. Pearls inserted under the skin of the penis are thought to increase potency and partner pleasure. Silicone beads are a common substitute for pearls.

7. While a desire for circumcising grows in Japan, Americans are beginning to question assumptions about its supposed benefits, and rates have dropped during recent decades from 90 percent of men to 64 percent (Lowen 1998).

8. A few people have told me that men's magazines sometimes carry advertisements for home circumcision kits made up of a sterile tissue cutter, antiseptic ointment, and instructions. However, I have never seen these and do not have any data on their use or efficacy.

9. According to Connell (2001), young women are also having cosmetic genital surgery done, ostensibly to boost self-confidence. The majority of the surgeries, sought by women in their twenties, involve labia reduction. Those who had the surgery say they want to look like the women they see in adult videos.

10. See also the article on eyelid surgery in *Time Asia* (2002).

11. This contrasts with Brownell's (2003) Chinese informants, who did not express any interest in the evolutionary history of physical traits such as eyelid shape.

12. Brownell (2003) also finds a variety of names for eye shapes in China.

## Chapter 5. Male Beauty Work

1. See *An An* (1999, 2000) for similar assessments.

2. The use of the address term *kun,* an intimate form that replaces *san* (Mr.),

is intended to establish the reader as a peer of the just-one-of-the-guys undergoing the esute treatment.

3. A preference for smooth chests appears to a limited extent in American youth culture and media as well. A journalist noted that *Men's Health* magazine had not had a hairy male chest on its cover since 1995 (Gomes 2001).

4. Decades ago the label *tsurutusru* was used to mean someone who is bald.

5. This anecdote is from a chapter on contrived female speech (Miller 2004a).

6. A news show once aired a special segment on the contents of junior and high school male students' bags. Reporters expected to find knives but instead pulled out oil-blotting papers, eyebrow-shaping kits, hair gel, and cologne (Carolyn Stevens, personal communication).

7. Frühstück (2003: 172) found that in the 1930s hormone products were pitched to men and women: to men for sexual problems and to women for beauty improvement and health issues.

8. The Itami assessment is from a conversation I had with him on October 17, 1997.

9. Sexual selection is one of the reasons Bovin (2001) offers as an explanation for the high value placed on male beauty among the Wodaabe of Niger, where men are taught to aspire to physical beauty and to wear makeup.

10. Thanks to Hiroko Hirakawa for helping me to frame these ideas.

## Chapter 6. The Well-Behaved Appetite

1. For other research on eating disorders and weight obsession among Japanese women, see Mukai, Crago, and Shisslak (1994) and Nakamura et al. (1999).

2. See Aoyama (1999) for more on women's writing about food.

3. Despite common assumptions to the contrary, the diet supplement industry in the United States is also unregulated and results in similarly dubious claims (*Consumer Reports* 2004).

4. Shiseido also created a "fat-burning" gel named Body Creator, made with pepper and grapefruit oil, which it claims will eliminate body fat without diet or exercise.

5. Many of the diets described here were discussed in *Can Cam Beauty* (1997b) and *Ranking Dai Suki!* (2000b). Additional diet aides and diet fads are described in Spielvogel (2003).

6. Interestingly, Hanihara (1999) claims that changes in the Japanese body shape are linked to modern diets. The formerly square Japanese jaw has become softer from chewing more animal fat and dairy foods, somewhat opposite of the Small Face Diet's principles.

7. Spielvogel (2003: 108–109) describes the use of the daily diary as a method for controlling and disciplining fitness club workers through the imposition of shared values and norms.

## Chapter 7. The Language of Esute

1. Versions of this chapter have been presented as conference papers at the American Anthropological Association Annual Meeting in San Francisco in 1996 and at the Midwest Conference on Asian Affairs in October 1996.

2. The widespread use of *up* in Japanese product names has resulted in its being emulated elsewhere in Asia; one can now find a Korean face makeup called "White Up" and a Chinese line of hair-care products from Sasa named "UP Ultraplus."

3. *Up* occurs in other nonbeauty product names as well. A perhaps unintended but felicitous nuance resulted when *up* was used on the package of Popchan-brand condoms, which said *tomodachi hakobu UP* ("Up and on the way to becoming friends"). An information section of *Can Cam Beauty* magazine is entitled "Step Up Information," and a psychological counseling service in Osaka goes by the name Self Up.

4. "Scientific" imagery is also a key staple of the American cosmetics industry. An early example was Estée Lauder's Swiss Performing Extract campaign (Tringal 2004: 36).

5. This seems to be the idea behind the Clinique line of cosmetics in the United States, which uses scrub green and chrome, colors associated with surgery.

6. For a discussion of marked-up photo-stickers or "graffiti photos" in girls' culture, see Miller (2003d, 2005).

7. For more on the use of *get* in Japanese, see Horie and Occhi (2001).

8. Stanlaw (2004) devotes a chapter to exploring the complex and creative use of multiple scripts in Japanese popular culture.

9. Japanese meta-consciousness about packaging and wrapping for commodities is also well known (Hendry 1994).

## Chapter 8. Esute Power

1. The euphemism *soap lady (sōpu redii)* is derived from *soapland (sōpu rando)*, the term for a brothel in a sauna setting.

2. A short evangelistic leaflet published by the New Life League in Saitama, Japan.

3. Beauty industries elsewhere are generally recession- and war-proof as well.

4 Slyomovic (1993) thought of American women's visits to spas in just this way. Of note is the increase in American "medical tourism," cosmetic surgery as part of an overseas travel package. See Andrews (2004).

5. Korean scholar Okpyo Moon of the Academy of Korean Studies is also investigating Japanese esute tourism to Korea.

6. In the early twenty-first century, the popularity of Korea extended to a huge fan following for Korean actor Bae Young-Jun, known as Yon-sama in Japan.

7. I brazenly pilfer Plath's (1966: 165) idea of "moral possibilism" as a springboard for my subheading.

8. Boone (1986) found this also in Mende conceptions of beauty.

# Bibliography

*Across.* 1989. "Otoko no taimō to sengo nihonjin" (Men's body hair and the post-war Japanese). *Across* (August): 47–61.

———. 1992. "Nijū-seiki no shika kyōsei" (Orthodontia in the twentieth century). *Across* (January): 78–85.

Adrian, Bonnie. 2003. *Framing the Bride: Globalizing Beauty and Romance in Taiwan's Bridal Industry.* Berkeley: University of California Press.

*Akita Sakigawa Shimbun.* 1996. "Otoko datte kirei ni" (Even men go after beauty). *Akita Sakigawa Shimbun,* 26 July.

Akiyama, T. 1958. "Basic problems of medical use of dimethylpolysiloxane." *Japan Journal of Plastic Reconstructive Surgery* 1: 244.

Allison, Anne. 1996. *Permitted and Prohibited Desires: Mothers, Comics, and Censorship in Japan.* Boulder, CO: Westview Press.

———. 1998. "Cutting the fringes: Pubic hair at the margins of Japanese censorship laws." In *Hair: Its Power and Meaning in Asian Cultures,* edited by A. Hiltebeitel and B. D. Miller, 195–217. New York: State University of New York Press.

Amanuma Kaoru. 1987. *"Gambari" no kōzō* (The structure of "endurance"). Tokyo: Yoshikawa Kōbundō.

American Society for Aesthetic Plastic Surgery. 2004. "Silicone Implants Press Kit: ASPS Supports FDA Regulatory Process Regarding Silicone Breast Implants." Arlington Heights, IL: American Society for Aesthetic Plastic Surgery.

*An An.* 1997. "An An ga erabu dakitai otoko, dakaretai otoko" (Selected by *An An* subscribers, men they want to embrace, men they want to be embraced by). *An An,* 20 June, 10–25.

———. 1999. "Suki na otoko, kirai na otoko" (Men we like, men we hate). *An An,* 25 June, 54.

———. 2000. "Dokusha ga eranda suki na otoko, kirai na otoko" (Readers' choice for men we like, men we hate). *An An,* 7 August, 53–67.

Anderson, Judith L. 1988. "Comment: Breasts, hips, and buttocks revisited." *Ethnology and Sociobiology* 9: 319–24.

Andrews, Michelle. 2004. "Vacation makeovers." *U.S. News and World Report,* 19 January, D2–D4.

Aoki, R., K. Mitsuhashi, and H. Hyakusoku. 1997. "Immediate reaugmentation of the breasts using bilaterally divided TRAM flaps after removing injected silicone gel and granulomas." *Aesthetic Plastic Surgery* 21 (4): 276–79.

Aoyama, Tomoko. 1999. "Food and gender in contemporary Japanese women's literature." *U.S.-Japan Women's Journal* 17: 111–36.

Appadurai, Arjun. 1991. "Global ethnoscapes: Notes and queries for a transnational anthropology." In *Recapturing Anthropology: Working in the Present,* edited by R. Fox, 190–216. Santa Fe, NM: School of American Research Press.

———. 1996. *Modernity at Large: Cultural Dimensions of Globalization.* Minneapolis: University of Minnesota Press.

Applbaum, Kalman. 1995. "Marriage with the proper stranger: Arranged marriage in metropolitan Japan." *Ethnology* 34: 37–51.

*Apple Tsūshin.* 1990. "Jotai kaibō jikenshitsu" (Laboratory analysis of woman's body). *Apple Tsūshin* (June): 87–95.

*Asahi Shimbun.* 1997a. "Karada de shuchō? Bodii āto" (Affirmation through the body? Body art). *Asahi Shimbun,* 26 August.

———. 1997b. "Dansei mo aiyō abura torigami" (Men also habitually use oil-blotting paper). *Asahi Shimbun,* 4 September.

———. 1997c. "Datsumō esute de higai" (Casualties from electrolysis treatments). *Asahi Shimbun,* 25 August.

———. 1998a. "'98 Tōkyo kyūji dēta fairu" (98 Tokyo [high school] ballplayers' data file). *Asahi Shimbun,* 14 July.

———. 1998b. "Kawaii otoko ga tsuide kureru no yo" (Cute boys pour drinks for us). *Asahi Shimbun,* 18 December.

———. 1998c. "Chūkōnen ni ninki" (Popular with the middle-aged). *Asahi Shimbun,* 16 April.

———. 1998d. "Biyō seikei" (Aesthetic surgery). *Asahi Shimbun,* 21 May.

———. 1999a. "Kirei na otoko ni naru" (In order to become a beautiful man). *Asahi Shimbun,* 10 July.

———. 1999b. "Boku, hanayome yori kirei desu" (Me, I'm more beautiful than my bride). *Asahi Shimbun,* 10 June.

———. 1999c. "Otoku o kirei ni hirogaru biyō shijō" (The expanding beauty market for male beauty work). *Asahi Shimbun,* 5 June.

———. 2002. *Japan Almanac 2003.* Tokyo: Asahi Shimbun Publishing Co.

———. 2003. *Asahi kiiwādo 2003* (Asahi keywords 2003). Tokyo: Asahi Shimbun Publishing Co.

Asami Yoshiyasu. 1997. *Basuto appu no senmon kurinikku* (Bust-up special clinic). Tokyo: Gendai Shorin.

Ashikari, Mikiko. 2003. "Urban middle-class Japanese women and their white faces: Gender, ideology and representation." *Ethos* 31 (1): 3–37.

Baba Junko. 1997. "Sekai no esute o tanoshimu" (Let's enjoy the world's body aesthetics). *Chérie* 1 (Spring): 16–19.

Bacon, Alice Mabel. 1891. *Japanese Girls and Women*. London: Gay and Bird. Revised and enlarged edition published 1919, Boston: Houghton, Mifflin.

Balsamo, Anne. 1996. *Technologies of the Gendered Body*. Durham, NC: Duke University Press.

Barber, Benjamin. 1995. *Jihad vs. McWorld*. New York: Times Books.

Baumslag, Naomi, and Dia Michels. 1995. *Milk, Money, and Madness: The Culture and Politics of Breastfeeding*. Westport, CT: Greenwood Publishing Group.

Bellah, Robert. 1957. *Tokugawa Religion*. New York: Free Press.

———, ed. 1965. *Religion and Progress in Modern Asia*. New York: Free Press.

Benson, Bob, and Melinda Elliott. 1999. "The massage industry mosaic." *Massage and Bodywork* (February/March): 76–124.

Bestor, Theodore. 1989. *Neighborhood Tokyo*. Stanford, CA: Stanford University Press.

*Bidan*. 1997a. "Pōchi no naka no byūtii guzzu o misete kure!" (Show me what beauty goods you have inside the pouch!). *Bidan*, no. 7 (August): 30–31.

———. 1997b. "Mayu mēku no tatsujin daishūgō" (Gathering of experts on eyebrow shaping). *Bidan*, no. 7 (August): 35–38.

———. 1997c. Horoscope. *Bidan*, no. 6 (July): 118.

———. 1997d. Editorial advertisement. *Bidan*, no. 6 (July): 157.

———. 1997e. Editorial advertisement. *Bidan*, no. 7 (August): 143.

Blumhagen, Dan. 1979. "The doctor's white coat: The image of the physician in modern America." *Annals of Internal Medicine* 91: 111–16.

Boone, Sylvia A. 1986. *Radiance from the Waters: Ideals of Feminine Beauty in Mende Art*. New Haven, CT: Yale University Press.

Bordo, Susan. 1985. "Anorexia nervosa: Psychopathology as the crystallization of culture." *Philosophical Forum* 17 (2): 73–103.

———. 1993. *Unbearable Weight: Feminism, Western Culture, and the Body*. Berkeley: University of California Press.

———. 1997. *Twilight Zone: The Hidden Life of Cultural Images from Plato to OJ*. Berkeley: University of California Press.

———. 1999. "Feminism, Foucault, and the politics of the body." In *Feminist Theory and the Body*, edited by J. Price and M. Shildrick, 246–57. New York: Routledge.

Bornoff, Nicholas. 1991. *Pink Samurai: Love, Marriage and Sex in Contemporary Japan*. New York: Pocket Books.

*Bounce*. 1999. "Hitoe's 57 Move." *Bounce*, no. 200 (July): 120–22.

Bourdieu, Pierre. 1984. *Distinction: A Social Critique of the Judgement of Taste*. Translated by Richard Nice. London: Routledge.

———. 1991. *Language and Symbolic Power*. Translated by Gino Raymond and Matthew Adamson. Cambridge: Polity Press.

Bovin, Mette. 2001. *Nomads Who Cultivate Beauty: Wodaabe Dances and Visual Arts in Niger*. Uppsala, Sweden: Nordiska Afrikainstitutet (Nordic Africa Institute).

Brown, Kendall H. 2001. "Flowers of Taishō." In *Taishō Chic: Japanese Modernity, Nostalgia and Deco,* edited by K. Brown and S. Minichiello, 17–28. Seattle: University of Washington Press.

Brownell, Susan. 2003. "The 'Oriental eye': The legacy of nineteenth-century western racism in contemporary Chinese cosmetic surgery." Paper presented at the American Anthropological Association, Chicago, November.

Bruch, Hilde. 1978. *The Golden Cage: The Enigma of Anorexia Nervosa.* New York: Vintage.

Brumberg, Joan Jacobs. 1997. *The Body Project: An Intimate History of American Girls.* New York: Vintage Books.

Buruma, Ian. 1984. *Behind the Mask.* New York: Penguin Books.

Butler, Judith. 1990. *Gender Trouble.* New York: Routledge.

Butler, Steven. 1998. "Japan's baby bust: Are unmarried 30-somethings 'parasites' on society?" *U.S. News & World Report,* 5 October, 42–44.

Byrd, Patricia. 1982. "The Hairbender Beauty Salon de Paris of Ethel." *American Speech* 57 (3): 183–89.

Byrne, John A. 1996a. *Informed Consent.* New York: McGraw Hill.

———. 1996b. "Beauty and the breast: How industry sold implants to women." *MS Magazine* (June): 45–46.

Campbell, Bernard G. 1970. *Human Evolution: An Introduction to Man's Adaptation.* Chicago: Aldine.

*Can Cam.* 1999. "Shitagi dō shimashō!?" (What to do about underwear!?). *Can Cam* (July): 113–20.

*Can Cam Beauty.* 1996. "Saizu ga tadashii" (The size is right). *Can Cam Beauty* (June): 400.

———. 1997a. "Katachi no ii basuto ni naru" (To get a nice-shaped bust). *Can Cam Beauty* (Summer): 59–69.

———. 1997b. "Tariki hongan daietto vs. jiryoku tassei daietto" (Reliance on the outside diets vs. self-achievement diets). *Can Cam Beauty* (Summer): 163–74.

———. 1997c. "Kirei ni naru gokuraku Bari esute" (Become beautiful with Bali paradise *esute*). *Can Cam Beauty* (Summer): special pull-out section.

Cant, J. G. H. 1981. "Hypothesis for the evolution of human breasts and buttocks." *American Naturalist* 117: 199–204.

Carlson, Richard. 1999. *Chiisai koto ni kuyokuyo surunai!* (Don't sweat the small stuff). Translated by M. Ozawa. Tokyo: Sanmaku Shuppan.

Casal, U. A. 1966. "Japanese cosmetics and teeth blackening." *Transactions of the Asiatic Society of Japan* 9: 5–27.

Caudill, William, and David W. Plath. 1966. "Who sleeps by whom? Parent-child involvement in urban Japanese families." *Psychiatry* 29: 344–66.

Center for Science in the Public Interest. 1998. "Functional foods: Public health boon or 21st century quackery." The International Association of Consumer Food Organizations Report. Electronic document, www.cspinet.org/reports/functional-foods/japan-market.html [accessed January 2001].

Chapkis, Wendy. 1986. *Beauty Secrets: Women and the Politics of Appearance.* Boston: South End Press.

Chapman, Rowena. 1988. "The great pretender: Variations on the New Man theme." In *Male Order: Unwrapping Masculinity,* edited by R. Chapman and J. Rutherford, 225–48. London: Lawrence and Wishart.

Chernin, Kim. 1981. *The Obsession: Reflections on the Tyranny of Slenderness.* New York: Harper and Row.

Cherry, Kittredge. 1987. *Womansword: What Japanese Words Say about Women.* Tokyo: Kodansha International.

Chow, Rey. 1995. *Primitive Passions: Visuality, Sexuality, Ethnography, and Contemporary Chinese Cinema.* New York: Columbia University Press.

Clammer, John. 1995. "Consuming bodies: Constructing and representing the female body in contemporary Japanese print media." In *Women, Media and Consumption in Japan,* edited by L. Skov and B. Moeran, 197–219. Honolulu: University of Hawai'i Press.

———. 1997. *Contemporary Urban Japan: A Sociology of Consumption.* Oxford: Blackwell.

Clark, Scott. 1994. *Japan: A View from the Bath.* Honolulu: University of Hawai'i Press.

CNN. 2004. "Japan cashes in on pretty boys." Aired 11 March 2004.

Cohen, Colleen Ballerino, Richard Wilk, and Beverly Stoeltje, eds. 1996. *Beauty Queens on the Global Stage: Gender, Contests, and Power.* New York: Routledge.

Condry, Ian. 2000. "The social production of difference: Imitation and authenticity in Japanese rap music." In *Transactions, Transgressions, Transformations: American Culture in Western Europe and Japan,* edited by U. Poiger and H. Fehrenbach, 166–84. New York: Berghan Books.

Connell, Ryann. 2001. "Plastic surgery gives lip service to women's worries." *Mainichi Interactive Wai Wai,* 5 May. Electronic document, mdn.mainichi .co.jp/waiwai/face/index.html [accessed July 2003].

———. 2004. "Men's beauty clinics—Enough to make you pull your hair out." *Mainichi Interactive Wai Wai,* 3 June. Electronic document, http://mdn.mainichi .co.jp/waiwai/0406/0603mensesthe.html [accessed December 2004].

Constantine, Peter. 1994. *Japanese Slang Uncensored.* Tokyo: Yenbooks.

*Consumer Reports.* 2004. "Dangerous supplements." *Consumer Reports* (May): 12–17.

Corson, Richard. 1972. *Fashions in Makeup: From Ancient to Modern Times.* New York: Universe Books.

Cortazzi, Hugh. 2001. "The curse of shikata ga nai." *Japan Times,* 16 April.

Counihan, Carole M. 1999. *The Anthropology of Food and Body: Gender, Meaning, and Power.* New York: Routledge.

Cowley, Geoffrey. 1996. "The biology of beauty." *Newsweek,* 3 June, 60–69.

Creighton, Millie. 1995. "Imaging the Other in Japanese advertising campaigns." In *Occidentalism: Images of the West,* edited by J. G. Carrier, 135–60. Oxford: Clarendon Press.

———. 1997. "Soto others and uchi others: Imaging racial diversity, imaging homogenous Japan." In *Japan's Minorities: The Illusion of Homogeneity,* edited by M. Weiner, 211–38. New York: Routledge.

Cullen, Lisa. 2002. "Changing faces." *Time Asia* 160, no. 4 (5 August).

*Daily Yomiuri.* 1992. "Ministry likely to ban use of breast silicone." *Daily Yomiuri,* 16 June.

Dalby, Liza. 1983. *Geisha.* Berkeley: University of California Press.

Darwin, Charles. 1859. *On the Origin of Species by Means of Natural Selection.* London: John Murray.

Datamonitor. 2003. "Make-Up in Japan Industry Profile." Unpublished report. Williamstown, MA: MindBranch.

Davenport, William. 1976. "Sex in cross-cultural perspective." In *Human Sexuality in Four Perspectives,* edited by F. Beach, 113–63. Baltimore, MD: Johns Hopkins University Press.

Davis, Kathy. 1995. *Reshaping the Female Body: The Dilemma of Cosmetic Surgery.* New York: Routledge.

De Beauvoir, Simone. 1968. *The Second Sex.* New York: Bantam Books.

Diamond, Irene, and Lee Quinby, eds. 1988. *Feminism and Foucault: Reflections on Resistance.* Boston: Northeastern University Press.

Diamond, Jared. 1992. *The Third Chimpanzee: The Evolution and Future of the Human Animal.* New York: HarperCollins.

Dikötter, Frank. 1998. "Hairy barbarians, furry primates, and wild men: Medical science and cultural representations of hair in China." In *Hair: Its Power and Meaning in Asian Cultures,* edited by A. Hiltebeitel and B. D. Miller, 51–74. New York: State University of New York Press.

Dore, Ronald. 1973. *City Life in Japan: A Study of a Tokyo Ward.* Berkeley: University of California Press.

Douglas, Susan J. 1994. *Where the Girls Are: Growing Up Female with the Mass Media.* New York: Time Books.

Downs, James F. 1990. "Nudity in Japanese visual media." *Archives of Sexual Behavior* 19: 583–94.

Dransart, Peggy. 1987. "Women and ritual conflict in Inka society." In *Images of Women in Peace and War: Cross-Cultural and Historical Perspectives,* edited by S. Macdonald, P. Holden, and S. Ardener, 62–77. Madison: University of Wisconsin Press.

Dutton, Kenneth. 1995. *The Perfectible Body: The Western Ideal of Male Physical Development.* New York: Continuum.

Eck, Diana. 1996. *Darśán: Seeing the Divine Image in India.* New York: Columbia University Press.

Edwards, Tim. 1997. *Men in the Mirror: Men's Fashion, Masculinity, and Consumer Society.* London: Cassell.

Edwards, Walter. 1989. *Modern Japan through Its Weddings.* Stanford, CA: Stanford University Press.

Efron, Sonni. 1997. "Women's eating disorders go global." *Los Angeles Times,* 18 October.

*Egg.* 2000. "Eroero dai kenkyū" (Major research on the erotic). *Egg,* no. 46 (August): 50–54.

Enchi Fumiko. 1997. *Hanakui uba* (The flower-eating hag). Tokyo: Bungei Bunko.

Endo, Shusaku. 1995. *The Sea and Poison (Umi to dokuyaku)*. First published 1958. Translated by Michael Gallagher. London: Peter Owen Publishing.

Erlich, Julie. 1995. "Giving drugs a good name." *New York Times Magazine,* 3 September, 36–37.

Ewing, Elizabeth. 1971. *Fashion in Underwear.* London: B. T. Batsford.

———. 1978. *Dress and Undress: A History of Women's Underwear.* New York: Drama Book Specialists.

Fallon, April. 1990. "Culture in the mirror: Sociocultural determinants of body image." In *Body-Images: Development, Deviance and Change,* edited by T. Cash and T. Pruzinsky, 80–109. New York: Guilford Press.

Featherstone, Mike. 1991. "The body in consumer culture." In *The Body: Social Process and Cultural Theory,* edited by M. Hepworth, B. Turner, and M. Featherstone, 170–96. London: Sage Publications.

Fetters, Michael. 1997. "Cultural clashes: Japanese patients and U.S. maternity care." *Journal of the International Institute* 4 (2) (Winter). Electronic document, www.umich.edu/~iinet/journal/vol4no2/medcult.html#top [accessed March 2000].

Fields, George. 1985. *From Bonsai to Levis.* New York: Mentor Books.

*Fine Boys.* 1997. "Otoko datte neiru o tsukereba kakkoi no da" (If men do their nails, it's cool!). *Fine Boys,* no. 137 (September): 107.

———. 1998. "Bokura no raifusutairu hakushō" (White paper on our lifestyles). *Fine Boys,* no. 142 (February): 183–90.

*Fine Surf & Street Magazine.* 1999a. "Ikasho jibun no karada ga naoseru to shitara, doko o dochi suru?"(If you could correct one place on your body, where would you do what?). *Fine Surf & Street Magazine,* no. 251 (May): 42.

———. 1999b. "Kono natsu watashi wa Miss Surf!" (This summer I'm gonna be Miss Surf!). *Fine Surf & Street Magazine,* no. 251 (May): 146–47.

———. 1999c. "Hayashi mono hyaku nin anketto" (Quick survey of 100 people). *Fine Surf & Street Magazine,* no. 251 (May): 39–43.

Ford, Clellan S., and Frank A. Beach. 1951. *Patterns of Sexual Behavior.* New York: Harper and Row.

Foucault, Michel. 1978. *The History of Sexuality.* Translated by R. Hurley. Harmondsworth: Penguin.

Fox, Richard Wrightman, and T. Jackson Lears, eds. 1983. *The Culture of Consumption: Critical Essays in American History, 1880–1980.* New York: Pantheon Books.

Fraser, James, Steven Heller, and Seymour Chwast. 1996. *Japan Modern: Graphic Design between the Wars.* San Francisco: Chronicle Books.

Friedan, Betty. 1982. *The Feminine Mystique.* First published in 1963. London: Penguin Books.

Frühstück, Sabine. 2000. "Treating the body as a commodity: 'Body projects' in contemporary Japan." In *Consumption and Material Culture in Contemporary Japan,* edited by M. Ashkenazi and J. Clammer, 143–62. London: Kegan Paul International.

———. 2003. *Colonizing Sex: Sexology and Social Control in Modern Japan.* Berkeley: University of California Press.

Fujimoto, Yukari. 2004. "Transgender: Female hermaphrodites and male androgynes." *U.S.- Japan Women's Journal* 27: 36–117.

Furman, Frida Kerner. 1997. *Facing the Mirror: Older Women and Beauty Shop Culture*. New York: Routledge.

Fuss, Diana. 1995. "Fashion and the homospectatorial look." In *Identities*, edited by K. A. Appiah and H. L. Gates, Jr., 90–110. Chicago: University of Chicago Press.

Gakken. 2000. *Menzu body manyuaru: Face and Body Grade Up Manual for Men* (Men's body manual: Face and body grade up manual for men). Tokyo: Gakken.

Galer, Sara. 1999. "Why is thin so in?" *Tokyo Journal* 18 (212): 13–18.

Gallup, Gordon G. 1982. "Permanent breast enlargement in human females: A sociobiological analysis." *Journal of Human Evolution* 11: 597–601.

Garon, Sheldon. 1997. *Molding Japanese Minds: The State in Everyday Life*. Princeton, NJ: Princeton University Press.

Gavenas, Mary Lisa. 2002. *Color Stories: Behind the Scenes of America's Billion-Dollar Beauty Industry*. New York: Simon & Schuster.

Giddens, Anthony. 1991. *Modernity and Self-Identity: Self and Society in the Late Modern Age*. Stanford, CA: Stanford University Press.

Gillmore, David. 1994. "The beauty of the beast: Male body imagery in anthropological perspective." In *The Good Body: Aestheticism in Contemporary Culture*, edited by M. G. Winkler and L. B. Cole, 191–214. New Haven, CT: Yale University Press.

Gilman, Sander L. 1999. *Making the Body Beautiful: A Cultural History of Aesthetic Surgery*. Princeton, NJ: Princeton University Press.

Goldman, Robert. 1992. *Reading Ads Socially*. New York: Routledge.

Goldstein-Gidoni, Ofra. 1997. *Packaged Japaneseness: Weddings, Business and Brides*. Honolulu: University of Hawai'i Press.

———. 1999. "Kimono and the construction of gendered and cultural identities." *Ethnology* 38: 351–70.

———. 2001. "The making and marking of the 'Japanese' and the 'Western' in Japanese contemporary material culture." *Journal of Material Culture* 6 (1): 67–90.

Goldwyn, Robert M. 1980. "The paraffin story." *Plastic and Reconstructive Surgery* 65 (4): 517–24.

Gomes, Lee. 2001. "Chest shaving is going mainstream." *Wall Street Journal*, 5 September.

Gottdiener, Marc. 1997. *The Theming of America: Dreams, Visions and Commercial Space*. Boulder, CO: Westview Press.

Gray, Blake. 1997. "The *chaptsu* syndrome." *Mangajin*, no. 66: 12–16.

Greenfeld, Karl Taro. 1994. *Speed Tribe: Days and Nights with Japan's Next Generation*. New York: HarperCollins.

Greer, Germaine. 1970. *The Female Eunuch*. New York: McGraw Hill.

Gumpert, Lynn, ed. 2000. *Face to Face: Shiseido and the Manufacture of Beauty*. New York: New York University Press.

Haarman, Harald. 1989. *Symbolic Values of Foreign Language Use.* Berlin: Mouton de Gruyter.

Haiken, Elizabeth. 1997. *Venus Envy: A History of Cosmetic Surgery.* Baltimore, MD: Johns Hopkins University Press.

Hakuhōdo Institute of Life and Living. 1987. *Jiryū wa joryū* (Women's trends are trends of the times). Tokyo: Nihon Keizai Shimbunsha.

Halberstam, Judith. 1999. "F2M: The making of female masculinity." In *Feminist Theory and the Body,* edited by J. Price and M. Shildrick, 125–33. New York: Routledge.

Hall, Christine Iijima. 1995. "Asian eyes: Body image and eating disorders of Asian and Asian American women." *Eating Disorders: The Journal of Treatment and Prevention* 3 (1): 8–19.

Hall, Stuart. 1977. "Culture, the media and the 'ideological effect.'" In *Mass Communication and Society,* edited by J. Curran, M. Gurevitch, and J. Woollacott, 315–48. London: Sage.

Hamanaka, Shinji, and Amy Reigle Newland. 2000. *The Female Image: Twentieth Century Prints of Japanese Beauties.* Leiden: Hotei Publishing.

Hamilton, M. E. 1984. "Revising evolutionary narrative: A consideration of alternative assumptions about sexual selection and competition for males." *American Anthropologist* 86 (3): 651–62.

Handler, Richard, and Jocelyn Linnekin. 1984. "Tradition, genuine or spurious." *Journal of American Folklore* 97 (385): 273–90.

Hanihara Kasurō. 1999. *Nihonjin no kao: Kogao, bijingao wa shinka na no ka* (The Japanese face: Has there been a change to thinner faces, beautiful faces?). Tokyo: Kōdansha, Sophia Books.

Hannerz, Ulf. 1987. "The world in creolisation." *Africa* 57 (4): 546–59.

Hansen, Joseph, and Evelyn Reed. 1986. *Cosmetics, Fashions, and the Exploitation of Women.* New York: Pathfinders Press.

Hashimoto, Akiko. 2004. "Culture, power, and the discourse of filial piety in Japan." In *Filial Piety: Practice and Discourse in Contemporary East Asia,* edited by C. Ikels, 182–97. Stanford, CA: Stanford University Press.

Hashimoto Osamu. 1994. *Bidan e no resson* (Lessons for beautiful men). Tokyo: Chūō Kōronsha.

Hebdige, Dick. 1979. *Subculture: The Meaning of Style.* London: Routledge.

Hendry, Joy. 1994. *Wrapping Culture: Politeness, Presentation, and Power in Japan and Other Societies.* Oxford: Clarendon Press.

Hickey, Gary. 1998. *Beauty and Desire in Edo Period Japan.* Canberra: National Gallery of Australia.

Higa, Masanori. 1979. "Sociolinguistic aspects of word-borrowing." In *Sociolinguistic Studies in Language Contact,* edited by W. Mackey and J. Ornstein, 277–94. The Hague: Mouton.

Higgins, Beth. 1984. "Office lady? Base-up? Thinking about Japanese English." *Eigo Kyōiku* 32 (11): 29–31.

Hiltebeitel, Alf, and Barbara D. Miller, eds. 1998. *Hair: Its Power and Meaning in Asian Cultures.* New York: State University of New York Press.

Hirota, Akiko. 1997. "The *Tale of Genji:* From Heian classic to Heisei comic." *Journal of Popular Culture* 31 (2): 29–68.

*Hokkoku Shimbun.* 1995. "Edo mo Meiji mo gendai mo bijin no kijun kawaranai" (During the Edo period, the Meiji period, and even now, beauty criteria are unchanged). *Hokkoku Shimbun,* 16 May.

Hollander, Anne. 1993. *Seeing through Clothes.* Berkeley: University of California Press.

Hooks, Bell. 1995. "Madonna: Plantation mistress or soul sister." Reprinted in *Rock She Wrote: Women Write about Rock, Pop, and Rap,* edited by E. McDonnell and A. Powers, 318–25. New York: Cooper Square Press.

Horie, Kaoru, and Debra J. Occhi. 2001. "Cognitive linguistics meets language contact: A case study of getto-suru in Japanese." In *Cognitive-Functional Linguistics in an East Asian Context,* edited by S. Sato and K. Horie, 13–34. Tokyo: Kurosio Publishers.

Horrocks, Roger. 1995. *Male Myths and Icons: Masculinity in Popular Culture.* New York: St. Martin's Press.

Horvat, Andrew. 1970. "On the uses of useless words." *Japan Quarterly* 18 (3): 324–26.

Howes, David, ed. 1996. *Cross-Cultural Consumption: Global Markets, Local Realities.* London: Routledge.

Hrdy, Sarah Blaffer. 1986. "Empathy, polyandry, and the myth of the coy female." In *Feminist Approaches to Science,* edited by R. Bleiser, 119–46. New York: Pergamon.

Hurley, Dan. 2004. "With new science, hair restoration improves." *New York Times,* 15 June.

Iigarashi, Eimi. 2002. "Expensive face creams worth their weight in gold." *Mainichi Shimbun,* 13 July.

Ikeda Riyoko. 1972. *Berusaiyu no bara* (The rose of Versailles). Tokyo: Shūeisha.

Ikegami, Naoki. 1989. "Health technology development in Japan." *Technology Assessment in Health Care* 4: 239–54.

Imamura I. 2000. "Kakkoii koto wa, nante kakko waruin darō" (Coolness can somehow be unhip). *J-Pop Hikyō* 479: 48.

Inoue, Mariko. 1998. "The gaze of the café waitress: From selling eroticism to construing autonomy." *U.S.-Japan Women's Journal* 15: 78–106.

InterNet Bankruptcy Library. 2000. Troubled Company Reporter: Asia Pacific 3, no. 249 (22 December 2000). Electronic document, http://bankrupt.com/TCRAP_Public/001222.MBX [accessed June 2003].

Ishino Hiroshi. 1985. "Yokomoji ga minna no mono ni natta" (The roman alphabet now belongs to everyone). *Gengo* 17 (9): 38–44.

Itoh, Kyoko. 1996. "Seizing control of your facial destiny." *Japan Times.* Electronic document, www/japantimes.co.jp/ [accessed July 1999].

———. 1997. "High price to pay for smooth skin." *Japan Times,* 22 May.

Itō Kimio. 1993. *"Otokorashisa" no yukue: Dansei bunka no bunkashakaigaku* (The location of "manliness": The cultural sociology of male culture). Tokyo: Shinyōsha.

Ivy, Marilyn. 1988. "Tradition and difference in the Japanese mass media." *Public Culture Bulletin* 1 (1): 21–29.

Iwabuchi, Koichi. 2002. *Recentering Globalization: Popular Culture and Japanese Transnationalism.* Durham, NC: Duke University Press.

Izbicki, Joanne. 1997. "The shape of freedom: The female body in post-surrender Japanese cinema." *U.S.-Japan Women's Journal* 12: 109–53.

*Japan Echo.* 1999. "Karaoke diet: Singing your way to slimness." *Japan Echo,* 23 July.

Japan External Trade Organization. 2003. "Market Information: Cosmetics." Electronic document, www.jetro.go.jp/ec/e/market/category6.html [accessed July 2004].

*Japan Now.* 2000. "Birth rate still declining." *Japan Now,* 4 February, 4.

Japan Soap and Detergent Association. 2004. "45th Clean Survey No. 18." Electronic document, http://64.233.161.104/search?q=cache:1Kt1lCIXO1IJ:www.jsda.org/e_news19.html+Japan+aesthetic+salon&hl=en&ie=UTF-8 [accessed August 2004].

*Japan Times.* 1997. "Girls' average weight on the decline, data shows." *Japan Times,* 9 December.

———. 2002. "Shaver demanded for detainees." *Japan Times,* 3 July.

Jenkins, Emily. 1998. *Tongue First: Adventurers in Physical Culture.* New York: Henry Holt.

Jolivet, Muriel. 1997. *Japan: The Childless Society?* Translated by Anne-Marie Glasheen. London: Routledge.

*Junion.* 2003. "2003 nen watashitachi no 'Besuto obu ii otoko' rankingu daihappyō" (Grand presentation of our ranking of the "best of the good guys" for the year 2003). *Junion* (March): 21–55.

Kagan, Harvey. 1963. "Sakurai injectable silicone formula." *Archives of Otolaryngology* 78: 663–68.

Kajihara Chion. 1998. *Kirei ni naritai itsusu no taipu* (Five types who want to become beautiful). Tokyo: Nesco.

Kashiwagi Hiroshi. 1987. *Shōzō no naka no kenryoku* (Power in the portraits). Tokyo: Heibonsha.

Kasulis, Thomas P. 1993. "The body—Japanese style." In *Self as Body in Asian Theory and Practice,* edited by T. P. Kasulis, 299–319. New York: State University of New York Press.

Katayama, Kazumichi. 1996. "The Japanese as an Asia-Pacific population." In *Multicultural Japan: Palaeolithic to Postmodern,* edited by D. Denoon, M. Hudson, G. McCormack, and T. Morris-Suzuki, 19–30. Cambridge: Cambridge University Press.

Kaw, Eugenia. 1993. "Medicalization of racial features: Asian American women and cosmetic surgery." *Medical Anthropology Quarterly* 7 (1): 74–89.

Kawashima, Terry. 2002. "Seeing faces, making races: Challenging visual tropes of racial difference." *Meridians* 3 (1): 161–90.

Kawazoe, Hiroko. 1997. An Anthropological Study of Contemporary Mutilation: A Case Study of Aesthetic Surgery in Japan. M.A. thesis, Tokyo University of Foreign Studies.

———. 2004. "Futsū o nozomu no hito tachi" (People who aspire to be "ordinary"). In *Gendai iro no minzoku-shi* (Ethnographic research in contemporary medicine), edited by T. Uchitakuya, M. Ikuko, and T. Hideo, 87–121. Tokyo: Akashi Shoten.

Keene, Donald. 1969. *The Japanese Discovery of Europe, 1720–1830*. Stanford, CA: Stanford University Press.

Keizai Yakumu Torihiki Tekiseika Kenkyūkai. 1994. *Sābisu keiyaku 110-ban* (Service contracts number 110). Tokyo: Tsūshō Sangyō Chōsakai Shuppanbu.

Kelly, William. 1986. "Rationalization and nostalgia: Cultural dynamics of new middle-class Japan." *American Ethnologist* 13 (4): 603–18.

Kelsky, Karen. 2001. *Women on the Verge: Japanese Women, Western Dreams*. Durham, NC: Duke University Press.

Kenkō Shimbunsha. 1994. *Basuto appu no hiketsu* (The key to bust-up). Tokyo: Bunbun Shobō.

Kilbourne, Jean. 1999. *Deadly Persuasion: Why Women and Girls Must Fight the Addictive Power of Advertising*. New York: Free Press.

Kinmouth, Earl H. 1981. *The Self Made Man in Meiji Japanese Thought: From Samurai to Salary Man*. Berkeley: University of California Press.

Kinsella, Sharon. 1995. "Cuties in Japan." In *Women, Media and Consumption in Japan*, edited by L. Skov and B. Moeran, 220–54. Honolulu: University of Hawai'i Press.

———. 2002. "What's behind the fetishism of Japanese school uniforms." *Fashion Theory* 6 (1): 1–24.

———. 2005. "Black faces, witches, and racism against girls." In *Bad Girls of Japan*, edited by L. Miller and J. Bardsley, 143–57. New York: Palgrave Macmillan.

Kiriike, N., T. Nagata, M. Tanaka, S. Nishiwaki, N. Takeuchi, and Y. Kawakita. 1988. "Prevalence of binge-eating and bulimia among adolescent women in Japan." *Psychiatry Research* 26: 163–69.

Klippensteen, Kate, and Everett Brown. 2000. *Ganguro Girls: The Japanese "Black Face"* Budapest: Könemann.

Kobayashi, S., H. Iwase, S. Karamatsu, A. Masaoka, and T. Nakamura. 1988. "A case of stromal sarcoma of the breast occurring after augmentation mammoplasty." *Japanese Journal of Cancer Clinics* 34 (4): 467–72.

Kobayashi Yoshinori. 1998. *Sensō ron* (An essay on war). Tokyo: Gentōsha.

Kojima, Kasuo. 1999. "Pepper diet burning up many young women." *Mainichi Shimbun,* 15 October.

Kokumin Seikatsu Center. 1992. *Esuteteikku toraburu* (Aesthetics trouble). Tokyo: Kokumin Seikatsu Center.

Komoto, Shigekazu. 1996. "Traditional medicine in modern Japan." *Keio Journal of Medicine* 45: 352–53.

Koren, Leonard. 1990. *Success Stories: How Eleven of Japan's Most Interesting Businesses Came to Be*. Tokyo: Chronicle Books.

Kosover, Toni. 1972. "Fill her up." *W,* 3 November, 20.

Kotani, Satoshi. 2004. "Why are Japanese youth today so passive?" In *Japan's Changing Generations: Are Young People Creating a New Society?*, edited by G. Mathews and G. White, 31–46. London: Routledge Curzon.

Kowner, R., and T. Ogawa. 1993. "The contrast effect of physical attractiveness in Japan." *Journal of Psychology* 127: 51–64.

Kristof, Nicholas D. 1999. "Out of the mist looms, maybe, the first Japanese." *New York Times,* 11 April.

Kubomura, Kiyoko. 1999. "Food ingredient trends in Japan." Report delivered at the International Food Ingredients and Additives Exhibiting and Conference, Tokyo, June 1999. Electronic document, www.worldfood scince.org/vol11/feature1-1.html [accessed July 2001].

Kumagai, Yasuo, Yukichi Shiokawa, Thomas A. Medscer, and Gerald P. Rodnan. 1984. "Clinical spectrum of connective tissue disease after cosmetic surgery: Observation on eighteen patients and a review of the Japanese literature." *Arthritis and Rheumatism* 27 (1): 1–12.

Kyōdō Kōkoku Kikaku Kyoku LIPS. 1989. *It's OL Show Time! Torendii OL no 24 jikan o yomu 42 kō* (42 lectures for understanding a trendy OL's 24-hour day). Tokyo: PHP Kenkyūjo.

Langman, Lauren. 1992. "Neon cages: Shopping for subjectivity." In *Lifestyle Shopping: The Subject of Consumption,* edited by R. Shields, 40–82. London: Routledge.

Larned, Deborah. 1977. "A shot—or two or three—in the breast." *Ms.* (September): 55.

Larrabee, Hart. 1994. "Orthography and affect: Roman text in Japanese magazine advertisements." M.A. thesis, University of Pennsylvania.

Leblanc, Lauraine. 2000. *Pretty in Punk: Girls' Gender Resistance in a Boys' Subculture.* New Brunswick, NJ: Rutgers University Press.

Lebra, Takie Sugiyama. 1976. *Japanese Patterns of Behavior.* Honolulu: University of Hawai'i Press.

———. 1984. *Japanese Women: Constraint and Fulfillment.* Honolulu: University of Hawai'i Press.

Lee, Charles. 2005. "Asian blephorplasty." Electronic document, www.emedicine.com/plastic/topic425.htm [accessed 25 March 2005].

Levitt, Theodore. 1983. "The globalization of markets." *Harvard Business Review* 61 (3): 92–102.

Levy, Howard. 1971. *Sex, Love and the Japanese.* Washington, DC: Warm-Soft.

Lock, Margaret. 1993. *Encounters with Aging: Mythologies of Menopause in Japan and North America.* Berkeley: University of California Press.

———. 1995. "Contesting the natural in Japan: Moral dilemmas and technologies of dying." *Culture, Medicine and Psychiatry* 19: 1–38.

*Look Japan.* 1998. "Apatite for success keeps Sangi smiling." *Look Japan* (March): 18–19.

Loveday, Leo. 1996. *Language Contact in Japan.* New York: Oxford University Press.

Low, Bobbi S. 1979. "Sexual selection and human ornamentation." In *Evolutionary Biology and Human Social Behavior,* edited by N. A. Chagnon and W. Irons, 462–87. North Scituate, MA: Duxbury.

Low, Bobbi S., R. D. Alexander, and K. M. Noonan. 1987. "Human hips, breasts, and buttocks: Is fat deceptive?" *Ethnology and Sociobiology* 8: 249–57.

Lowen, Sara. 1998. "Rethinking a custom." *U.S. News and World Report,* 15 June, 66.

Lunsing, Wim. 1997. "Gay boom in Japan: Changing views of homosexuality?" *Thamyris* 4 (2): 267–93.

Lutz, Catherine A., and Jane Collins. 1993. *Reading National Geographic*. Chicago: University of Chicago Press.

Machida Shinobu. 1997. *Jintan wa, naze nigai?* (Why is Jintan bitter?). Tokyo: Boranteia Jōhō Nettowāku.

Maeda T. 1956. "Organogen ni tsuite" (About Organogen). *Geka no Ryōiki* 4: 800.

*Mainichi Daily News*. 2002a. "Diet supplement business booming." *Mainichi Daily News*, 7 May.

———. 2002b. "Deadly diet pills claim 5th victim." *Mainichi Daily News*, 1 August.

*Mainichi Daily News Interactive*. 2002. "Woman wins payout over beauty parlor hernia." *Mainichi Daily News Interactive*, 24 April. Electronic document, http://mdn.mainichi.co.jp/news/archive/200204/24/20020424p2a00m0fp003 001c.html [accessed August 2004].

———. 2003a. "Mole-reading 'psychic' busted over restaurant beauty parlor." *Mainichi Daily News Interactive*, 20 August. Electronic document, www12 .mainichi.co.jp/news/mdn/search-news/912021/mole-0-2.html [accessed May 2004].

———. 2003b. "Beauty parlor boss busted over hair removal." *Mainichi Daily News Interactive*, 11 March. Electronic document, http://mdn.mainichi.co.jp/news/ archive/200303/11/20030311p2a00m0dm010000c.html [accessed June 2002].

———. 2003c. "Women busted for unqualified colon cleansing." *Mainichi Daily News Interactive*, 15 January. Electronic document, http://mdn.mainichi.co.jp/ news/archive/200301/15/20030115p2a00m0dm031000c.html [accessed June 2004].

*Mainichi Shimbun*. 1991. "Riyō shite mitai ga . . . : Esuteteikku no saron ryokin ya gijutsu ni fuan ankētto chōsa de wakaru" (I want to try it but . . . : Anxiety about aesthetic salon fees and technology seen in public opinion poll). *Mainichi Shimbun*, 1 June.

———. 1995. "Kimutaku genshō o saguru: Kawaii otoko ga suki?" (Probing into the Kimutaku phenomenon: Do you like cute boys?). *Mainichi Shimbun*, 7 November.

———. 1996. "Binanron josetsu: Shakai ga dansei ni mo 'bi' o motomeru jidai" (Commentary on male beauty: The era in which society demands "beauty" even from men). *Mainichi Shimbun*, 19 August.

———. 2003. "Puchi seiki būmu" (The petite surgery boom). *Mainichi Shimbun*, 16 May.

Malinowski, Bronislaw. 1979. *Coral Gardens and Their Magic*. New York: Dover.

Mascia-Lees, Frances, John H. Relethford, and Tom Sorger. 1986. "Evolutionary perspectives on permanent breast enlargement in human females." *American Anthropologist* 88: 423–29.

Matsuba, T., T. Sujiura, M. Irei, N. Kunishima, H. Uchima, S. Miyagi, Y. Iwata, and K. Matsuba. 1994. "Acute pneumonitis presumed to be silicone embolism." *Internal Medicine* 8: 481–83.

Matsui, Midori. 1993. "Little girls were little boys: Displaced femininity in the representation of homosexuality in Japanese girls' comics." In *Feminism and the Politics of Difference,* S. Gunew and A. Yeatman, eds., 176–96. Boulder, CO: Westview Press.

Matsumoto Yūko. 1991. *Kyoshokushō no akenai yoake* (Daybreak is not another day for bulimic me). Tokyo: Shūeisha Bunko.

McCombe, Mel. 1995. "Barbie benders." *Women's Review of Books* 12 (9): 10–12.

McCracken, Grant. 1988. *Culture and Consumption: New Approaches to the Symbolic Character of Consumer Goods and Activities.* Bloomington: Indiana University Press.

McLelland, Mark. 1999. "Gay men as women's ideal partners in Japanese popular culture: Are gay men really a girl's best friend?" *U.S.-Japan Women's Journal* 17: 77–110.

———. 2001. "Why are Japanese girls' comics full of boys bonking?" *Intensities, Journal of Cult Media* 1 (Spring/Summer). Electronic document, www.cultmedia.com/issue1/CMRmcle.htm [accessed August 2002].

McVeigh, Brian J. 1997. *Life in a Japanese Women's College: Learning to Be Ladylike.* Nissan Institute/Routledge Japanese Studies Series. New York: Routledge.

———. 2000. *Wearing Ideology: State, Schooling and Self-Presentation in Japan.* Oxford: Berg.

Mellican, Eugene. 1995. "Breast implants, the cult of beauty, and a culturally constructed 'disease.'" *Journal of Popular Culture* 28 (4): 7–17.

Menand, Louis. 2004. "Game theory." *New Yorker,* 1 March, 87–89.

Mercer, Kobena. 1990. "Black hair/style politics." In *Out There: Marginalization and Contemporary Cultures,* edited by F. Russell, M. Gever, M. Trinh, and C. West, 247–64. Cambridge, MA: MIT Press.

Mertz, John. 1996. "Close encounters of the first kind: Jippensha Ikku, Kanagaki Robun, and the literary construction of national identity." *Asian Cultural Studies* 22: 43–58.

Mi, Huang-Fu. 2004. *The Systematic Classic of Acupuncture and Moxibustion: A Translation of the Jia Yi Jing by Huang-Fu Mi.* Translated by Yang Shou-zhong and Charles Chace. Boulder, CO: Blue Poppy Press.

Mikamo, M. 1896. "Plastic operation of the eyelid." *Chugaii Jishimpō* 17: 1197.

Miller, Daniel. 1995. *Worlds Apart: Modernity through the Prism of the Local.* London: Routledge.

Miller, Laura. 1994. "Japanese and American indirectness." *Journal of Asian and Pacific Communication* 5, nos. 1–2: 37–55.

———. 1995. "Introduction: Beyond the *sarariiman* folk model." *American Asian Review* 13 (2): 19–27.

———. 1997. "*Wasei eigo:* English 'loanwords' coined in Japan." In *The Life of Language: Papers in Linguistics in Honor of William Bright,* edited by J. Hill, P. J. Mistry, and L. Campbell, 123–39. The Hague: Mouton/De Gruyter.

———. 1998a. "Hidden assets: Japan's social transformations for the 21st century." *American Asian Review* 16 (3): 43–63.

———. 1998b. "People types: Personality classification in Japanese women's magazines." *Journal of Popular Culture* 31 (2): 133–50.

——. 1998c. "Visual pedagogy of male beauty work in Japan." *Newsletter of the American Anthropological Association* 39 (9): 51–52.

——. 1998d. "Bad girls: Representations of unsuitable, unfit, and unsatisfactory women in magazines." *U.S.-Japan Women's Journal* 15: 31–51.

——. 2000. "Media typifications and hip *bijin*." *U.S.-Japan Women's Journal* 19: 176–205.

——. 2003a. "Male beauty work in Japan." In *Men and Masculinities in Contemporary Japan: Dislocating the Salaryman Doxa,* edited by J. Roberson and N. Suzuki, 37–58. New York: Routledge/Curzon Press.

——. 2003b. "Mammary mania in Japan." *Positions: East Asia Cultures Critique* 11 (2): 271–300.

——. 2003c. "Consuming Japanese print media in Chicago." In *Ethnolinguistic Chicago: Language and Literacy in Chicago's Neighborhoods,* edited by Marcia Farr, 357–80. Mahwah, NJ: Lawrence Erlbaum.

——. 2003d. "Graffiti photos: Expressive art in Japanese girls' culture." *Harvard Asia Quarterly* 7 (3): 31–42.

——. 2004a. "You are doing *burikko!*: Censoring/scrutinizing artificers of cute femininity in Japanese." In *Japanese Language, Gender, and Ideology: Cultural Models and Real People,* edited by J. Shibamoto Smith and S. Okamoto, 146–65. New York: Oxford University Press.

——. 2004b. "Youth fashion and changing beautification practices." In *Japan's Changing Generations: Are Young People Creating a New Society?,* edited by G. Matthews and B. White, 83–97. New York: Routledge/Curzon Press.

——. 2004c. "Those naughty teenage girls: Japanese Kogals, slang and media assessments." *Journal of Linguistic Anthropology* 14 (2): 225–47.

——. 2004d. "No body is exempt: Beauty compulsion and resistance in Japan." In *Storytelling Sociology: Narrative as Social Inquiry,* edited by by R. Berger and R. Quinney, 107–17. Boulder, CO: Lynne Rienner Publishers.

——. 2005. "Bad girl photography." In *Bad Girls of Japan,* edited by L. Miller and J. Bardsley, 127–41. New York: Palgrave Macmillan.

Miller, Mara. 1998. "Art and the construction of self and subject in Japan." In *Self as Image in Asian Theory and Practice,* edited by E. Ames, T. Kasulis, and W. Dissanayke, 421–60. Albany: State University of New York Press.

Mills, C. Wright. 1959. *The Sociological Imagination.* New York: Oxford University Press.

Miner, Horace. 1956. "Body ritual among the Nacirema." *American Anthropologist* 58 (3): 503–507.

Ministry of Economy, Trade and Industry. 2004. *Esuteteikku sangyō no tekiseika ni kansuru hōkokushō* (Report concerning the optimization of the aesthetic industry). Electronic document, www.meti.go.jp/kohosys/press/0004103/ [accessed August 2004].

Ministry of Health, Labor and Welfare. 2001. Vital Statistics. Electronic document, www.mhlw.go.jp/english/index.html [accessed June 2001].

Ministry of Public Management, Home Affairs, Posts, and Telecommunications. 2002. "Japan Standard Industrial Classification: Historical Background and

Revision No. 11, March." Electronic document, www.stat.go.jp/english/index/seido/sangyo/1.htm [accessed July 2004].

Mintier, Tom. 1996. "'Diet' means more than 'parliament' in Japan: Japanese women spend millions on weight loss fads." *CNN Interactive Food and Health*. Electronic document, www.cnn.com/HEALTH/9607/01/japan.diet/ [accessed July 1999].

Miura Kentarō. 1990. *Beruseruku* (Berserk). Tokyo: Hakusensha.

Miyata, Y., R. Okano, and Y. Kuratomi. 1997. "Interstitial pneumonia associated with human adjuvant disease which developed thirty years after silicone augmentation mammoplasty." *Nippon Kyōbu Shikkan Gakkai Zasshi* 35 (10): 1093–98.

Miyoshi, K., T. Tomioka, and Y. Kobayashi. 1964. "Hypergammagobulinemia by prolonged adjuvanticity in man. Disorders developed after augmentation mammaplasty." *Nihon Ijishimpō*, no. 2122: 9–14.

Mizuki Shukei. 1991. *Onna no ko māketingu* (The female market). Tokyo: PHP Kenkyūjo.

Moeran, Brian. 1985. "When the poetics of advertising become the advertising of poetics: Syntactical and semantic parallelism in English and Japanese advertising." *Language and Communication* 5 (1): 29–44.

——. 1993. "A tournament of values: Strategies of presentation in Japanese advertising." *Ethnos* 58 (1–2): 73–93.

——. 1996a. *A Japanese Advertising Agency: An Anthropology of Media and Markets*. Honolulu: University of Hawai'i Press.

——. 1996b. "The Orient strikes back: Advertising and imagining Japan." *Theory, Culture & Society* 13 (3): 77–112.

Moore, Robert E. 2001. "Indian dandies: Sartorial finesse and self-presentation along the Columbia River, 1790–1855." In *Dandies: Fashion and Finesse in Art and Culture,* edited by Susan Fillin-Yeh, 59–100. New York: New York University Press.

Morgan, David. 1993. "You too can have a body like mine: Reflections on the male body and masculinities." In *Body Matters: Essays on the Sociology of the Body,* edited by S. Scott and D. Morgan, 69–88. London: Falmer Press.

Morgan, Elaine. 1972. *The Descent of Woman*. New York: Bantam.

Mori, Kyoko. 1999. *Polite Lies: On Being a Woman Caught between Cultures*. New York: Fawcett Books.

Morohashi Taiki. 1993. *Zasshi bunka no naka no joseigaku* (A study of women found in the culture of magazines). Tokyo: Meiseki Shoten.

Morris, Desmond. 1994. *The Human Animal*. New York: Crown Publishing.

Morris, Ivan. 1964. *The World of the Shining Prince: Court Life in Ancient Japan*. Tokyo: Charles E. Tuttle.

Mukai, T., M. Crago, and C. M. Shisslak. 1994. "Eating attitudes and weight preoccupation among female high school students in Japan." *Child Psychology and Psychiatry* 35 (4): 677–88.

Mukai, Takayo, Akiko Kambara, and Yuji Sasaki. 1998. "Body dissatisfaction, need for social approval, and eating disorders among Japanese and American college women." *Sex Roles: A Journal of Research* 39 (9/10): 751–63.

Mulvey, Laura. 1975. "Visual pleasure and narrative cinema." *Screen* 16 (3): 6–18.

Mutou, Y. 1980. "Augmentation mammoplasty in Japan." *Nihon Biyō Geka Gakkai Kaihō* 2 (2): 67–77.

*Myōjō*. 1990. "Watashi, narushisuto nan desu" (Me, I'm a narcissist). *Myōjō* (August): 59.

Nakamura, K., Y. Hoshino, A. Watanabe, K. Honda, S. Niwa, K. Tominaga, S. Shimai, and M. Yamamoto. 1999. "Eating problems in female Japanese high school students: A prevalence study." *International Journal of Eating Disorders* 26: 91–95.

Nakamura Tanio. 1980. *Kaiga ni miru Nihon no bijo* (Japanese beauties from the perspective of paintings). Osaka: Hoikusha.

Nakashima, Tamiji, and Takayuki Matsushita. 2004. "Gender and hierarchical differences in lead-contaminated Japanese bones from the Edo period." *Dai 104-kai Nihon Kaibōgaku Gakkai Sōkai Intānetto Sesshon* (The 104th Japan Anatomy Association general meeting internet session). Electronic document, www.vit.or.jp/~tamiji/ [accessed August 2004].

Nardini, Gloria. 1999. *Che Bella Figura! The Power of Performance in an Italian Ladies' Club in Chicago*. New York: State University of New York Press.

*Nihon Keizai Shimbun*. 1989a. "Otoko rashisa yori subesube ohada wakamono ni takamaru eikyū datsumō" (Smooth skin before manliness: The increase in electrolysis among young men). *Nihon Keizai Shimbun*, 16 August.

———. 1989b. "Otokogokoro o sasō biyō saron" (Beauty salons tempt the inner man). *Nihon Keizai Shimbun*, 12 November.

———. 1990. "Konshūmā jōhō: Datsumō, bigan no kujō ōi esuteteikku 100 ban" (Consumer report: Many complaints about hair removal and facials at the aesthetic "911" hotline). *Nihon Keizai Shimbun*, 13 March.

———. 1999. "Chūnen dansei esutegayoi" (Middle-aged men frequent *esute* salons). *Nihon Keizai Shimbun*, 3 May.

*Nikkei Trendy*. 1997. "Chapatsu, piasu no tsugi wa mayu no teire" (After *chapatsu* and piercing, eyebrow care). *Nikkei Trendy*, no. 117 (February): 164–65.

———. 1998. "Petto wa kodomo yori kawaii!" (Pets are cuter than kids!). *Nikkei Trendy*, no. 133 (April): 74–75.

Nishihata, T. 1923. "Augmentation rhinoplasty using ivory." *Clinical Photography* 7: 8.

*Nishi Nihon Shimbun*. 1995. "Meiji omoshiro hakurankai" (Exhibition of Meiji amusements). *Nishi Nihon Shimbun*, 27 September.

Nogami, Y., K. Monma, Y. Izumiya, and Y. Kawakita. 1987. "A study on binge-eating among female students." *Seishin Igaku* 29: 155.

Nomura, Masaichi. 1990. "Remodeling the Japanese body." In *Culture Embodied*, edited by M. Moerman and M. Nomura, 259–74. Osaka: National Museum of Ethnology.

Ochiai, Emiko. 1997. "Decent housewives and sensual white women: Representation of women in postwar Japanese magazines." *Japan Review* 9: 151–69.

Ogawa Yōko. 1991. *Shugā taimu* (Sugar time). Tokyo: Chūō Kōronsha.

Ohnuki-Tierney, Emiko. 1984. *Illness and Culture in Contemporary Japan*. Cambridge: Cambridge University Press.

———. 1994. "Brain death and organ transplantation." *Current Anthropology* 35 (3): 233–54.

———. 1997. "McDonald's in Japan: Changing manners and etiquette." In *Golden Arches East: McDonald's in East Asia,* edited by J. L. Watson, 161–82. Stanford, CA: Stanford University Press.

Ohtake, Naoyuki, Yasumi Koganei, Masatsugu Itoh, and Nobuyuki Shioya. 1989. "Postoperative sequelae of augmentation mammaplasty by injection method in Japan." *Aesthetic Plastic Surgery* 13: 67–74.

Onishi, Norimitsu. 2005. "It's 3:30 a.m. The off-duty hostesses relax. With hosts." *New York Times International,* 5 April, A4.

Ono, Yumiko. 1999. "Beautifying the Japanese male." *Wall Street Journal,* 11 March.

Orbaugh, Sharalyn. 2003. "Busty battlin' babes: The evolution of the shojo in 1990s visual culture." In *Gender and Power in the Japanese Visual Field,* edited by J. Mostow, N. Bryson, and M. Graybill, 201–28. Honolulu: University of Hawai'i Press.

Orenstein, Peggy. 2001. "Parasites in prêt-à-porter." *New York Times Magazine,* 1 July, 31–35.

Ortner, Sherry, and Harriet Whitehead. 1981. *Sexual Meanings: The Cultural Construction of Gender and Sexuality.* Cambridge: Cambridge University Press.

Ossman, Susan. 2002. *Three Faces of Beauty: Casablanca, Paris, Cairo.* Durham, NC: Duke University Press.

Peiss, Kathy. 1998. *Hope in a Jar: The Making of America's Beauty Culture.* New York: Henry Holt.

———. 2001. "On beauty . . . and the history of business." In *Beauty and Business: Commerce, Gender, and Culture in Modern America,* edited by P. Scranton, 7–22. New York: Routledge.

*PHP Intersect.* 1987. "You handsome hunk of man, you." *PHP Intersect* (January): 4.

Plath, David W. 1966. "Japan and the ethics of fatalism." *Anthropological Quarterly* 39 (3): 161–70.

———. 1980. *Long Engagements: Maturity in Modern Japan.* Stanford, CA: Stanford University Press.

Pollack, Andrew. 1996. "Barbie's journey in Japan." *New York Times,* 22 December.

Pollock, Griselda. 1988. *Vision and Difference: Femininity, Feminism and Histories of Art.* London: Routledge.

Postman, Neil. 1993. *Technopoly: The Surrender of Culture to Technology.* New York: Vintage Books.

Poston, Carol H. 1988. *Mary Wollstonecraft: A Vindication of the Rights of Woman: An Authoritative Text, Backgrounds, the Wollstonecraft Debate, Criticism.* New York: W. W. Norton.

Pyles, Thomas. 1957. Review of *A Concise Dictionary of the American Language,* by Arthur Waldhorn. *American Speech* 32: 125–28.

Quackenbush, Edward. 1974. "How Japanese borrows English words." *Linguistics* 131: 59–75.

*Ranking Dai Suki!* 1999a. "Karada o teire de ichiban ki o tsukatte iru koto" (The things about my body I most attend to repairing). *Ranking Dai Suki!* (March): 91.

———. 1999b. "Anata no hada no iro wa?" (What skin color do you have?). *Ranking Dai Suki!* (March): 54.

———. 1999c. "Otoko no ko no karada ni tsuite, kore wa yurusen! to omou koto" (Women think that, as for the male body, this is not allowed!). *Ranking Dai Suki!* (March): 91.

———. 1999d. "Onna no ko no karada no naka de, ichiban sukina bubun" (The most favorite part of all of a woman's body). *Ranking Dai Suki!* (March): 91.

———. 1999e. "Onna no ko ni kikimashita" (The girls were asked). *Ranking Dai Suki!* (March): 39.

———. 1999f. "Pantsu no chūshin dō natteruno?!" (What's it like inside your undies?!). *Ranking Dai Suki!* (March): 45.

———. 1999g. "Iketeru no wa kore!" (This is what's in!). *Ranking Dai Suki!* (March): 112.

———. 2000a. "Mezase! Muteki no natsu Gals sutairu" (Take aim! Unrivaled Gals summer style). *Ranking Dai Suki!* (July): 102.

———. 2000b. "Uwasa ni daietto o tameshi daichōsa" (Sampling of a huge survey of rumored diets). *Ranking Dai Suki!* (July): 73–79.

*Ray.* 1997a. "Meronpai bura" (Melon boobs bra). *Ray,* no. 114 (October): 174–75.

———. 1997b. "Me kara uroko no ketsueki-gata daietto" (Watching the scale with a blood-typology diet). *Ray,* no. 114 (October): 199–210.

Reader, Ian, and George Tanabe. 1998. *Practically Religious: Worldly Beliefs and the Common Religion of Japan.* Honolulu: University of Hawai'i Press.

Ribeiro, Jorge. 1987. "Wacoal: Dynamic company, bionic bras." *PHP Intersect* (February): 44–45.

Richie, Donald. 2001. *The Donald Richie Reader: 50 Years of Writing on Japan.* Compiled by Artuo Silva. Berkeley, CA: Stone Bridge Press.

Ritzer, George. 1993. *The McDonaldization of Society: An Investigation into the Changing Character of Contemporary Social Life.* Thousand Oaks, CA: Pine Forge Press.

Roberson, James E., and Nobue Suzuki. 2003. "Introduction" In *Men and Masculinities in Contemporary Japan: Dislocating the Salaryman Doxa,* edited by J. Roberson and N. Suzuki, 1–19. New York: Routledge/Curzon Press.

Robertson, Jennifer. 1991. *Native and Newcomer: Making and Remaking of a Japanese City.* Berkeley: University of California Press.

———. 1998. *Takarazuka: Sexual Politics and Popular Culture in Modern Japan.* Berkeley: University of California Press.

———. 2001. "Japan's first cyborg? Miss Nippon eugenics and wartime technologies of beauty, body and blood." *Body and Society* 7 (1): 1–34.

———. 2002. "Reflexivity redux: A pithy polemic on 'positionality.'" *Anthropological Quarterly* 75 (4): 785–92.

Root, Deborah. 1996. *Cannibal Culture: Art, Appreciation, and the Commodification of Difference.* Boulder, CO: Westview Press.

Rosenberger, Nancy. 2000. *Gambling with Virtue: Japanese Women and the Search for Self in a Changing Nation*. Honolulu: University of Hawai'i Press.

Rubinfein, Louise. 1995. "Commodity to brand." Paper presented at the Davis Center Colloquium on Business, Enterprise and Culture in Japan, Princeton University.

Russell, Jack. 1995. "Balanced beauty." *Advertising Age*, 17 April, 1–19.

Russell, John. 1998. "Consuming passions: Spectacle, self-transformation, and the commodification of Blackness in Japan." *Positions: East Asia Cultures Critique* 6 (1): 113–78.

Rybczynski, Witold. 1986. *Home: A Short History of an Idea*. New York: Penguin Books.

*Saitama Shimbun*. 1997. "Kankoku-shiki esute de tekihatsu" (Exposing Korean-style *esute*). *Saitama Shimbun*, 19 July.

*Sankei Shimbun*. 1994. "Kankoku taiken tsuā" (Korean experience tour). *Sankei Shimbun*, 21 December.

———. 1997. "Karada no nayami, kiite kiku" (Let's ask about body worries). *Sankei Shimbun*, 6 February.

Sato, Barbara Hamill. 2003. *The New Japanese Woman: Modernity, Media, and Women in Interwar Japan*. Durham, NC: Duke University Press.

Sato, Ikuya. 1991. *Kamikaze Biker: Parody and Anomy in Affluent Japan*. Chicago: University of Chicago Press.

Satō Ayako. 1999. *Ippunkan de jibun o kaeru* (Change yourself in one minute). Tokyo: Sanryū Shoten.

———. 2000. *Sukina jibun ni naru 55 no hōhō* (55 ways to have a likeable self ). Tokyo: Kōdansha.

Schaefer, Gary. 2003. "Japanese women flock to cosmetic surgery." *Wisconsin State Journal*, 13 October, A7.

Schalk, Deborah N. 1988. "The history of augmentation mammoplasty." *Plastic Surgical Nursing* 8 (3): 88.

Schilling, Mark. 1992. "Worshiping the naked goddess: The media, mores, and Miyazawa Rie." *Japan Quarterly* 105 (23): 218–24.

Schreiber, Mark. 2002. "Cosmetic surgery on virile member comes at stiff price." *Mainichi Daily News*, 5 May.

Screech, Timon. 1999. *Sex and the Floating World*. Honolulu: University of Hawai'i Press.

Sebba, Mark. 1986. "The -ex ending in product names." *American Speech* 4: 318–26.

Sedgwick, Eve. 1991. *Epistemology in the Closet*. London: Harvester Wheatsheaf.

Seidensticker, Edward. 1983. *Low City, High City*. New York: Alfred A. Knopf.

———. 1990. *Tokyo Rising: The City since the Great Earthquake*. New York: Alfred A. Knopf.

Seki Osamu. 1996. *Bidanron josetsu* (Introduction to theories of male beauty). Tokyo: Natsume Shobō.

*Self.* 1995. "Bras through the ages." *Self* (March): 149–50.

Sergile, S. L., and K. Obata. 1997. "Mikamo's double eyelid operation: The advent of Japanese aesthetic surgery." *Plastic Reconstructive Surgery* 99 (3): 662–67.

*Seventeen.* 2001a. "Onna no ko ga shiritakatta otoko no ko karada no himitsu" (Boys' body secrets the girls wanted to know about). *Seventeen,* no. 6 (February): 123–25.

———. 2001b. "Otoko no ko no kahanshin Q & A" (Q & A about a boy's lower body region). *Seventeen,* no. 6 (February): 126–27.

———. 2001c. "Oppai bijin ni naru!" (Become a big-breasted beauty!). *Seventeen,* no. 6 (February): 71–75.

*Shanghai Star.* 2001. "Eating disorders plague young Japanese women." *Shanghai Star,* 28 June.

Shibusawa, Keizō. 1958. *Japanese Life and Culture in the Meiji Era.* Translated by Charles Terry. Tokyo: Ōbunsha.

Shilling, Chris. 1993. *The Body and Social Theory.* London: Sage.

Shinbutsu Goriyaku Kenkyūkai, ed. 1989. *Jinja, otera goriyakuchō* (Guidebook to supplications at temples and shrines). Tokyo: KK Rongu Serāzu.

Shiokawa, Kanako. 1999. "Cute but deadly: Women and violence in Japanese comics." In *Themes and Issues in Asian Cartooning: Cute, Cheap, Mad, and Sexy,* edited by J. Lent, 93–125. Bowling Green, OH: Bowling Green State University Popular Press.

Shirakabe, Yukio. 1990. "The development of aesthetic facial surgery in Japan." *Aesthetic Plastic Surgery* 14: 215–21.

Shiseidō Hanatsubaki. 1979. *Shiseidō sendenshi* (History of Shiseido). Tokyo: Shiseidō.

*Shizuoka Shimbun.* 1997. "Esute kaisūken ya hosei shidaigi wakai josei no sōdan zōka" (Increase in consultations with young women who are victims of *esute* scams). *Shizuoka Shimbun,* 29 August.

Shōgakukan. 1999. *Dētaparu: Saishin jōhō, yōgo jiten* (DataPal: Up-to Date Information and Encyclopedia of Terms). Tokyo: Shōgakukan.

Short, Roger V. 1976. "The evolution of human reproduction." *Proceedings of the Royal Society of London* 195: 3–24.

Silverberg, Miriam. 1992. "Constructing the Japanese ethnography of modernity." *Journal of Asian Studies* 5 (1): 30–54.

Simmel, Georg. 1957. "Fashion." *American Journal of Sociology* 62 (6): 541–58.

Sims, Calvin. 1999. "Be tall and chic as you wobble to the orthopedist." *New York Times International,* 26 November.

Singleton, John. 1993. "*Gambaru:* A Japanese cultural theory of learning." In *Japanese Schooling: Patterns of Socialization, Equality and Political Control,* edited by J. Shields, 8–15. University Park: Pennsylvania State University Press.

Skov, Lise, 1996. "Fashion trends, Japonisme and postmodernism, Or, 'What is so Japanese about Comme des Garçons?'" *Theory, Culture & Society* 13 (3): 129–51.

Skov, Lise, and Brian Moeran. 1995. "Introduction: Hiding in the light: From Oshin to Yoshimoto Banana." In *Women, Media and Consumption in Japan,* edited by L. Skov and B. Moeran, 1–74. Honolulu: University of Hawai'i Press.

Slyomovic, Susan. 1993. "The body in water: Women in American spa culture." In *Bodylore,* edited by K. Young, 35–56. Knoxville: University of Tennessee Press.

Sobo, Elisa J. 1997. "The sweetness of fat: Health, procreation and sociability in rural Jamaica." In *Food and Culture: A Reader,* edited by C. Counihan and P. Van Esterik, 256–71. New York: Routledge.

Société Centrale d'Echanges Techniques Internationaux. 2004. "The specificity of the Japanese aesthetic market." Report issued by Société Centrale d'Echanges Techniques Internationaux, Tokyo.

Spiegler, Marc. 1996. "Business reports: Health care, breast implants." *American Demographics* 18 (1): 13.

Spielvogel, Laura. 2003. *Working Out in Japan: Shaping the Female Body in Tokyo Fitness Clubs.* Durham, NC: Duke University Press.

Stanlaw, James. 1992. "'For beautiful human life': The use of English in Japan." In *Remade in Japan: Everyday Life and Consumer Taste in a Changing Society,* edited by J. Tobin, 58–76. New Haven, CT: Yale University Press.

——. 2000. "Open your file, open your mind: Women, English, and changing role and voices in Japanese pop music." In *Japan Pop! Inside the World of Japanese Popular Culture,* edited by T. J. Craig, 75–100. London: M. E. Sharpe.

——. 2004. *Japanese English: Language and Culture Contact.* Hong Kong: Hong Kong University Press.

Steinbeck, John. 1947. *The Wayward Bus.* New York: Viking Press.

Steinem, Gloria. 1983. "If men could menstruate." In *Outrageous Acts and Everyday Rebellions,* 337–40. New York: Holt, Reinhart and Winston.

Stevenson, Seth. 2002. "I'd like to buy the world a shelf-safe children's lactic drink." *New York Times Magazine,* 10 March, 38–43.

Strom, Stephanie. 1998. "Luxury in recession land." *New York Times,* 29 October.

Stuhlman, Andreas. 1999. "See the world through different eyes." *Tokyo Journal* 18 (212): 15.

Suematsu, H., H. Ishikawa, T. Kuboki, and T. Ito. 1985. "Statistical studies on anorexia nervosa in Japan." *Psychotherapy and Psychosomatics* 43: 96.

Sugimoto, Yoshio. 1997. *An Introduction to Japanese Society.* Cambridge: Cambridge University Press.

Suzuki Sonoko. 1980. *Yasetai hito wa tabenasai* (If you want to lose weight, eat!). Tokyo: Shōdensha.

Swartz, Mimi. 1995. "Silicone City." *Texas Monthly* 2 (8): 69–100.

Takahashi, Eiji. 1986. "Secular trend of female body shape in Japan." *Human Biology* 58 (2): 293–301.

Tanaka, Keiko. 1994. *Advertising Language: A Pragmatic Approach to Advertisements in Britain and Japan.* London: Routledge.

Tanaka, Rieko. 1991. "Aesthetic boom brings complaints." *Japan Times Weekly International Edition,* 19 August.

Tanizaki Jun'ichiro. 1970. *Tanizaki Jun'ichiro zenshū* (Collected works of Tanizaki Jun'ichiro). Vol. 14: *Ren'ai oyobi shikijō* (Love and passion), published in 1931. Tokyo: Chūō Kōronsha.

Tanja Yujiro. 2003. *F.U.C.K. I Love Japan.* Tokyo: Shufu no Tomo.

Terry, Jennifer. 1989. "The body invaded: Medical surveillance of women as reproducers." *Socialist Review* 19 (2): 13–43.

*Time Asia.* 2005. "Non-incisional technique to create double eyelids gains favor among Asian patients." *Time Asia* 160, no. 4 (5 August).

Tobin, Joseph J. 1992. "Introduction: Domesticating the West." In *Remade in Japan: Everyday Life and Consumer Taste in a Changing Society,* edited by J. Tobin, 1–41. New Haven, CT: Yale University Press.

*Tokyo Shimbun.* 1996. "Riyū kō no 'bi' jin" (The eyebrow "beauty" trend). *Tokyo Shimbun,* 31 May.

Tomlinson, John. 1991. *Cultural Imperialism.* Baltimore, MD: Johns Hopkins University Press.

Torgovnich, Marianna. 1996. *Primitive Passions.* New York: Knopf.

Treat, John Whittier. 1996. "Introduction: Japanese studies into cultural studies." In *Contemporary Japan and Popular Culture,* edited by J. Treat, 1–14. Honolulu: University of Hawai'i Press.

Tringal, Juliana. 2004. "Beauty and the feast: The cosmetic industry's female feeding frenzy." *Bitch: Feminist Response to Pop Culture* 23 (Winter): 35–37, 89–90.

Trumble, Angus. 2004. *A Brief History of the Smile.* New York: Basic Books.

Tsuda Noriyo. 1985. *Mayu no bunkashi* (A cultural history of eyebrows). Tokyo: Pōra Bunka Kenkyūkai.

Tsutamori T. 1990. *Otoko datte kirei ni naritai* (Even men want to become beautiful). Tokyo: Keisō Shobō.

Turner, Terence. 1980. "The social skin." In *Not Work Alone: A Cross-Cultural View of Activities Superfluous to Survival,* edited by J. Cherfas and R. Lewin, 112–40. Beverly Hills: Sage.

Turner, Victor. 1967. *The Forest of Symbols: Aspects of Ndembu Ritual.* Ithaca, NY: Cornell University Press.

Uemori Mio. 1997. *Dō shitemo yasetai kijo* (You got thin no matter what). Tokyo: Sanichi Shinsha.

Ueno, Chizuko. 1997. "In the feminine guise: A trap of reverse orientalism." *US-Japan Women's Journal* 13: 3–25.

*U.S. News and World Report.* 1999. "Multiple Mr. Rights." *U.S. News and World Report,* 5 July, 56.

Veblen, Thorstein. 1925. *The Theory of the Leisure Class: An Economic Study of Institutions.* London: Allen and Unwin.

Wagatsuma Hiroshi and Hiroko Hara. 1974. *Shitsuke* (Upbringing). Tokyo: Kōbundō.

Washburn, Sherwood L. 1978. "Human behaviors and the behavior of animals." *American Psychologist* 33: 405–18.

Watson, James L., ed. 1997. *Golden Arches East: McDonald's in East Asia.* Stanford, CA: Stanford University Press.

White, Emily. 1992. "Revolution girl style now." *LA Weekly,* 10–16 July. Republished in *Rock She Wrote: Women Write about Rock, Pop, and Rap,* edited by E. McDonnell and A. Powers, 96–408. New York: Cooper Square Press.

White, Merry. 1993. *The Material Child: Coming of Age in Japan and America.* New York: Free Press.

Wilk, Richard. 1995. "Learning to be local in Belize: Global systems of common difference." In *Worlds Apart: Modernity through the Prism of the Local,* edited by D. Miller, 110–33. London: Routledge.

Williams, Tom. 1996. *The Complete Illustrated Guide to Chinese Medicine.* New York: Barnes and Noble.

Williamson, Judith. 1978. *Decoding Advertisements.* London: Marion Boyars.

Willis, Judith. 1982. "About body wraps, pills and other magic wands for losing weight." *FDA Consumer.* Washington, DC: U.S. Food and Drug Administration.

*With.* 1992. "People: *Akai Hidekazu.*" *With,* no. 132 (September): 28–29.

Wolf, Naomi. 1992. *The Beauty Myth: How Images of Beauty Are Used against Women.* New York: Anchor Books.

Wolfren, Karl Van. 1989. *The Enigma of Japanese Power.* New York: Alfred A. Knopf.

Wood, Joe. 1999. "The Yellow Negro." *Transition* 7 (73): 40–66.

Yalom, Marilyn. 1997. *A History of the Breast.* New York: Alfred A. Knopf.

Yamada Toyoko. 2000. *Burando no seiki* (The century of brands). Tokyo: Magazine House.

Yamamoto T. 2001. *Nonpara: Parasaito shinai onna tachi no "hontō"* (Nonparasites: The truth about women who are not parasites). Tokyo: Magazine House.

Yamazaki, T., T. Kinjo, H. Terada, Y. Nakano, N. Tei, and M. Kitamura. 1977. "Experience with mammography of augmentation mammoplasty in relation to breast cancer detection." *Rinsho Hōshasen* 22: 861–67.

Yamazaki Kōichi. 1993. *Danjō ron* (Theroizing male and female). Tokyo: Kinōkuniya Shoten.

Yano, Christine. 2002. *Tears of Longing: Nostalgia and the Nation in Japanese Popular Song.* Cambridge, MA: Harvard University Press.

Yasumaru Yoshio. 1981. *Deguchi nao* (A further way out). 2d ed. Tokyo: Shimbunsha.

Yayoi, K. 1982. "Treatment of foreign body in the breast." *Geka Chiryō* 47: 562–69.

*Yomiuri Shimbun.* 1989. "Zenshin biyō saron: 'Esute' no toraburu tahatsu" (Whole body beauty salon: *Esute*'s frequent problems). *Yomiuri Shimbun,* 19 August.

———. 1997a. "Surimu na kao e 'henshin' guzzu ninki" ("Mask" goods popular for face slimming). *Yomiuri Shimbun,* 5 March.

———. 1997b. "Mayuge binan: 'Kimutaku mitai ni' biyōshitsu ni kayō dankai" (Beautifully eyebrowed men: The crowd who visits beauty salons in order to "look like Kimutaku"). *Yomiuri Shimbun,* 17 April.

———. 1997c. "Mō obasan nante yobasenai, shōhi o hipparu midei pawā" (Don't call us old bags anymore: Middle-aged power creates consumption patterns). *Yomiuri Shimbun,* 17 February.

Yoshida, T., M. Tanaka, K. Okamoto, and S. Hirai. 1996. "Neurosarcoidosis following augmentation mammoplasty with silicone." *Neurological Research* 18 (4): 319–20.

Young, Katharine. 1997. *Presence in the Flesh: The Body in Medicine.* Cambridge, MA: Harvard University Press.

# Index

*Page references in italics refer to illustrations or tables.*

Abhyanga (oil treatment), 65
acupoints, electro-stimulation of, 63–64
acupuncture, 62, 69
advertising, 17; by aesthetic salons, 49,
209n4; awards for, 193; for breast
enhancement, 71, 75, 91, *95,* 190, 210n1;
creative language in, 179, 192–93;
decoding of, 193–94; for dieting, 174;
English in, 177, 178–79, 191–92, 194;
explicit, 191; exploitation of anxiety
by, 97, 191; for eyelid surgery, 119;
fashion, 30; food language in, 193;
for hair removal, *107,* 133, 134; orthographic code-switching in, 192, *192;*
polygraphic, 192; print, 177; reassur-
ance in, 190; by Shiseido, 68, 178;
social function of, 194; testimonials
in, 190; of Tokyo Beauty Center, 104,
203; in youth culture, 177–78. *See also*
esute language
aesthetics: Asian, 61–66; bar-hostess, 28,
54; of cuteness, 25–26, *25,* 27, 31, 32,
75; dental, 31; divination, 197; ethnic
borrowing in, 32–34; mental, 10; syncretic, 122–24; world expos in, 66.
*See also* esute
aesthetics, body: Chinese, 195–96; culture
of, 2; internal, 112; male, 136; Oriental, 63; in prewar Japan, 23–24; "raw,"
81; transnational, 5, 66–70

aesthetic salons, 3; advertising by, 49,
209n4; after care *(afutā kea)* of, 180;
Asian treatments at, 61–66; breast
enhancement treatments at, 86–91;
bridal treatments at, 44, *45;* chains,
42, 43; complaints against, 52–53;
consumer abuse in, 16, 41, 50, 52–53,
70; contests of, 49; cost of, 44, *45;*
counseling rooms of, 30, 57; cupping
treatment at, 62–63, *62;* customers
of, 45–46; customers' experience at,
54–61; dieting treatments at, 167;
downturn in, 198; electrolysis at,
43, 45, 46, 50, 52, 106–7; employees
of, 51–52, 53, 55; ethnography of, 15;
facials at, 44, 45, 46; facilities of,
42–43, 60–61; French Antique decor
of, 54–55, 209n10; hair removal at,
41, 44, 52, 60, 100; as health-care
experience, 56; home products of,
58, 61; ideology of, 41; international,
199–200; in Japanese economy, 41–
42; legitimacy of, 49–54; locations
of, 55; marketing by, 30, 46, 57–58, 61;
names of, 55, 209n11; numbers of, 2,
42, 209n2; ownership of, 42; pleasure from, 60; purpose of, 43, 60–61;
reasons for visiting, 59; regulation of,
50; revenue from, 42, 209n1; services
of, 44; slimming treatments at, 56;

241

| | |
|---:|:---|
| Text: | 10/13 Galliard |
| Display: | Galliard |
| Compositor: | Integrated Composition Systems |
| Printer and Binder: | Thomson-Shore, Inc. |